IEA Studies in European Union

JUSTICE COOPERATION IN THE EU

THE CREATION OF A EUROPEAN LEGAL SPACE

Reflections on the growing role of the European Union in cooperation in justice and home affairs

Edited by GAVIN BARRETT

INSTITUTE OF EUROPEAN AFFAIRS

Published by the
Institute of European Affairs
Europe House
8 North Great George's Street
Dublin 1, Ireland
Tel: (01) 874 6756 Fax: (01) 878 6880
e-mail: iea@connect.ie

ISSN 0791-588
ISBN 1-874109-33-8

Cover design and typography by
Butler Claffey Design

Originated and printed by
Brunswick Press Limited
Dublin, Ireland

◼ CONTENTS

◾ CONTRIBUTORS

- Eamonn Barnes is one of Ireland's best-known lawyers, having for many years held the office of Director of Public Prosecutions. He has written widely on a variety of legal topics.

- Dr Gavin Barrett is leader of the Third-Pillar Project in the Institute of European Affairs and has published articles in that area and on other legal topics and issues related to European integration. He has also spoken at various conferences on themes relating to justice and home affairs cooperation. In addition to being the editor of this volume, he is the author of *Economic and Monetary Union – the Third Stage,* published in April 1997 by the Institute of European Affairs. From August 1997 he will be taking up a position with the Academy of European Law in Trier, Germany.

- Patrick Cooney is Chairman of the Third-Pillar Project in the Institute of European Affairs and a former Dáil Deputy and Minister for Justice. He was for several years a Member of the European Parliament where he played an active part in its activities relating to justice and home-affairs matters.

- Eileen Barrington is a practising barrister and lecturer who has published on legal topics relating to European integration, in particular combating fraud in the European Union. Called to the French Bar in 1994, she has worked as a lawyer in Paris and Brussels.

- Professor William Duncan is Professor of Law and Jurisprudence at the University of Dublin (Trinity College) and a former member of Ireland's Law Reform Commission. He is the Irish member of the Committee on Racism and Xenophobia and has written widely including a well-known legal textbook in the field of family law.

- Val Flynn is an official working with the Security Bureau of the European Commission and has published articles on the topic of police cooperation.

- Dr Michael Forde is a Senior Counsel, barrister, university lecturer and the author of a large number of articles and leading textbooks on legal subjects, including constitutional law, arbitration law, company law, commercial law and extradition law.

- Dermot Gilroy is a senior official in the Irish Revenue Commissioners who has particular expertise in the field of customs cooperation.

- Paul Gormley works as a Head of Sector for the European Commission Representation in Ireland.

- Diarmaid McGuinness is a practising barrister and was a member of the Constitutional Review Group appointed by the Government to review the operation of the Irish Constitution.

- Bill Shipsey is a Senior Counsel, practising barrister and noted expert in the field of asylum law.

- Dr Ben Tonra is Research Fellow in the Institute of European Affairs and a lecturer in political science in the University of Dublin (Trinity College). He has published widely in the field of political studies.

- Dr Brian Walsh is one of Ireland's most distinguished jurists. For many years the Senior Judge in Ireland's Supreme Court, where he delivered the judgments in many landmark cases, he is now a Judge of the European Court of Human Rights and has written extensively on a number of legal topics.

- Anthony Whelan is a *référendaire* in the European Court of Justice and a former lecturer in law in the University of Dublin (Trinity College). He was co-author of a book of cases and materials on European integration, and of *Citizenship of the European Union* (IEA Occasional Paper, No. 6, 1995), in addition to writing extensively on other legal topics.

- Seamus Woulfe is a practising barrister who has acted in a number of leading cases and has written widely on legal topics.

▣ INTRODUCTION

The very beginning of the European Union on 9 May 1950, with the Schuman Declaration, embraced the twofold aspiration of economic and political union. Merging the coal and steel industries of the founding member states had obvious economic implications and ceding control of them to a supranational institution was hugely politically significant.

The journey to economic union is nearly complete, with the single market achieved and a single currency looming inevitably closer. The road to political union still stretches ahead with a considerable distance to be traversed.

The first formally legal steps on that road were taken with the Single European Act of 1986 – the fruit, we should recall, of the Dooge Committee. The Act, when there were ten member states, enabled the Treaty on European Union (Maastricht) to be signed in February 1992, though it did not come into force until November 1993 when finally ratified by the then twelve member states.

That Treaty, with its optimistic title, represented progress on the road to political union insofar as it incorporated a political dimension by providing for two new forms of cooperation, in foreign and security policy and in the fields of justice and home affairs. Unfortunately, the mechanisms for achieving this cooperation, though involving the Community institutions of Council, Commission and Parliament, have been disappointing in what they have achieved, with the result that progress towards further integration or deepening, which is what Union means, has been disappointing.

The 1996-97 intergovernmental conference had the crucial role of redressing this lack of progress. This role is urgent too. because of the growing pressure for enlargement. It is essential for the future stability of the European Union, if not for its very continuance, that significant political integration take place before any further enlargement. To negotiate further progress will be extremely difficult with fifteen member states, but with any more it could be well-nigh impossible.

This is particularly true in the sensitive areas of justice and home affairs. Being conscious of this, the Institute of European Affairs has arranged for the publication of this volume in the hope that it will be useful in creating a wider awareness of this important policy field.

Patrick Cooney

▪ PREFACE

> Action in the fields of Justice and Home Affairs shall have as its objective
> to maintain and develop the Union as an area of freedom, security and
> justice in accordance with the principle of the rule of law.[1]

For a number of reasons, the present time seems opportune for the
publication of a volume of reflections on European Union activity in the field
of justice and home affairs. In the first place, five years have elapsed since
agreement was reached on the text of the Treaty on European Union at
Maastricht in February, 1992 – a Treaty which conferred substantive
jurisdiction on the European Union in the field of justice and interior affairs.
Such a period is arguably sufficient to permit a fair assessment of what has
taken place in this policy area at EU level, and perhaps also to permit
reflection on possible directions for a future evolution of European-level
cooperation in justice and home affairs matters.

A second reason why the publication of this volume appears timely is the
fact that the fifteen member states of the Union have been engaged in
ongoing discussions on the revision of the Treaties since the intergovernmental conference commenced under the Italian Presidency in the first half
of 1996. The importance of these negotiations to the future shape of the
European Union makes the maximum level of understanding of the issues
involved on the part of all interested Europeans highly desirable, to say the
least. This is particularly the case in view of the fact that the results of these
deliberations are likely to take the form of a revised Treaty, which will have
to be submitted to popular referendum in several member states of the
Union – including the state in which the present volume is being published,
Ireland.

The final factor which arguably makes examination of the field of justice and
home affairs timely is linked to the second, and consists of the fact that in
many respects Ireland, in common with the other member states of the EU,
is faced with important choices as to how it should proceed in this policy
area. Ireland's interests as a small open economy have been well served to
date by a favourable approach towards various initiatives promoting further
European economic integration in the context of the European Community.
However, integration in the field of justice and home affairs is not primarily
economic in nature.[2] And in the policy area of justice and home affairs there
are considerations tending to pull Ireland in a different direction to that of
further integration with Europe.

Through its border with Northern Ireland, the Irish state is geographically contiguous with another member state, the United Kingdom, which has for long been a champion of resistance to communitarisation and seen itself as a resolute defender of state sovereignty and by and large as an opponent of increases in competence or jurisdiction on the part of the institutions of the European Union. It is not just geographical adjacency that links Ireland and the UK in the field of justice matters, but also such factors as the shared and otherwise unique feature in the European Union of being two island states, the fact of sharing a common law legal system, and the high level of cooperation which already exists between Ireland and the UK in relation to many justice policy areas, such as the well-developed extradition arrangements and above all the passport-free common travel area which operates throughout Ireland and Great Britain. With links such as these, choices may have to be made in the field of justice and home affairs between involvement in the further process of European integration and retaining all the features of the present system of cooperation with our nearest neighbour. This, then, is another reason – albeit a somewhat "hibernocentric" one – for careful deliberation to be given to this area of cooperation in justice and home affairs.

One of the most idiosyncratic features of Britain's position in relation to internal security cooperation has been its approach relating to border controls. Under the aegis of the Schengen Agreement (ironically, a non-European Union initiative, although one which has close links to the EU in various ways) every member state of the Union, with the exception of the United Kingdom and Ireland, either has abolished border controls or is committed to doing so in the very near future. With over seventy per cent of all travel in and out of the Republic of Ireland reputedly involving the United Kingdom as place of origin, a place of destination or a transit point, the practical implications of Irish adherence to the Schengen accord for those travelling in and out of Ireland would undoubtedly be considerable, and indeed almost certainly disproportionately so were this to involve an end to the Ireland–UK passport-free zone. Official pronouncements to date have thus, unsuprisingly, attached priority to the maintenance of the common travel area.[3]

However, the difficult position in which UK opposition to the abolition of border controls places Ireland regarding adherence to Schengen should not mean that proper debate within Ireland as to the merits or otherwise of the maintenance of border controls should simply be forgone. It should also be borne in mind that as European integration in justice and home affairs deepens in *other* respects (i.e. apart from border controls), proper debate and consideration of the appropriate policy response by this state to other kinds of initiative will be necessary. If this volume assists in either initiating or furthering any such discussion or debate, it will have achieved its principal goal.

The objective of the publication of this work is to promote understanding of both the realities and the possibilities of cooperation at European Union level in justice and interior (or home) affairs. Apart from Part I and Part V of the book (which address, respectively, the general framework of EU-level cooperation in justice matters and its implications for the fundamental rights of the individual citizen) the general approach has been a theme-based one, with writers having been asked to address particular aspects of the nine areas of justice policy listed by the member states as "matters of common interest" in the Treaty on European Union.[4] Some contributors have chosen to focus on the possibilities for future cooperation, others have concentrated on what has been achieved to date and still others have sought both to report developments and to anticipate future changes. The approaches taken by the writers vary from the approving to the heavily critical. No attempt has been made to censor the various authors' views, and it is hoped that the varied approach may both maintain the reader's interest and assist in furthering knowledge and debate in this area.

Although many of the contributors to this work are lawyers, it is hoped that its readership will go beyond the members of this profession. Ongoing cooperation at European level in justice and home affairs has implications for democracy, for the rule of law, for human rights, for the security and the sovereignty of states, and for the protection from crime of the citizen. Such matters affect everyone, not merely lawyers. It follows that the manner of the present evolution of a European legal space should rightly be the concern of every European citizen.

Before concluding, it is appropriate to thank a number of individuals. Brendan Halligan, Chairperson of the Institute of European Affairs, was of very great help in relation to many aspects of the editorship of this book. The editor is further indebted to both the present director of the Institute, Terry Stewart and his predecessor, Professor Brian Farrell, for their help. The various members of the Third Pillar Steering Committee, the Lawyers' Group, the Intergovernmental Conference Monitoring Group and of course, the Author's Group, too numerous to be thanked individually, were all of assistance. Particular mention needs to be made here, however, of the present Chairperson, Patrick Cooney, Dermot Cole of the Department of Justice, Tom Haughey of Aer Rianta, the Honourable Mr Justice Paul Carney of the High Court, and Professor Patrick Keatinge of Trinity College, Dublin. On the administrative and publications side, Siobhán Couser and latterly Margaret Ahearne were of indispensable assistance. It is also wished to acknowledge the considerable help provided by Odran Reid, Jean Barker and the remaining staff of the Institute of European Affairs, as well as the indispensable and time-consuming work carried out by Iain MacAulay and the Publications Committee in bringing matters to the point of publication. Finally, and on a more personal note, I would like to thank Della and Michael Barrett and Madeleine Roussel-Coumont for their invaluable assistance at all times in the editing of this volume. Without them it would simply not have come about, and to them in consequence – insofar as the present writer has had a role to play in its writing and editing – it is affectionately dedicated.

Gavin Barrett
St Patrick's Day, 1997

NOTES
1. Excerpt from Article K of the draft Treaty put forward by the Irish Presidency in December 1996 as a general outline for a draft revision of the Treaties. See *Adapting the European Union for the Benefit of its Peoples and Preparing it for the Future* (CONF 2500/96)(Brussels, 5 December, 1996).
2. Although at least part of the reason why it is necessary derives from the process of European economic integration.
3. See e.g. reported comments of Mr Gay Mitchell in J. Downing, "UK blocks border-free Europe", *Irish Independent,* 25 February 1997. See more generally in relation to the United Kingdom position on Europe, P. Gillespie, *Britain's European Question – The Issues for Ireland* (Institute of European Affairs, 1996).
4. See Article K.1 of Title VI of the Treaty on European Union. The area of racism and xenophobia has been included as appropriate subject-matter for a chapter in this volume even though it is not included in Title VI of the Treaty on European Union as a matter of common interest (see chapter by W. Duncan). This is because the role which the EU should play here has to date been the focus of much interest. It may be added that if the recent draft Irish Treaty is an accurate guide, this is a policy field which may in the future be made one of the justice and home affairs areas of common interest. (See Article K.1(4) thereof.) In addition, 1997 has been designated the European Year against Racism. (See Chapter 11, *infra.*)

PART I

COOPERATION IN JUSTICE MATTERS IN THE EUROPEAN UNION – THE GENERAL FRAMEWORK

Chapter 1
Cooperation in Justice and Home Affairs in the European Union – an Overview and a Critique

Gavin Barrett

Part I: An overview of cooperation in Justice and Home Affairs

Introduction

Cooperation in the field of justice and home affairs is rapidly assuming prominence as one of the key areas of cooperation in the European Union. It is an area in which interest is heightened by virtue of the very direct impact which the issues coming within this policy area have on individual citizens throughout Europe. Cooperation in justice and home affairs affects such issues as the fight against organised crime, drug addiction and fraud as well as "free movement" policy areas, e.g. immigration, asylum, visa and border controls. Topics such as these have the common feature that they all relate in some way to the question of internal security. This is an area which has for long been perceived as the more-or-less exclusive preserve of the individual nation-state. Indeed the state's capacity to act in this field has been regarded to some extent as being one of its *raisons d'être*. The question may justifiably be asked, therefore, why it has been seen as desirable that the European Union involve itself in such matters. The reasons are, in reality, several. The most important factor, however, has undoubtedly been that of simple practical necessity. In other words, European-level cooperation is taking place because in order to ensure that action taken in relation to any of these issues is effective, much of it *must* take place at European level. The point has been well made that one will inevitably see greater cooperation between countries in tackling internal security problems, regardless of the involvement of the European Union. As Cullen has observed:

> The EU would of course be useful in providing a more coordinated forum for cooperation. The point that should be emphasised, however, is that it is not only because of the EU that countries will decide to cooperate in these areas.[1]

This necessity for European level cooperation merits further explanation. It has its origin in two separate sources. The first source is one which is only indirectly linked with the process of European integration. It consists of the fact that Europe has in recent times been hit by a wave of challenges and problems which either can *only* be dealt with by a concerted effort from the member states or can *best* be dealt with by such action. The streams and currents of world migratory flows pressing on the southern and eastern flanks of the Union are one such challenge. Population movements have been exacerbated in recent times by the economic difficulties of states which border the EU in these regions. Increased numbers of refugees and asylum seekers over the past two decades are a second such challenge. In 1972 there were 13,000 asylum applications in Europe. By 1992 the figure had risen to 550,000.[2] A different kind of problem – but one which is also Continent-wide in its scale – has been the rise since the 1970s of political violence, transfrontier crime, and racist incidents.

Individual European states acting in isolation are frequently too weak to tackle effectively many of these Continent-wide phenomena. Large-scale migratory flows, for example, can be best dealt with through united action. Quite apart from law enforcement measures, it is clearly only on this level that it becomes possible to envisage attempts to address root causes in countries of origin, through, for example, trade assistance or cooperation. Again, a united front on the question of asylum is plainly more advantageous both to the member states themselves and to the asylum seeker. Here there is another reason for common action: to prevent the development of a Europe with fifteen different asylum policies, a Europe in which refugees will be forced to gravitate to the jurisdiction which demonstrates the most tolerance for them, and thus a Europe in which there will be an economic incentive for states to adopt ever more severe admission standards – in other words, the policies of the lowest common denominator.[3] In the long term individual action by states in this area can arguably lead only to beggar-thy-neighbour policies with a generalised lowering of standards of treatment for asylum seekers.[4]

Apart from the interdependences of the member states, and the common threats faced by them, the second factor which has made cooperation at EU level in the field of justice and home affairs a practical necessity has been the very success which has been enjoyed by various aspects of the process of European integration, and in particular the success with which the EU has pursued its goals of the abolition of obstacles to the "four freedoms" – free movement of goods, persons, services and capital.[5] Inevitably, along with the enormous economic benefits which such steps have brought in their wake, have come some disadvantages – in the shape of increased cross-border criminal activity such as drug smuggling, political violence and international fraud. The member states have also been faced with the reality of the increased ease of movement of illegal immigrants. Such Europe-wide challenges, brought about in part by the very process of increased European integration, have been seen to require European-wide solutions. A specific example is that the relaxation of border controls has been deemed to require compensatory measures to be taken in terms of increased police cooperation. (Indeed, any future abolition of such measures will arguably render a common immigration and visa policy on the part of affected states a practical necessity.)

The "expectation that integration in one social-economic sphere would lead to pressure for integration in associated areas" is a recognised phenomenon.[6] Cooperation in the field of justice and home affairs is accurately seen as at least in part the "functional spillover" of the earlier successful attempt to establish the internal market.[7]

There are of course other reasons for European-level involvement in justice and home affairs matters. It is arguable, for example, that increased integration in justice matters has been made more imperative by the continued process of the enlargement of the European Union. It has been observed that

> the events of 1989 have expanded the boundaries of democracy to encompass Central and Eastern Europe and thereby extended the number of potential members to a point where a Union of up to 30 members is feasible. The change from the EEC of the sixties with only six members to the wider Europe in prospect for the next century is best characterised as one from a compact region to an amorphous continent whose eastern and southern borders have yet to be determined.[8]

Two particular consequences of enlargement stand out as being of interest from the justice and home affairs point of view. The first is that eastward expansion will create the prospect of potential large-scale immigration into the EU from the former Soviet Union and the Balkan states as well as increasing the prospect of internal migration from east to west within the EU itself (i.e. with the addition of new states).[9] The second consequence of enlargement will be massively increased commercial contact on the part of the existing member states of the EU with post-communist societies whose business communities have been infiltrated to an alarming extent by organised crime. Germany, geographically contiguous to the former Eastern bloc and economically the most powerful state in Europe, is particularly concerned with the dangers here. But the problems are European-wide in their ramifications and are probably best resolved by concerted action on the part of European states.

Agreement on further enhancement of the EU role in the field of internal security is likely in at least some measure to stem from a further factor – the belief that progress in the area could help to restore the confidence of European electorates in the process of European integration. Thus, in Germany, progress in justice and home affairs is to some extent seen as a *quid pro quo* necessary to counter any negative political consequences which might result from the sacrifice of the Deutschmark in the process of European Monetary Union. As long ago as September 1994, the Lamers-Schäuble Paper called for efforts to combat organised crime and to establish a common policy on migration "with a view to enhancing public acceptance of European integration".[10] The need to win public acceptance is an important factor, given that amendments to the TEU that have resulted from the 1997 intergovernmental conference (IGC) will have to be ratified in all fifteen member states, and be subjected to popular referendum in several of these.

The final point may be made that on the theoretical plane, at least, increased integration in internal security matters and the creation of a European legal space can be argued to be the logical consequence of the ideals which motivated the foundation of the European Communities, and perhaps a way of giving effect to the idea of citizenship of the European Union as conceived in the Treaty of Maastricht.[11] How great a part this particular consideration played in reality in securing the present role of the EU in internal security matters is not clear, however, and it probably formed no part at all in the thinking of at least some member states.

THE FIRST GENERATION OF COOPERATION – THE PRE-MAASTRICHT SCENARIO

The 1970s marked the emergence of major internal security problems, the solutions to which – or at least the optimum solutions to which – clearly lay in the sphere of collective action by the member states. This gave rise to a dilemma, for no structures existed for such collective action, and the European Communities Treaties certainly provided no legal bases for it. The result was the proliferation starting in the mid-1970s and continuing up to at least the end of the 1980s of a series of *ad hoc* structures and groups without any treaty basis, each one designed to constitute the forum for the resolution of particular problems.[12] Thus the TREVI group was set up on the basis of a decision of the Council of Justice and Interior Ministers in October, 1976.[13]

Although operating without permanent staff and without European Commission involvement and although its working groups met only twice a year, TREVI continued to govern police cooperation between the Community partners right up to 1993 (including preparing for the establishment of Europol). Its main focus was on combating terrorism and drug-related and organised crime.

Another important group originating in the 1970s promoting cooperation in the criminal civil law field was the Working Party on Cooperation in the Field of Law. In the 1980s, the issue of immigration forced its way into the agenda. Partly because of this, and partly because of the objections on the part of some member states to the use of Community structures to tackle the issues raised here, yet more *ad hoc* structures were set up. One such structure was the Schengen Group, which, modelling itself on the Franco-German Saarbrücken Agreement of 1984, signed the Schengen Agreement on the gradual implementation of border controls in June 1985, and followed this with the far more extensive Schengen Implementation Agreement of 1991. (At the time of writing, seven states of the EU have applied its terms,[14] a further three are likely to do so in the near future,[15] and the Nordic member states have recently acceded – with the non-EU states of Iceland and Norway having concluded Association Agreements. Only the United Kingdom, and perforce Ireland, have remained outside.)

A further important body, the Ad Hoc Immigration Group, was founded at a meeting in London in 1986 under the British Presidency. In essence, this was an intergovernmental body, but with some involvement allowed to two institutions – the Community and the General Secretariat.[16] The confusingly large number of groups dealing with the free movement of persons led to the setting up of what was called the "Free Movement Coordinators" Group to coordinate their activities at the end of 1988. Meeting once a month and reporting to the Council, this group proved its effectiveness by *inter alia* speedily sowing the seeds of two major initiatives. One of these was the 1990 Dublin Convention Determining the State Responsible for Examining Applications for Asylum Lodged in One of the Member States of the European Communities – a vital initiative intended to govern the treatment of asylum applications in Europe (and, incidentally, the only "positive law" measure to result directly from the "first generation" of cooperation between Community member states).[17] The other major initiative (which has so far fared less well) was the 1991 draft Convention between the Member States of the European Communities on the Crossing of their External Borders (the

"External Borders" Convention). Six years after its initial proposal, agreement in this measure is still not forthcoming – principally, although not exclusively, by virtue of a dispute between Spain and the United Kingdom on whether or not Gibraltar should be included in the area of application of the Convention.

Overall, the first generation of European cooperation in the field of internal security can be seen as the period in which member states discovered the advantages to be derived from pooling their sovereignty in this area. Within this period there were produced not alone several valuable concrete initiatives in the justice field but also the embryonic form of many later initiatives and indeed the skeleton of the administrative model of the next phase of cooperation in justice and home affairs. Less positively, this period can be criticised as having produced a somewhat chaotic and disorganised constellation of working groups, coordinating groups and committees, some of which lacked efficiency, many of which had overlapping jurisdiction and lacked an administrative driving mechanism, and not all of which involved *all* the member states. The system, if it can be called that, cried out for reform, and this was a task undertaken by the Treaty of Maastricht.

THE SECOND GENERATION OF COOPERATION – THE TREATY ON EUROPEAN UNION

The Treaty on European Union (henceforth referred to as the TEU) signed at Maastricht in February 1992 and brought into force in November the following year, contained within its provisions the first comprehensive effort by all the member states to deal with internal security matters. These provisions are set out in Title VI of the TEU, under the heading "Provisions on Cooperation in the Fields of Justice and Home Affairs". Title VI provides no general definition of "justice" or of "home affairs"; instead it deals with nine areas which are to be of common interest. Thus Article K.1 provides that, without prejudice to the powers of the European Community,[18] member states are to regard as matters of common interest: (1) asylum policy, (2) rules governing the crossing by persons of the external borders of the member states and the exercise of controls thereon, (3) immigration policy and policy regarding nationals of third countries, (4) combating drug addiction, (5) combating fraud on an international scale, (6) judicial cooperation in civil matters, (7) judicial cooperation in criminal matters, (8) customs cooperation and (9) police cooperation for the purposes of preventing and combating terrorism, unlawful drug trafficking and other serious forms of international crime. A further nine Articles were also included under Title VI dealing with such questions as, *inter alia*, the instruments to be used to achieve objectives in this area, and the legal structures available to attain these goals. However, the member states' jealous protection of their national sovereignty meant that concessions to supranationalism were minimised. Thus the radical step of bringing cooperation in this area within the existing Community structure was not taken. Indeed, it has been observed by one commentator of Title VI that "its provisions are not amendments to any of the three Treaties establishing the European Communities, hence they are not part of the Community law"[19] and by another that its legal nature "can be described most accurately as being public international law".[20]

Far from *communitarising* cooperation in this area, therefore (in other words, subjecting it to the established system of the European Communities), the basic approach of Title VI has been to continue the intergovernmental approach of pre-Maastricht cooperation, albeit in a more streamlined, intensified and centralised manner.

To the pure waters of this intergovernmentalism were added just a little of the wine of communitarisation, however. Thus Title VI "borrows" some of the institutions of the European Community for its intergovernmental activities viz., the Council, the Commission and the Parliament (the Court of Justice being expressly excluded);[21] but the functions of these institutions are very different to their respective roles in the Community structure. Thus, for example, it is to the Council of (Justice and Interior) Ministers that most of the real power in Title VI is given. This body is the main successor of the ministers who, before the coming into force of the TEU, would have met in the framework of intergovernmental cooperation.[22] The Commission, by contrast, enjoys no role as the exclusive proposer of legislation (a function it enjoys in the Community structure). Rather, it is merely the sharer (with the member states) of a joint right of initiative – except in the field of customs cooperation, police cooperation and judicial cooperation in criminal matters, where the member states have the field to themselves.[23] The European Parliament, again in sharp contrast to its status in the Community sphere, where it enjoys a legislative role – is given very limited rights to be informed, to be consulted and to have its views taken into consideration.[24]

There is, of course, no denying that the Commission and the Parliament have at least some role to play in Title VI. Attaining this was in itself a considerable achievement for these institutions in a policy area in which the dominant wish appeared to be to keep matters intergovernmental. It is an achievement which has been ascribed to a number of factors: the growing political weight of the institutions at the time of the conclusion of the Maastricht accord, the need for apparent consistency of action on the part of the member states which were asserting the existence of a single institutional framework elsewhere in the Treaty on European Union[25] and the role already played by the Commission in some elements of intergovernmental cooperation and in related areas of Community law (e.g. the free movement of persons).[26] In the case of the Commission, its "place at the table" here can probably also be seen as a vindication of its pragmatic decision (taken long before the reaching of agreement at Maastricht), to associate itself with intergovernmental cooperation, rather than to insist intransigently on a communitarisation of justice and home affairs cooperation which the member states would plainly not agree to.[27]

The point may be added that the role played by the Community institutions is not the only link between Title VI and the European Community structure. Another bridge between the two systems is constituted by the provision in the TEU of a "passerelle" procedure – effectively a one-way bridge facilitating the transfer to the Community system of some of the subject matter of Title VI.[28] However, it was always likely that any use of this "passerelle" procedure would be controversial and the fact that the TEU subjects the use of the passerelle to the "double lock" requirements of (a) a unanimous Council vote, plus (b) the adoption of a decision to transfer by the member states in accordance with their respective constitutional requirements made it as good as completely impracticable. The end result of these and other factors has been that the "passerelle" has never been used.[29]

Both institutionally and otherwise, therefore, the links and common features shared by Title VI on the one hand and the Community system laid down in the Treaty of Rome (as amended by the TEU) on the other, remain weak. It is on this basis that Curtin has opined that

> the putative claim ... that the Union shall be served "by a single institutional framework" can, in the light of the substantive provisions of the Treaty, be described, not too unkindly, as mere lip-service to an ideal. It is single only in the sense that the intergovernmental pillars do not have institutions of their own.[30]

Similarly, the point has been made that the European Union has more of "an institutional *géométrie variable* than a single framework".[31]

One should not be too critical. Title VI has plainly led to a valuable intensification of cooperation between the member states. Nonetheless, for a proper understanding of this area one must realise that what is taking place is intensified cooperation on the outer fringe of the Community's institutional system.[32] This "second generation" of joint activity by the member states in the field of internal security can no longer accurately be described as pure intergovermentalism – but it is not unfair to characterise it (as one observer has done) as "improved intergovernmentalism".[33]

Title VI is frequently described as the "third pillar" of the European Union, the image being that of the portal of a Doric temple, with the first and second pillars of the entrance being, respectively, the European Communities and the system of cooperation in foreign and security policy. It follows from the foregoing, however, that this image is somewhat misleading as it purports to give the impression of uniformity in the shape or structure of cooperation that goes on within, for example, the European Community on the one hand and under Title VI on the other. The European Union (which to date, unlike the European Community, has been conferred with no legal personality and thus, for example, has no capacity to conclude international treaties in its own right)[34] has been more accurately compared to a tarpaulin-like structure or an umbrella, covering the very widely differing structures of, first, the European Communities,[35] secondly, the Common Foreign and Security Policy,[36] and thirdly, Title VI.[37]

Such a description is not intended to decry the level of cooperation which has been attained in the European Union, however. On the contrary, the frequency of meetings of experts in justice and home affairs matters at European Union level has, by the time of writing, reached a very high level, by any standard. During the Irish Presidency in the latter half of 1996, the number of meetings on such issues reportedly extended into three figures. As Morgan has accurately pointed out:

> It appears that within the legal framework of an intergovernmental set-up, we may be seeing some of the actual practice conforming more to an integrated mode of behaviour and of policy making, even though it is not formally a supranational one.[38]

Furthermore, sight should not be lost of a second major point: that political preconditions exist for cooperation in this field which do not exist in other policy areas. In internal security matters, politicians may enhance their prestige by announcements that cooperation with the forces of law and order in other countries has led to successful joint police operations or the more successful combating of crime. By contrast, forays by individual national leaderships of member states in the field of the Middle East or in the former Yugoslavia have demonstrated the belief of politicians that in the foreign policy area individual initiatives can yield more profitable dividends in terms of political kudos than does joint action with other member states.[39]

Cooperation in Justice and Home Affairs Outside Title VI

Before proceeding to a critique of the operation of Title VI in practice, mention should be made of a point which has considerable potential for confusion. This is the fact that although cooperation in internal security matters now takes place *primarily* in the framework of Title VI, it does not take place *exclusively* there.

Cooperation in the Sphere of the Community's Activities

As mentioned earlier, the jealously protective attitude of the member states of their sovereignty prevented much jurisdiction being conferred on the Community in internal security matters in the Maastricht Treaty, or indeed in the negotiations of the Single European Act which preceded it. Nevertheless, such opposition did not extend to preventing *any* Community involvement in justice and home affairs issues.

Thus the European Community Treaty includes among the activities of the Community the abolition of obstacles to the free movement of persons.[40] The Treaty further stipulates that the internal market is to comprise an area without internal frontiers in which, *inter alia*, the free movement of persons is ensured in accordance with the provisions of the Treaty.[41] An even clearer example of Community competence in what can be characterised as internal security matters is constituted by the Treaty's conferring of jurisdiction on the Community to determine the third countries whose nationals must be in possession of a visa when crossing the external border of the member states[42] – a power which was duly exercised, although after lengthy political wrangling, with the adoption of a Council Regulation doing just that in September 1995.[43] The Community also has jurisdiction in the field of the prevention of drug dependence,[44] and has competence in the area of fraud.[45] In terms of secondary legislation, Community Directives have been adopted on matters ranging from money laundering, to data protection, to insider dealing, to firearms, as well as including a Council Regulation aimed at discouraging the use of certain substances.[46]

Having said this, the Community's role should not be exaggerated. In visa policy, for example, it goes little further than the power to compile a uniform visa list, and, as Niemeier has somewhat scathingly characterised it, "the design of a visa sticker".[47]

The existence of competences on the part of the Community on the one hand and Title VI structures on the other can be said to give rise to at least one potential problem. This consists of the danger of overlapping jurisdiction. Frontier regulation, data protection, fraud prevention and the prevention of drug addiction are topics which all straddle the divide between the European Community and the Title VI system, creating the risk of overlapping or even conflict between Community legislation on the one hand and Title VI measures on the other.[48] It is somewhat puzzling to note the somewhat peculiar fashion in which competence of the European Community on the one hand and the Title VI system on the other were fixed by the TEU. Great care was taken to ensure that, within the Title VI structure, neither the "passerelle" procedure nor the Commission joint right of initiative would apply to customs cooperation, judicial cooperation and criminal matters or police cooperation.[49] But this approach ignored the reality that certain topics under these headings *already* fall squarely within the jurisdiction of the European Community – with the very considerable involvement of the European Parliament, the European Court of Justice and the European Commission – which Community competence in any policy area involves. Examples of such topics are the Community's competences in relation to, for example, money-laundering [50] and customs cooperation.[51]

Overall, however, notwithstanding this unsatisfactory overlap, and notwithstanding the untidiness of having some justice and home affairs matters dealt with in the Community sphere and some, indeed most, catered for within the structure of Title VI, it must be acknowledged that the present distribution of competences is, to some extent, a reflection of the political reality that communitarisation of this entire sphere of European level internal security cooperation is simply not on the agenda for most (if not all) member states of the Union. Advocates of communitarisation will therefore have to content themselves for the foreseeable future with a situation in which competence to act in this area is carried out only to a limited extent within the Community structure. However, a somewhat less artificial demarcation line between Community competence and Title VI system competence would clearly be desirable.

Flexible or Differentiated Integration in Internal Security Matters

Apart from the fact that both the Title VI system and (to a more limited extent) the Community have jurisdiction in sometimes overlapping areas of internal security, another potential source of confusion exists in that there is yet another tier of European-level cooperation in this field. This tier consists of the Schengen system – a group of states whose intergovernmental cooperation here forms a surviving remnant of the "first generation" of *ad hoc* intergovernmental cooperation in justice and home affairs. The adherents to the Schengen Agreement of 14 June 1985 on the gradual implementation of border controls at the common frontiers and the Implementing Convention of 19 June 1990 have now expanded to include all of the member states of the EU except Ireland and the United Kingdom. With the effective absorption by the Schengen system of the Nordic common transport area at the end of 1996, even two non-EU member states, Norway and Iceland, were added to this system through the device of Associated Agreements. This has created the remarkable phenomenon of an area either free of border controls or soon to be free of border controls from the Mediterranean to the Arctic Circle and from the eastern end of the territory of the European Union to the furthest western point of the European mainland.

It is important to realise that, unlike Title VI and the European Community, the Schengen system is not a part of the structure of the European Union. However, there are both legal and operational links between the two structures. Thus, for example, only member states of the EU can formally accede to the Schengen accords.[52] Furthermore, by its own terms, the provisions of the Schengen Implementing Convention of 1990 are specifically made to apply only insofar as they are compatible with Community law.[53] Links like these are not confined to the terms of the Schengen treaties. There is also the provision of Article K.7 in Title VI of the Treaty on European Union itself that

> the provisions of this Title shall not prevent the establishment or development of closer cooperation between two or more member states in so far as such cooperation does not conflict with, or impede, that provided for in this Title.

This was included in the Treaty of Maastricht with the specific objective of facilitating the continued existence of the Schengen system and initiatives like it.

In reality, the links go even further than the contents of the above provisions would indicate. The deepest link of all is the reality that the Schengen system has effectively acted as a substitute for reform at EU level in the area of border controls. Negotiations on the EU's own External Borders Convention long ago reached deadlock, and Community proposals in the area of free movement of persons have no "immediate prospect of adoption".[54]

The constitutional significance of this substitute development should not be underestimated. Much ink has been spilt and much debate occasioned on the topic of "differentiated integration" and "flexibility" within the European

Union and on the need for interested states to be permitted to proceed with further integration within the EU structure where a unanimous desire on the part of *all* member states to cooperate on a deeper level is lacking. Schengen is of importance as the example *par excellence* of what can happen if such pressures for differentiation are not accommodated within the structure of the European Union itself. It is an example which has both positive and retrospective aspects. The tremendous achievement of the extra-EU development constituted by Schengen is not to be underestimated, namely, the abolition of frontier controls (or their imminent abolition) in the greater part of the territory of western Europe. But not all of the features of the system used to bring this about are equally praiseworthy. Thus, the secretive nature of the workings of the Schengen executive committee – a body set up to administer the working of the Schengen Agreement – and the fact that this committee arguably operates without adequate democratic and judicial scrutiny, have rightly given rise to grave misgivings.[55] Developments such as the abolition of border controls effected by Schengen, as well as the operation on information-sharing and of rules governing asylum – aspects which also form part of that accord – should be brought about in a structure which provides adequate controls.

Overall, it may be concluded that outright opposition on the part of a minority of member states to the abolition of internal border controls being brought about within an EU context has not stopped this very phenomenon being made to come about throughout most of the territory of the EU. All such opposition has achieved [56] is merely to have driven the mechanism for effecting the abolition into the field of *ad hoc* intergovernmentalism, where it has arguably acquired some of the most undesirable features of this method of cooperation. It is submitted that there are lessons to be learned here which are of general significance for the constitutional structure of the European Union. In the specific context of justice and home affairs, Schengen constitutes visible proof (if any was needed) that the era of differentiated integration and "variable geometry" has already arrived. The form such differentiated integration takes in future developments in this area, as well as the question of whether it takes place inside or outside the existing structures of the EU, remain to be seen, however.

With the passage of time, optimistic predictions that Schengen might be superseded by Community or Title VI initiatives are coming to seem less likely.[57] Another possibility, however, is the absorption of some of the Schengen *acquis* itself into the structure of the European Union.[58] The explanatory comments on the draft Treaty which was presented by the Irish Presidency in December 1996 mentioned that an important issue requiring further consideration by the Conference is whether the Schengen Agreement should be incorporated into the Treaty on European Union. It has been suggested that this might be done in a phased way with a provision for opt-outs.[59]

However, whether this particular suggested Treaty reform will be acceptable to all fifteen member states negotiating the revision of the Treaties is as yet unclear.

PART II: A CRITIQUE OF THE OPERATION OF TITLE VI

As has already been indicated, the bulk of cooperation in justice and home affairs matters at European Union level takes place within the structure of Title VI of the TEU. The remainder of the present chapter is therefore devoted to a brief critique of the operation of Title VI from two separate but interlinked perspectives:

- the efficiency and effectiveness of the Title VI system in achieving cooperation in the area of justice and home affairs

- the level of openness and democratic and judicial control in the Title VI structure.

The general point may be made at the outset that the coming into effect of Title VI brought improvements on both of these fronts. Thus the centralisation and streamlining of the greater part of the web of *ad hoc* intergovernmental bodies into a hierarchical structure with the Council of Ministers at the summit clearly enhanced the efficiency (and indeed the capacity) of the member states in taking effective action in internal security matters. Testimony has arguably been borne to this point by the fact that it was possible for the draft Treaty drawn up by the Irish Presidency at the end of 1996 to suggest the expansion of EU cooperation in the justice and home affairs field to include a broad range of new activities – *all* forms of police cooperation, combating trafficking in persons and offences against children, combating illegal drug trafficking,[60] preventing and combating racism and xenophobia, judicial cooperation in civil and commercial matters,[61] preventing and combating corruption and "ensuring consistency in the rules applicable to the member states on conflicts of law and jurisdiction in civil and commercial matters".[62] The boldness of this proposal bespeaks a certain level of satisfaction on the part of member states with the progress achieved to date in relation to existing "matters of common interest".[63]

The level of openness, as well as democratic control, in the field of cooperation in justice and home affairs matters was also upgraded with the adoption of the TEU – although, as shall be argued, to a level still unacceptably low – by conferring through Title VI of at least some role, however minimal in practice, on the European Parliament, the European Commission and, at least potentially, the European Court of Justice.

Having noted that Title VI constitutes an improvement, under both headings, on the pre-existing situation, the case should not be overstated. As shall be seen below, there is much to be criticised in the operation of Title VI. The apparently obvious answer is a radical structural change.

But many reforms that might seem obvious at first sight are in practice extremely difficult to achieve because of the strong links between the right of action in the internal security field and what some member states perceive to be the appropriate level of retention of their sovereign rights here. Title VI has been accurately described as "hybrid: essentially intergovernmental but with a dash of the supranational, mainly pooling sovereignty but also partly transferring it".[64] The compromise between intergovernmentalism and communitarisation constitutes one which member states can be reluctant to see altered in favour of European Union institutions and away from themselves. This factor overshadows much of the discussion of this area of policy cooperation.

EFFICIENCY AND EFFECTIVENESS OF TITLE VI

As has already been observed, from the perspective of effectiveness and efficiency, the operation of Title VI must be counted as a success if compared with the first generation of cooperation in this area. The work, in particular of the Coordinating Committee of senior officials set up by Article K.4 of Title VI, has ensured that collective initiatives in this area are now more systematic, better coordinated and more rational in their approach. With the number of meetings in the area of justice and home affairs running into several hundred a year, cooperation in this area is now at a much more intensified level than was formerly the case. Nonetheless, this relative success must be characterised as highly qualified in nature. On the legislative front, in particular, activity has been pitifully slow for most of the existence of Title VI – with initiatives in key areas such as border controls, police cooperation, asylum, bankruptcy, fraud and customs either having been blocked for inordinately lengthy periods of time or, when finally agreed, having taken, without any obvious justification, a similarly long time to develop into any form of rule which is enforceable within the legal systems of the member states.[65] Progress in this respect has compared very unfavourably with the level of activity which has been capable of being achieved in the context of the European Community.

Some of the reasons for the difficulties which exist are structural, and it is intended to return to these presently. But it is important to realise that the blame for any slowness in decision-making under Title VI cannot all be attributed to structural factors.

POLITICALLY SENSITIVE NATURE

The particular nature of the subject matter of Title VI counts for a great deal. This includes the highly politically sensitive nature of some of the issues involved in internal security matters.[66]

JUSTICE OFFICIALS WORKING TOGETHER

A second unique feature of EU cooperation in this policy area is that it involves officials in various national ministries of justice and interior affairs working together on a frequent basis. The significance of this point should not be overlooked. Unlike national government departments dealing with matters such as agriculture, industry and trade, there was little tradition of either cooperation at international level or the sharing of information by such departments at European level prior to the coming into force of the TEU. Writing in 1995, Fortescue cited as one of the features of the present system which has been most unconducive to progress:

> the fact that in these early days, the ministers and ministries involved are not yet sufficiently accustomed to the working methods and disciplines of the Council to seek actively ways of making decision-making possible with any kind of urgency.[67]

INEVITABLE NEED FOR TIME

National departments of justice and interior ministries have a tendency to be among the institutions least likely to be wedded to a tradition of openness and information-sharing. Indeed, although the learning process may be lengthier in the case of justice ministries than elsewhere, the reality has been acknowledged that it takes time for an institutional tradition and heritage to grow in any new area of cooperation. In the member states' cooperation in relation to matters governed by Title VI, a process of trust-building has therefore had to take place. In other words, member states have to learn by experience (and continue to do so) that it is possible to cooperate and rely both on other member states and on EU institutions such as the Commission in relation to the sensitive matters dealt with under Title VI.

CAUSE AND EFFECT

A third factor which has to be borne in mind in order to avoid putting any undue blame for law-making inertia on the structures of Title VI is the danger of confusing cause and effect. Some of the blame for the lack of activity in justice and home affairs cooperation can rightly be attributed to a lack of a unanimous political will on the part of the member states themselves. This much said, however, the structures of Title VI can be rightly criticised if an inappropriate balance is struck between the protection of the interests of each individual member state and the efficient working of cooperation in this area. Thus the question of the requirement of unanimity which must be met prior to the taking of most action under Title VI is examined further below.

Notwithstanding the above-listed excusing factors, it is nonetheless arguable that several serious structural flaws exist in Title VI which tend to decrease the efficiency and effectiveness of cooperation in this policy area over and above the extent to which proper working of Title VI ought to have been affected. It is now proposed to enumerate briefly these argued-for flaws. In doing so, it is worth pointing out that since administrative efficiency within the EU tends to be popular with a broad spectrum of opinion, ranging from its most hostile critics to its most ardent supporters, it is likely that the correction of at least some of the following contended-for defects will result from the intergovernmental conference. This much, as shall be seen presently, is something which cannot be said for many of the flaws which affect the level of openness and democracy in Title VI rather than merely its short-term efficiency.

STRUCTURAL FLAWS IN TITLE VI

LACK OF SPECIFIED OBJECTIVES

Some of the legislative lethargy in the area of Title VI may be attributed to the failure of the member states to have specified either precise objectives or deadlines under this Title. In contrast to the activities of the Community listed in the EC Treaty (which stipulates such aims as the creation of common agricultural, transport and commercial policies as well as of an internal market) the list of matters coming within Title VI are described by Article K.1 of Title VI as merely to be regarded as "matters of common interest ... for the purposes of achieving the objectives of the Union, in particular the free movement of persons". This is a formulation which binds member states to no specific course of action in relation to such matters.[68]

There is an absence not just of broad overall policy goals here, but also of objectives within particular policy areas. Achermann has posed the question:

What is the common interest in immigration and asylum policies? The interest appears "common" insofar as cooperation is better for member states than uncoordinated action and because most of the states have the same or similar problems with immigration and asylum. But interests are not exactly the same for all states, nor is the need for action equally urgent. Some states, for example, have less asylum seekers or serve only as transit states. Besides the common interest, there are – as in most other political fields – conflicting national interests. Member states with a high number of asylum seekers and refugees, for instance, call for fair burden sharing, which, of course, other states are not willing to accept.[69]

While this may underestimate the potential for compromise, it is certainly true that, to some extent, the member states are only gradually arriving at agreement on the goals which they ought to pursue in the field of justice and home affairs. The 1997 intergovernmental conference may have accelerated this process of agreement on appropriate objectives. The draft Treaty prepared by the Irish Presidency at the end of 1996 stipulates the broad objective, in the justice and home affairs policy area, of the development of the European Union as an area of freedom, security and justice, in accordance with the principle of the rule of law (even suggesting the setting of an overall target date to achieve this aim) and contains an extensive setting-out of objectives in many particular areas in this policy field.[70]

THE REQUIREMENT OF UNANIMITY

It is difficult to know whether an element as crucial to the existence of Title VI as is the requirement of unanimity can be termed a "flaw" – for without the safeguard of the requirement of a unanimous vote in respect of most matters arising under Title VI, it is clear that not all member states would have been prepared to adhere to this Title at Maastricht.[71] Nonetheless, the question which we are at present addressing is the efficient and effective operation of the regime for cooperation in internal security and there can be no doubt that the requirement of unanimity constitutes a serious impediment to action here. Indeed, it is worthy of note that certain measures, e.g. the adoption of conventions and the use of the above-mentioned "passerelle" procedure, are subjected not alone to the requirements of unanimity, but to what has been termed a "double-lock" in the form of requirement of unanimity *plus* approval by all member states in accordance with their respective constitutional requirements; this may involve anything from the sanction of national parliaments to approval in popular referenda.[72]

The unanimity requirement leads to several consequences, not all of them immediately obvious. At worst, where common ground cannot be found by all fifteen member states, a requirement of unanimity will obviously lead to paralysis in progress in the relevant area. But even where it is eventually possible to reach the agreement of all parties, the need to comply with the unanimity requirement can lead to a watering down of the provisions so as to reach the level of the lowest common denominator.[73] Alternatively, the requirement of unanimity may give rise to the necessity to adopt a non-binding text. The unanimity requirement rule is said to have a particularly paralysing effect in justice and home affairs matters, by reason of the lack of a long tradition between the various ministries (such as that which exists in the case of, e.g. finance ministries) of acknowledging the need to seek compromise and make concessions.[74]

This much said, the perceived link between the requirements of unanimity and national sovereignty means that the rule of unanimity is far from a guaranteed candidate for removal from any area at present covered by Title VI. It is difficult to envisage each and every one of the fifteen states being ready to agree to anything other than a unanimity requirement in relation to all or indeed any areas at present coming within the subject area of Title VI, when the results of the 1997 IGC emerge, unless some kind of variable geometry can be constructed so as to exempt the states with the most serious concerns here, from the application of qualified majority voting.

However, the needs of efficiency in Title VI may make change from the requirement of unanimity imperative. This is especially so in view of the prospect of the enlargement of the Union which is now looming. For if the unanimous agreement of the fifteen member states is now difficult to secure, what would it be like to secure unanimity in an enlarged European Union of twenty states or more?

CUMBERSOME DECISION-MAKING STRUCTURE

The operational structure for Title VI was set up by effectively superimposing extra administrative layers on top of structures which owed their existence to the days of pre-Maastricht *ad hoc* intergovernmentalism. The result of this has been that cooperation in justice and home affairs is now administered by a five-level bureaucratic structure consisting of (in descending order from the top of the structure) the Council of Justice and Interior Ministers, the Committee of Permanent Representatives ("Coreper"), the "Article K.4" Committee of senior officials, three Steering Groups,[75] and below these a large number of working groups. (See diagram on p. 92, *infra*.) Such a cumbersome structure (with one more level than in equivalent Community structures) seemed bound to slow down the rate of cooperation, and a considerable amount of friction within and between different levels

21

and confusion as to respective roles seems to have duly taken place. This was the case, for example, in the early stages of Title VI in clearly establishing the respective roles of Coreper and the K.4 Committee, although initial difficulties here seem to have resolved themselves into the working arrangement that Coreper now deals more with political problems while the K.4 Committee concerns itself more with difficulties which are of a primarily technical nature.

Reform of the decision-making apparatus seems to have been one of the few areas in which a consensus in favour of change clearly existed in the Reflection Group on the Intergovermental Conference which reported at the end of 1995.[76] It seems that steering committee level is the tier most likely to be removed from the Title VI decision-making structure as a result of the 1997 intergovernmental conference.

LACK OF A BODY WITH INITIATIVE-TAKING ROLE

The efficiency of EU cooperation in the field of justice and home affairs appears to suffer, to some extent at least, from the absence of a single body with an impetus-creating and initiative-taking role (along the lines of the role which the Commission fulfils in the European Community structure).

Under Title VI the Commission enjoys a right of initiative in most of the areas of internal security which are enumerated in that part of the Treaty. In reality, this right is not as impressive an entitlement as it might at first sight seem. In the case of customs cooperation, police cooperation and that limited form of police cooperation which comes within Title VI, a Commission role is excluded, and the right of initiative is lodged exclusively with the member states.[77] And even in the remaining areas, instead of enjoying an exclusive right of initiative as it does in the European Community structure, the Commission shares its right to initiate legislation with the member states.[78] In practice, this shared right of initiative is a very different creature to an exclusive right to put forward legislative proposals. For a start, instead of the Commission being able to set the agenda for debate (as it can in the Community sphere by virtue of the exclusive right of initiative which it enjoys there) in Title VI the Commission finds itself in competition with the member states insofar as it attempts to put forward proposals in the justice and home affairs policy field. Put another way, in the Community sphere, the Commission proposals are guaranteed to be the "only show in town" and the member states must base their approach either on supporting them (whether in their original or in a modified form) or opposing them, for they can put forward no alternative proposals of their own. This is not the case in internal security matters.

Thus there is no similar effective guarantee that whatever proposals the Commission puts forward will be seriously considered at all by the member states. Furthermore, from the date of coming into force of Title VI, the Commission has been at something of a disadvantage when it comes to putting forward initiatives in the field of justice and home affairs, in the sense that – unlike the member states themselves – it is relatively new to this area of cooperation between the member states (from which it was largely excluded, or, at most, given only observer status, prior to Maastricht). Thus it has found itself given no easy task in ensuring that its policy proposals here can offer member states added-value over and above those initiatives which they can table for themselves in this field.[79]

In practice, the Commission has been extremely reticent in putting forward proposals for legislation in this area. However, apart from the above considerations[80] it is submitted that there are strong reasons militating against the taking of any other approach by the Commission. First, there is the danger of alienating member states, some of whom, Fortescue has observed, "are almost pathological in their determination to keep the Community institutions out of the process".[81] In such circumstances, the Commission must obviously be careful to behave in a way of which the member states broadly approve. Otherwise, it is scarcely likely to see its competences extended by those same member states either now or at any point in the future. A second factor militating against activism on the part of the Commission is the fact that it must guard against the danger of alienating large swathes of public opinion. Such alienation could be quickly brought about by taking controversial positions in the justice and home affairs field, for this is an area of policy which is highly politicised, and in which public opinion is capable of dividing upon party and/or ideological lines. Taking strong stances in internal security matters can thus be seen as an approach fraught with danger for the Commission, and perhaps for the European Union itself. In these circumstances, it is scarcely surprising that the Commission has adopted a "softly-softly" approach in justice and home affairs, concentrating on enhancing its credibility, through, e.g. tabling communications, rather than tabling controversial legislative proposals.[82]

In conclusion, it may be observed that although the Title VI structure seems lacking in a body which would take the initiative in the field of justice and home affairs, and that this factor has inhibited its efficiency and effectiveness, the point should not be lost that there could potentially be dangers in creating a body with such a right of initiative without also adequately expanding democratic answerability in this area, so as to provide a pressure valve for any public disquiet that might arise because of the activities of such an initiative-taking body. In other words, it seems arguable that reform of the impediment to efficiency constituted by the lack of an initiative-taking body in Title VI should be addressed side-by-side with the reform of a different problem (discussed at a later point in this chapter) – the relative lack of responsiveness to democratic forces of the Title VI system.

LACK OF SUITABLE LEGAL INSTRUMENTS

The final structural problem in Title VI which has arguably had a retarding effect on the effectiveness and efficiency of justice and home affairs cooperation is the absence of a clearly defined and suitable legal instrument facilitating harmonisation in this area.

Article K.3 of Title VI introduced new legal instruments into this policy area, specifying that the Council could adopt joint positions, joint actions and conventions. Regrettably, however, it did not go on to specify the respective legal consequences of the former two instruments – and the predictable result of this has been that relatively little use has been made by the Council of ministers of joint actions and positions.

Joint positions, probably the least potentially useful of the three instruments, have been argued not to produce any legal effects as such.[83] Müller-Graff has opined that a "joint position is to be understood as a joint declaration or recommendation without a legally binding effect on member states".[84] If this is correct, it means that the joint position is an instrument which was never likely to be of much use in the field of justice and internal security.

Joint actions, on the other hand, may well produce legal effects – although the point of whether it *does* or not is far from clear one way or the other – which makes their use an unattractive option for member states.[85] Despite some increase in joint actions and joint positions, neither instrument could be described as having received any kind of extensive use since the TEU came into force.

The third type of instrument, and "the only instrument of cooperation clearly binding upon the member states" [86] is the *convention.* Reasonably extensive recourse has by now been had to the use of this instrument (by December 1996, sixteen such instruments were under discussion or had already been signed).[87] A convention – in other words, an international treaty – is a legal instrument, a process of agreement which has not materially changed since the time of its use in the early part of the twentieth century in the conclusion of e.g. the Treaty of Versailles. Conventions suffer from the defect of being slow, cumbersome means of achieving objectives. Even when they have been agreed by all member states, conventions must then be ratified by member states according to their respective constitutional requirements. This is itself a slow process, and one which is not guaranteed to be successful since national parliaments can refuse to ratify conventions. By December 1996, not even one convention under Title VI had completed its ratification process in all member states of the Union.

The point should be made before passing from this topic, however, that there may be some risk of confusing cause and effect in discussing the legal instruments available to be used in Title VI. While it seems desirable to have legal instruments capable of rapid adoption and which have clear legal consequences, in order to advance cooperation in justice and home affairs in the European Union (and indeed the draft revised Treaty put forward by the Irish Presidency at the end of 1996 contains proposals to this effect),[88] it is nonetheless far from clear that the member states will be prepared to use "hard law" measures of this type in a policy area of such sensitivity.[89] To date far more use has been made by the Council of non legally binding instruments such as resolutions, recommendations, statements, opinions and communications than has been made of joint actions, joint positions or conventions. The former category of instrument is regarded as having the advantage of flexibility and of being capable of speedy adoption. Such instruments also successfully influence the policy direction of member states without falling prey as easily as "hard law" measures to the accusation of being an infringement of national sovereignty (since they impose no legal compulsion on the member state). Cullen has maintained that

> steady progress can be achieved outside of the confining law-making framework now provided for in the First Pillar, without member states having to be overly coerced. Once this has been achieved, and only when there is greater confidence among member states in their ability to meet necessary criteria – can one consider embarking upon a more rigid form of harmonisation.[90]

However, the crucial caveat must be entered that although reliance on measures such as statements, opinions and communications may increase the efficiency of justice and home affairs cooperation, it is not without grave dangers too. Such measures are completely immune from scrutiny by either national parliaments or the European Parliament. However, the risks involved in this are more closely linked to the questions of democracy and openness than to the issues of efficiency and effectiveness. It is proposed to examine these issues in the context of the next section of this chapter.

OPENNESS, DEMOCRACY AND JUDICIAL REVIEW AND COOPERATION IN TITLE VI

Apart from analysing the performance of Title VI by reference to how effectively and efficiently it operates, it is possible to examine its performance against a second set of criteria, i.e. its legitimacy as judged by reference to such standards as openness, democracy and judicial review. Judged from this perspective, although the Title VI system is obviously an improvement on the pre-existing *ad hoc* intergovernmentalism, it is also the case that there is much to criticise here, and an urgent need for redesign.

JUDICIAL REVIEW – ROLE OF EUROPEAN COURT OF JUSTICE

Judicial control of what goes on in Title VI can best be described as minimal. National courts for their part have traditionally kept their distance from the kind of diplomatic activity and intergovernmental cooperation which was the essence of cooperation in justice matters prior to the agreement of the TEU at Maastricht (and which to a large extent is still the system that prevails). The distance between national courts and international cooperation may fairly be said to be particularly marked in Ireland and the United Kingdom. Both of these states have what are called "dualist" legal systems, which means that an international treaty must be enacted into national law before it can be invoked before the courts. Even within the purely domestic sphere, the role of national courts in certain issues coming within Title VI, e.g. immigration and visa policy, varies widely from state to state. In some fields the degree of intervention by the courts of some states has been slight indeed.

The advent of very extensive cooperation at EU level in the justice and home affairs area has now created additional reasons for judicial intervention of a sort which in some cases national courts are or will be unable to supply. An example here is the need which now exists to provide for a uniform interpretation of legal instruments such as conventions which are adopted under Title VI. A further such challenge is the need to impose judicial control on the structures of Title VI so as to counterbalance at least in some measure the lack of democratic accountability there. Alternatives to the European Court of Justice as institutions or bodies capable of assuming these tasks are in short supply. With recourse to other international tribunals such as the European Court of Human Rights or the International Court of Justice having its own disadvantages,[91] it might have been expected that representatives of the member states meeting at Maastricht would have conferred the same kind of jurisdiction on the Court of Justice in Title VI matters as it enjoys in the Community system. In reality, more or less the opposite happened: the Court of Justice was specifically excluded from a role in relation to the bulk of issues arising under Title VI.[92]

The work of the Court of Justice in relation to Title VI is confined to that of a kind of gatekeeper, with power merely to guarantee that member states do not deal with Community matters under Title VI and that Title VI measures do not violate Community law. Under Title VI, the Court has no jurisdiction in respect of joint positions, no jurisdiction in respect of joint actions, no jurisdiction in relation to the variety of non-binding legal instruments such as communications, statements and recommendations which the member states have employed in this policy field – and the Court has jurisdiction over conventions only if the member states decide to stipulate (on an individual basis) that it should have this.[93] The reasons given for the exclusion of the Court of Justice have been many, but opposition to a role for the Court seems to be based primarily on a generalised opposition to the extension of jurisdiction of Community institutions and on the sensitive nature of the areas of policy coming within Title VI (which, as has been noted, are not always the subject of extensive control even by the national courts).[94]

The exclusion of the European Court has created a dissymetry between Title VI and those aspects of justice and home cooperation which fall within the Community system, and can be said to have had several serious consequences for the operation of Title VI. Groenindijk has observed that in the Community system, the Court of Justice traditionally performs four different tasks, (a) stimulating compliance with the rules of Community law by the member states, (b) ensuring the uniform interpretation of Community law, (c) protecting the rights of individuals, and (d) deciding disputes between member states and Community institutions regarding Community law.[95]

The exclusion of the Court from Title VI, by contrast, has left a complete institutional void when it comes to the fulfilment of these tasks. Thus, for example, as a result, there is no tribunal or body in existence which is empowered to provide the member states with an answer to the question of the precise legal effect of joint actions.[96]

Further, the protection of individual rights – by reason of the lack of jurisdiction on the part of the European Court of Justice – is left entirely to the courts of the member states. This is despite the wide variations in the availability of formal procedures to challenge operational decisions in this area.[97]

Again, the exclusion of the European Court of Justice means that Title VI arguably suffers from the absence of adequate mechanisms to ensure that member states meet their obligations in timely fashion. The need for such mechanisms is met in the Community system through the provision of the possibility of infringement proceedings before the Court of Justice, and through the availability of the option (and sometimes the obligation) for national courts to refer questions of EC law to the European Court of Justice.[98] Whether such a rigid system would be appropriate to a policy area as sensitive as that of justice and home affairs may well be open to question, but the complete absence of the European Court of Justice from this area arguably sits uncomfortably with any idea of supposedly enforceable obligations in Title VI.

The failure to provide for the inclusion of the role for the Court also means that there is no guarantee of a uniform and consistent interpretation of measures adopted under Title VI.[99]

Finally, perhaps one of the most serious arguments in favour of the need for a role for the Court of Justice in this area is the legitimacy which this would add to the process of integration. Independent judicial control is fundamental to the rule of law in any governmental system.[100] Not alone is such control desirable *per se*, but it is rendered additionally necessary in the context of Title VI by the arguable absence of adequate democratic control of this area (a topic which shall be returned to presently) .

Notwithstanding the foregoing considerations, extension of the Court's jurisdiction to the areas falling within Title VI is a step which would seem to be wholly unlikely at present to win the unanimous assent of all member states. The precise results of the intergovernmental conference are difficult to predict. "Variable geometry" in this respect, i.e. different arrangements for different states, might be one possibility. Of interest in this regard is the system adopted (although only after a considerable period of political discussion and debate) in the Protocol to the Europol Convention, whereby each member state was given the option to declare that its national courts or only its higher courts may request a ruling from the Court of Justice.[101] This may not be an ideal solution to the problem of the lack of judicial control in Title VI, but it is, at least, some form of solution, and one which would certainly be a vast improvement on the present arrangements.

LACK OF PARLIAMENTARY CONTROL

The European Parliament was given no law-making role as such under Title VI of the TEU. (Although the Parliament does have a Committee on Civil

Liberties and Internal Affairs, the main role of this body has been described as drawing up own-initiative reports, opinions and resolutions.)[102] Perhaps in consequence of the fact (already touched on in the text above), that the basic approach of Title VI is an improved form of intergovernmentalism, the substantive entitlements conferred on the European Parliament by Title VI of the TEU are of a fairly weak nature. The Presidency, i.e. the member state holding, for the moment, the Presidency of the Council of Ministers, and the Commission are obliged to "regularly inform" the Parliament of discussions in the area covered in Title VI. Furthermore, the Presidency is required to consult the European Parliament "on the principal aspects of activities in the areas referred to (in Title VI) and shall ensure that the views of the European Parliament are duly taken into consideration".[103]

In practice even these few limited rights have been given virtually the narrowest construction possible. Thus the Council at an early stage decided that the duty to "inform" the European Parliament would involve merely "informally" forwarding Council documents to the Parliament – denying members the right to automatically receive the documents before Council meetings and thereby produce any kind of worthwhile opinion.[104] The complaint – remarkable in the attitude it reveals on the part of the Council – has been heard that even journalists and governments of third countries engaged in the work of the Council can at times be better informed than the European Parliament.[105] Monar has contrasted the more agreeable attitude of the Commission towards supplying information to the Parliament but has noted:

> In the areas of intergovernmental cooperation, however, it is the Presidency which is in the centre of the decision-making process, and most of the member states prefer to restrict information for the European Parliament to a minimum. Communications to the Parliament are usually vague and evasive, and it has happened frequently that Parliament has been left in the dark as regards the precise legal status of texts adopted by the governments or that texts have been forwarded with considerable delays or even not at all.[106]

Similarly Parliament's right to be consulted "on the principal aspects of activities" in Title VI areas has in practice resulted in nothing like the level of consultation which is the normal practice in the Community field. The reason for this appears straightforward. With no Court of Justice to enforce and delimit the extent of Parliament's right to be consulted, it is in practice entirely a matter for the Presidency to decide what precisely are the "principal aspects" upon which Parliament must be consulted. The results have been a regrettably predictable restrictive approach.

Finally, the obligation on the Presidency to take the views of the European Parliament into consideration has in practice yielded little benefit. It may be noted that it is a somewhat incompletely expressed obligation, since no indication is given as to how, or even in what forum, Parliament's views are to be taken into account.[107] In practice, this has in the past been described as having been a "purely symbolic provision"[108] (although there has been a gradual improvement here, so that Parliament's opinion is now reportedly asked on all Conventions which are proposed under Title VI).

It is not merely that Parliament has begun with a marginalised role under Title VI. It appears to have met with fairly persistent opposition on the part of the member states to any improvement of its lot. Use of the passerelle procedure to transfer issues into the Community system (where Parliament has a far more substantial role) was never really on the agenda for the Council. But Parliament also failed to secure the taking of other, less ambitious steps which would have improved or consolidated its role, e.g. securing the necessary support from the Council for an inter-institutional agreement which would serve the valuable function setting out Parliament's precise role in Title VI matters.[109] Member states had also avoided any possibility of Parliament using its very considerable powers over the European Community budget as an indirect means of gaining any control in this area, by the simple expedient of charging operational expenditure in Title VI directly to member states, rather than to the Community budget.[110]

In some respects Parliament has not always assisted its own case here. In the first place, its early doctrinaire insistence on communitarisation of all areas of Title VI – even when this was plainly not going to be on offer in the near future – was scarcely likely to endear it to member states concerned about the maintenance of their national sovereignty.[111] Secondly (as might have been expected) time has been needed for the Parliament to develop an expertise, and to demonstrate its efficiency, its commitment and its standing in relation to justice and home affairs issues.[112]

Any proposal to increase the jurisdiction of the European Parliament would be a controversial step within the 1997 intergovernmental conference [113] and yet it is difficult to see what other bodies would be capable of exercising adequate democratic control over activities in Title VI in the future. The suggestion that national parliaments could fulfil this task seems an unlikely one.

In the first place, for a variety of reasons, such bodies would be unable to exercise the required control. Many national parliaments have only a weak system by which to scrutinise European-level developments in justice and home affairs areas. Moreover, with few exceptions, as Monar has observed,

> (National) parliaments do not have the possibility to discuss major issues of justice and home affairs before their governments commit themselves at the European level. The information provided by the governments is usually not only scarce but rather late. Information on particularly important points on the agenda of cooperation frequently only results from good personal contacts of individual members with government circles or indiscretion revealed by journalists.[114]

It is of interest that Ireland has been mentioned by some commentators as one of the states with a particularly low level of information provided to its national parliament.[115] Even in states whose parliaments have relatively strong powers of scrutiny, however, there have been difficulties in the exercise of control here.[116] This much said, there is nonetheless doubt that national parliaments have an invaluable role to play in injecting an element of democracy and transparency into this policy area. Neither should an increase in the involvement of national parliaments be seen as an incursion into the territory of the European Parliament, or (and this is important) *vice versa*. The reality – regrettably often unappreciated by parliamentarians at either national or European level, who tend to be jealous of their own institutions' powers [117] – is that national parliaments and the European Parliament should have complementary roles in increasing the level of openness in decision-making. Rather than it being a question of the European Parliament taking over work which is presently carried out by national parliaments, or the latter bodies taking over the work of the former institution, the appropriate common aim is arguably the opening to democratic scrutiny by either body of those decisions which are at present unnecessarily carried out in a shroud of bureaucratic secrecy.

The further reality must be recognised, however, that no matter how effective its parliamentary powers of scrutiny, a national parliament can at best only exercise influence over one Minister out of fifteen at the Council of Ministers. Control over the Council as a collective entity is only capable of being exercised by a European-level institution, such as the European Parliament. At the moment, however, Parliament has not been given adequate tools to do this job.

The consequences of this situation for the democratic control of the government of the European Union are not to be underestimated. What has been created is something without parallel at national level in normal times – law creation by a Council of Ministers almost completely untrammelled by

Parliamentary scrutiny, and to a large degree untroubled by judicial control.[118] Although it is true that even the European Community system has never corresponded exactly to a simple separation of powers model, the exclusion of both the Court of Justice and the European Parliament from Title VI has produced a singular and worrisome absence of effective checks and balances in the structures of cooperation in justice and home affairs in the European Union.

The issue of sovereignty can be seen to have reared its head here. Some member states appear to have taken the view that the giving of additional powers to the European Parliament here is to be avoided as "communitarisation through the back door".[119] If democratic control is to be maintained over an increasingly significant area of activity of the European Union, however, the simple reality is that there will be little alternative for the member states to the further empowerment of the European Parliament.

ABSENCE OF DEMOCRATIC FEATURES IN TITLE VI

The fundamental objection to the present operation of the structures of Title VI in terms of their implications for democracy has been stated as follows: "Decisions with far-reaching consequences for individual rights and freedoms are made in secret by committees of ministers who are under no obligation at present to do more than announce their conclusions." [120]

Since democratic government is an ideal the desirability of which seems now largely unquestioned, and all member states of the Union are democracies, it seems fair to ask why it has been acceptable that Title VI should be so lacking in such obvious democratic features as, for example, the adequate involvement of an elected assembly. A number of reasons suggest themselves as likely explanations.

The most obvious has already been touched upon, and consists of the fact that member states, anxious to safeguard their sovereignty, were unwilling to contemplate further transfers of competence to the European Community. Steps such as the greater empowerment of the European Parliament in Title VI would have been regarded (perhaps with some justification) as leading to indirect communitarisation of justice and home affairs issues. However, much of such opposition to increased European Parliament involvement in justice and home affairs cooperation arguably involves the error of viewing the assignment of competences in this policy field as necessarily involving transfers of sovereignty from member states to the European Union. There can be a failure to see the synergy involved in cooperation at European level – in other words, the fact that by acting as a collective unit, member states have created, in the field of justice and home affairs, as in other policy areas, a new tier of sovereignty, acquiring the power to take action and to meet challenges which could not be addressed by them in isolation, and the power to do so in a way which is greater than the sum of the individual abilities of the member states added together. Infusion of democratic control by the European Parliament into cooperation in justice and home affairs at EU level arguably need not involve as large a transfer of sovereignty from national level as is sometimes thought, since to some extent at least, such empowerment of the European Parliament would merely be democratisation of competences which do not exist at national level. And indeed, as has already been seen, it may also be democratisation which it is simply not possible to effect at national level.

Apart from sensitivity about national sovereignty, three further factors appear to have played a role in the relative lack of democratic features in Title VI. One of these is that the field of internal security has always been one where, even at national level (and perhaps for sound practical reasons) there has been a higher degree of secrecy and discretion and "a strong tradition of discrete working methods of informing ministers only if they have to take responsibility and of keeping the information of parliaments (and the public) at the lowest possible level".[121] The continuation of this general approach when high levels of cooperation came to be demanded at European level was therefore perhaps to be expected. However, this is a mere historical reason for such an approach rather than a rational justification for it.

A third reason for the lack of obvious democratic features in Title VI may stem from its intergovernmental roots. The still basically intergovernmental structure of Title VI extends, as we have seen, to the use of the public international law instruments of conventions – in other words, international treaties – as the primary legislative instrument. Intergovernmental cooperation in general, and the negotiation of international treaties in particular, has, for reasons of efficiency, tended to be the preserve of the executive, with only weak controls imposed on them at national parliamentary and judicial level. This practical necessity can be put forward both as an historical and a theoretical justification for the absence of clear democratic elements in Title VI itself. The difficulty here however is that government is increasingly carried on at international level – and in the particular context of Europe, at European Union level. More and more aspects, including justice and home affairs, are coming to be dealt with on this plane. There is "a new European order in which large sections of national government are being transferred to executive bodies at European level'.[122] Curtin and Meijers have pointed out that when portions of government power are transferred to an international organisation,

> there will be a loss of democratic content if the international organisation does not have a parliamentary body which has as many powers as a national parliament, if there is no international court which has jurisdiction to review the legality of the acts of the international organisation, and if the openness which is observed at the national level in respect of the transferred areas of government is undermined as a result of the transfer of government to the closed international circuit.[123]

In the specific context of the European Union the former writer has elsewhere argued plausibly that

> from the point of view of liberal democracy the danger of democratic retrogression is real if matters are taken out of the national systems and intergovernmentalised, but not within the Community system (with its concomitant parliamentary and judicial control).[124]

Adherence to the traditional methods of intergovernmental cooperation has both its advantages (in terms of increased short-term efficiency in decision-making) and its advocates (particularly those individuals and states who are most anxious to prevent what they would see as the wholescale erosion of state sovereignty). But such advocates face an uphill struggle, it is submitted, insofar as they seek to deny the force of the argument that the subject matter of Title VI "is too important to be left to national civil servants and government ministers in the habit of operating – at least in the Union context – in the cushioned twilight of ministerial, diplomatic and administrative ante-chambers".[125]

A fourth historical reason (and indeed a theoretical justification) for the absence of obvious democratic features in Title VI is that the view has been taken by at least some states that even *without* any such features, inter-governmentalism in Title VI is nonetheless soundly based on democratic structures. According to this view, Title VI derives its legitimacy from the fact that decisions in its field of application are taken by the unanimous vote of government ministers each of whom is individually answerable to a national parliament.[126] This is an attractive view if one prefers to see nation states as the sole entity capable of conferring democratic legitimacy. But the practical reality seems to be that even if this kind of reasoning could be argued to provide some kind of theoretical democratic legitimacy for actions taken within Title VI continuing to be taken by intergovernmental decision-making structures, subject only to national parliamentary scrutiny, such an approach cannot provide real and adequate democratic control here.[127]

Possible methods for increasing the level of democracy in Title VI could include a greater role for the European Parliament (whether secured through Treaty amendment or through inter-institutional agreement). Other steps would also arguably help, however, such as increased effective scrutiny by national parliaments of Title VI activity, increased cooperation between the European Parliament and national parliaments, and an improvement in the level of openness and transparency in European-level cooperation in this field. The last point is a crucial one. It is proposed to focus upon it briefly.

OPENNESS AND TRANSPARENCY IN TITLE VI

TRANSPARENCY AS AN ESSENTIAL ELEMENT OF DEMOCRACY

The general rule in Western European-style democracies is that legislative assemblies perform their law-making task in the full glare of publicity, which in turn is provided by such features as the publication of draft legislation, the fact that they must meet in open session and the fact that parliamentary debates are reported. Indeed, the requirement of such publicity is generally seen as essential to the functioning of the democratic system.[128] It is therefore strongly arguable that in so far as a democratic deficit may be said to exist in the rule-making apparatus in Title VI, central to this elimination will be the sweeping away of the information and publicity deficit which exists to a large degree in relation to its law-making activities.

It is perhaps somewhat surprising to realise (given the difficulty which exists in discovering what precisely has been decided in relation to cooperation in justice and home affairs) that the member states explicitly acknowledged the importance of transparency to democratic government in the Maastricht text. In the Declaration on the Rights of Access to Information annexed to the Final Act of the TEU it was stated that transparency of the decision-making process strengthens the democratic nature of the institutions and the public's confidence in the administration.

In practice, however, the depth of the member states' conversion to this view is to be doubted, especially in view of what has been the well-documented resistance of the Council to the idea of releasing documents or information relating to deliberations on internal security matters.[129]

TRANSPARENCY AS A CIVIC RIGHT

Linked to the idea of publicity for law-making being essential to democratic government is the further argument that the right of access to information is appropriately viewed as a right of the citizen in a democratic society. However, opposition by member states to any linking of citizenship to such sensitive issues as border controls and the general policy areas of internal security meant that no such advanced notion of citizens' rights was adopted at Maastricht. Instead, the citizenship provided for in the Maastricht accord was one which focussed to the point of near-exclusivity on the rights of those citizens who opt to live and work in another member state of the Union.[130] Even in the wake of Maastricht, it has been noticeable that the focus of discussions of extensions of the concept of citizenship of the Union has tended to be mainly on formal legal rights and protections.[131] However, it seems arguable that, as de Búrca has put it, that

> if citizenship is to be a legitimating force in the context of the EU, it must constitute and make possible a genuine connection between the person and the polity. European Union citizens must at least have the possibility of a role to play in its system and institutions if they are to feel a sense of political commitment towards the Union.[132]

A certain level of confidentiality will obviously always be required in the policy area of internal affairs, e.g. in the interest of security or to protect the right to privacy or commercial confidentiality. But the degree of secrecy surrounding the meetings of the steering committees and working groups (whether the result of deliberately thought-out policy or not) and even the widespread ignorance among non-specialists as to the existence of these bodies and of the K.4 Committee itself, seems unnecessary. Yet there seems to be no good reason for this lack of openness. At national level, reforms to, e.g. immigration law or asylum regulation are debated in public fora. Why should this not be the case at European level?

At least some of the historical reasons for the lack of openness are undoubtedly the same as those adduced in the text above for the lack of democratic structures in Title VI. However, it seems possible that there are some additional factors at play here. Thus O'Keeffe for example has pointed out that the problem of an information deficit is more pronounced in the Title VI area than elsewhere in the structure of the European Union partly because the K.4 Committee, and its steering committees and working groups, "are not subject to the copious 'leaks' which occur at Community level and which are an unorthodox, but practical way of remedying the information deficit".[133] Secondly, there is probably also an element of spillover from the observance of high standards of secrecy in operational matters in internal security cooperation – where confidentiality is doubtless often important – to the use of the same approach in the taking of decisions in relation to policy matters. The problem is, however, that in the field of policy-making, secrecy is not alone generally unnecessary, but also positively undesirable.[134]

As matters stand, the lack of advance publicity and consequent lack of consultation with the public, with non-governmental organisations, as well as with national parliaments and with the European Parliament, has arguably had some degree of negative effect on the outcome of decision-making in Title VI. It is scarcely surprising, with decision-making being taken in this fashion at intergovernmental level, that many of the initiatives undertaken under Title VI appear to bear the hallmark of the search for maximised administrative or executive efficiency, rather than any wider political concerns. Thus, for example, in asylum policy the broad thrust of initiatives has been at ensuring that the fifteen different asylum policies of the Union are applied in a coordinated fashion rather than attempting to harmonise their substantive rules. This has been characterised by one commentator as starting reform at the wrong end, with member states being "prepared to recognise each other's negative decisions on (asylum) applications, in whatever way arrived at, and to reduce twelve asylum shops to one supermarket with near empty shelves".[135]

A culture of transparency is arguably needed in Title VI, and such a culture could be introduced into Title VI in a number of ways. The publication in the Official Journal of draft measures and final decisions alike would be of considerable value. And for as long as recourse is to be had to non-legally binding measures such as recommendations, communications and opinions in order to advance the policy agenda in Title VI, it is arguable that similar publication requirements should apply in relation to these measures. Institutional Codes of Conduct requiring extensive disclosure should also become the norm, particularly as regards the Council.[136] More fundamental reform, involving the European Parliament in the decision-making process, is arguably also needed. Apart from openness in government being a democratic imperative, and arguably a civil right, increased transparency would have a powerful legitimating effect on the structure of cooperation in justice and home affairs.

It may well be that more openness in Title VI could have a cost in terms of short-term administrative convenience and efficiency – but it would seem that rejection of an open approach to cooperation in justice and home affairs would ultimately cost more in terms of public alienation. Indeed, insofar as it is feared that too much exposure to the harsh glare of publicity might destabilise cooperation in Title VI, it is submitted that the appropriate response to this worry is the stabilisation of the Title VI edifice through the construction of democratically responsive structures within it – not the shrouding of important decisions in an atmosphere of confidentiality to an inappropriate degree. As has been argued by one commentator,

> A more open and wider process of consultation and information, even one which reveals the divisions over the nature and direction of European integration, needs to take place.[137]

CONCLUSION

By way of conclusion, a certain number of themes which have appeared either expressly or implicitly in the foregoing text may be mentioned here.

The first point is that it seems likely that continued increased cooperation at European level in justice and home affairs is likely to take place, whether or not the pressures for such cooperation are accommodated within the structure of the EU. Schengen has already been one example of such pressures having to be accommodated outside the structure of the EU.

Secondly, notwithstanding its structural flaws, dwelt upon at some length above, the limitations of the system of cooperation in justice and home affairs need to be seen in the context of its very considerable achievements. As many of the succeeding chapters in this volume testify, Title VI has proved of considerable benefit to the citizens of Europe, and will continue to do so as the various conventions and measures agreed under its aegis on a wide variety of themes come on stream.

Thirdly, it should not be forgotten that many of the argued-for structural flaws in the Title – such as the exclusion of a greater role for the European Parliament and the European Court of Justice, and the ubiquity of the requirement of unanimity – have simply been the price of consensus among the member states. In other words, they are concessions which had to be made to one or more member state in order to win an agreement on justice and home affairs in the Treaty on European Union. On this basis, Title VI may be said to be an example of an area in which strong attachment on the part of states to their sovereign rights is to some extent frustrating both (a) the efficient and effective operation of cooperation (i.e. by virtue of the all-encompassing nature of the unanimity requirement, regardless of its effect on the efficient working of Title VI) and (b) the potential for the infusion of legitimating elements into the structure of Title VI (such as a democratic input from the European Parliament, and judicial review by the European Court of Justice). In other words, Title VI appears to mark the location of a policy area where the requirements of state sovereignty, as presently interpreted by at least some member states, and those of the individual citizen, may well diverge to a certain extent.

Fourthly, Title VI now appears to be a policy area where, at European level, the checks and balances which are normally accepted as a necessity to restrain the powers of government are largely absent. Just as it was deemed necessary at a certain point in history for the power of the state to be divided up to prevent any danger of abuse of power, it seems arguable that a similar development should occur in relation to Title VI, and that the largely untrammelled power of the Council in this area be subjected to appropriate judicial and parliamentary control.

Fifthly, the opposition of the member states (with the United Kingdom tending to be in the vanguard here) to many of the reforms advocated in the text above makes it appear very likely that what is variously referred to as "variable geometry" or "differentiated integration" – i.e. a number of states of the Union proceeding ahead of the other member states along the road to further integration – will come about. It is very likely that this approach will be reflected in the results of the 1997 intergovernmental conference.

Sixthly, cooperation in justice and home affairs seems to be one area of the activities of the European Union which would benefit from greater openness. Transparency here would arguably improve the quality of the decision-making, as well as enhancing public acceptability of initiatives in this field. Quite apart from this, openness may be argued to be a necessary feature of a democratic government and a civic right of the individual citizen.

Seventhly, and linked to the question of openness, there is arguably a very great need to impress upon the citizens and electorates the value of current EU-level cooperation in justice and home affairs. This need stems from two sources. The first is that future deepening of beneficial cooperation and internal security matters will inevitably depend on such integration being acceptable to the public. The second is that the revisions to the Treaties which will be agreed upon by the 1997 intergovernmental conference will almost certainly have to be approved by the electorates in many of the EU states, including Ireland. Creating an awareness of the useful role played by EU-level cooperation here could be of considerable value in winning public acceptance of the merits of continued European integration.

By way of a final point, and on a broader level, it is submitted that in relation to Title VI there is an especially strong argument to be made that mainly bureaucratic intergovernmental methods of building an integrated Europe may now have exhausted their potential.[138]

Czech President Vaclav Havel has stated:

> If the citizens of Europe understand that it is not just an anonymous bureaucratic monster that wants to limit or even deny their autonomy, but simply a new type of human community that actually broadens that freedom significantly, then the European Union need not fear for its future.[139]

It is submitted that particular account needs to be taken of such comments in relation to cooperation in the fields of justice and home affairs in the European Union. They should serve both as a warning of the dangers which exist and as a guide to the choice of an appropriate future *modus operandi* for cooperation at European Union level in this policy area.

NOTES

1. D. Cullen, "Variable geometry and overlapping circles: in search of a suitable model for justice and home affairs" in R. Bieber and J. Monar (eds.) *Justice and Home Affairs in the European Union* (1995) at p. 91.
2. D. Joly, "The porous dam: European harmonisation on asylum in the nineties" (1994) *IJRL 159* at p. 163. Some of this increase would have been due to growing restrictions on legal immigration.
3. See here Amnesty International, "Europe: the need for minimum standards in asylum procedures " (AI Index EU Ass/01/94).
4. States which have generous policies towards refugees can argue with some justification that they should not be penalised for showing more regard for human rights than do their neighbours. An analogous process of logic led to the insertion of sex equality provisions relating to employment in the Treaty of Rome in 1957, the logic here being that the French did not want to be prejudiced economically by reason of their more progressive policies in this regard. See in relation to asylum, chapter 10 in this volume by B. Shipsey.
5. See Article 3 of the EC Treaty (as substituted by Article G(B)(3) of the Treaty on European Union).
6. See chapter 2 in this volume by B. Tonra, *infra.*
7. Note in this respect the reference in Article K.1 of the Treaty on European Union to the earlier established objective of free movement of persons. Morgan has argued that "the phenomena that have accompanied the liberalisation of the internal market lead to an internationalisation or transnationalisation of societies in Europe, including their problems. This is why we now face the question of the right sort of institutional set-up for the collective management of this range of problems." See R. Morgan, "The Third Pillar: an introduction" in J. Monar and R. Morgan, *The Third Pillar of the European Union* (European Interuniversity Press, 1994) at p. 15 thereof.
8. Institute of European Affairs, *1996 Intergovernmental Conference: Issues Options Implication* (1995) at p. 30 thereof.

9. It should be noted however that the question of immigration is not one solely raised on the eastern flank of the EU alone. See in relation to the demographic trends in the south of the EU *Mediterranean Partnerships* (Philip Morris Institute, 1995) at pp. 20-21.

10. This paper has been published as an annex to K. Lamers, *A German Agenda for the European Union* (Federal Trust for Education and Research, Konrad Adenauer Foundation, 1994).

11. See argument to this effect in P. Müller-Graff, "The legal bases of the Third Pillar and its position in the framework of the Union Treaty" in Monar and Morgan, *op. cit.,* at p. 30 thereof.

12. There was precedent for the lack of a legal basis for such bodies. Interpol, founded in 1923 in Vienna as the International Police Commission, has no treaty framework. (See M. Anderson, M. den Boer and G. Miller, "European citizenship and cooperation in justice and home affairs" in A. Duff, J. Pinder and R. Pryce, *Maastricht and Beyond* (Routledge, 1994) at p. 113 thereof.)

13. See European Parliament Directorate General for Research, *Cooperation in the Fields of Home Affairs and Justice* (PE162.500). TREVI allegedly stood for "Terrorisme, Radicalisme, Extremisme et Violence Internationale" although in reality it seems likely that the name's origins had as much to do with the group's place of birth. See generally in relation thereto, J. Peck, "International police cooperation within justified political and juridical frameworks: five theses on TREVI" in Monar and Morgan, *op. cit.*

14. Although France only incompletely, due to a long-standing dispute between that state and the Netherlands over the latter's drugs policy.

15. Viz. Austria, Italy and Greece.

16. W. de Lobkowicz, "Intergovernmental cooperation in the field of migration – From the Single European Act to Maastricht" in Monar and Morgan, *op. cit.,* at p. 107.

17. de Lobkowicz, *op. cit.,* at p. 110 and see generally here pp. 107-117.

18. As to which see text below.

19. Müller-Graff, *op. cit.,* p. 24.

20. F. Snyder, "Institutional development in the European Union: some implications of the Third Pillar" in Monar and Morgan, *op. cit.,* at p. 89 thereof.

21. Article L of the TEU.

22. See Müller-Graff, *op. cit.,* pp. 25 and 26 for an analysis of the Council role.

23. Article K.3(2) of the TEU.

24. Article K.6(2). The Parliament may in addition ask questions of the Council or make recommendations to it, although this guarantees neither that proper answers will be provided to the former, nor any real account taken of the latter.

25. See Article C of the TEU.

26. See here J. Monar, "The evolving role of the Union institutions in the framework of the Third Pillar" in Monar and Morgan, *op. cit.,* at pp. 69 and 70 thereof.

27. *Ibid.,* at pp. 71 and 72.

28. Article L. 9 of the TEU. The communitarisation of a subject as currently dealt with in Title VI can also take place by means of the normal process of Treaty amendment. This process is provided for in Article N.1 of the TEU.

29. See here, e.g. D. O'Keeffe, "Recasting the Third Pillar" (1995) *32 CML Rev. 893* at pp. 899-901, R. Bieber, "Links between the 'Third Pillar' (Title VI) and the European Community (Title II) of the Treaty on European Union", in Monar and Morgan, *op. cit.,* at pp. 43-47. It has been observed that, in the case of Denmark, use of the passerelle may well have required a constitutional amendment.

30. D. Curtin, "The constitutional structure of the Union: a Europe of bits and pieces" (1993), *30 CMLR 17* at p. 28.

31. Editorial Comments, "Post-Maastricht", *29 CMLR Rev. 199* at p. 202 quoted in Curtin, *loc. cit.*, See for an interesting analysis of the topic of variable geometry and cooperation in justice and home affairs, D. Cullen, *loc. cit.*, in Bieber and Monar, *op. cit.*, at p. 65 thereof.
32. Curtin, *loc. cit.*, at p. 19.
33. Terminology employed by de Lobkowicz, *op. cit.*, at p. 118.
34. Note the provision in Article K.5 of the TEU that "within international organisations and at international conferences in which they take part, member states" – rather than the Union itself – "shall defend the common positions adopted under the provisions of this Title."
35. i.e. the European Coal and Steel Community, the European Atomic Energy Community and the European Community (formerly the European Economic Community).
36. See Title V of the TEU.
37. See here Curtin, *loc. cit.*, at pp. 23-24.
38. Morgan, *op. cit.*, at p. 16.
39. A point made by Morgan, *op. cit.*, at p. 18.
40. See the reference in Article K.1 of Title VI to the objective of the free movement of persons. Article 3(c) of the EC Treaty (as inserted by the Article G(B)(3) of the TEU).
41. Article 7a of the EC Treaty. Article 7a was originally inserted as Article 8a of the Treaty of Rome by Article 13 of the Single European Act (SEA) and was renumbered Article 7a by Article G(B)(9) of the TEU. Note that there are strong disagreements on the topic whether Article 7a (when read together the reserve power conferred on the Community by Article 235 to take action necessary to attain the objectives of the Community) confers power on the Community to extend freedom of movement to third country nationals, and whether it requires the ultimate abolition of border controls. See here, e.g. K. Hailbronner, "Migration law and policy within the Third Pillar of the Union Treaty" in Bieber and Monar, *op. cit.*, at pp. 98-100. For a general study of this area see J. Handoll, *Free Movement of Persons in the EU* (Wiley, 1995).
42. Article 100c of the EC Treaty (as inserted by Article G(D)(23) of the TEU).
43. Council Regulation EC/2317/95 of 25 September, 1995, Determining the Third Countries whose Nationals must be in Possession of Visas when Crossing the External Borders of the member states.
44. Article 129 of the EC Treaty (as inserted by Article G(D)(38) of the TEU).
45. Article 209a of the EC Treaty (as inserted by Article G(E)(77) of the TEU).
46. See here Anderson, den Boer and Miller, *op. cit.*, at p. 113 thereof. In relation to e.g. money laundering, see Council Directive 91/308/EEC (10 June, 1991) (OJ L 166/77) and on its implementation into Irish law, see D. O'Neill, "Money laundering and the Criminal Justice Act, 1994", *Bar Review,* December 1996.
47. M. Niemeier, "The K.4 Committee and its position in the decision-making process" in Bieber and Monar, *op. cit.*, at p. 322.
48. See here O'Keeffe, "Recasting the Third Pillar" (1995) *32 CMLRev* at pp. 911 to 913.
49. See Article K.9 and Article K.3(2) of the TEU respectively.
50. As to which see footnote 46 *supra.*
51. As to which see, e.g. Council Regulation (EEC) No. 1468/81 (1981 Official Journal C144/1) as amended by Council Regulation (EEC) No. 945/87 (1987 Official Journal L90/3) and cf. chapter 6 in this volume by D. Gilroy.
52. Hence the need for Norway and Iceland to accede to the Schengen System through the mechanism of Association Agreements.
53. Article 134 of the Implementing Convention. Cf. Article 142 thereof which provides that when the member states of the European Communities have concluded conventions to achieve the area without internal frontiers, the Contracting Parties to Schengen will determine which provisions of the Schengen Convention require to be modified or replaced as a result.

54. Perhaps a side effect of this substitute role is the striking similarity in some respects of Schengen Agreement provisions and those of EU measures such as the Dublin Convention Determining the State Responsible for Examining Applications for Asylum Lodged in One of the Member States of the European Communities. This similarity has been remarked upon in the past. See, e.g. D. O'Keeffe and R. Piotrowicz, "Asylum law and practice in the United Kingdom" in K. Hailbronner, *Comparative Law of Asylum and Immigration in Europe* (Europäische Rechtsakademie, Trier, 1992) at p. 50.
55. See here D. Curtin and H. Meijers, "The principle of open government in Schengen and in the European Union: democratic retrogression?" (1995) *CML Rev 391* esp. at pp. 402-416 thereof.
56. That is, apart from the self-imposed exclusion of the United Kingdom which could arguably be achieved anyway at EU level.
57. See, e.g. Anderson, den Boer and Miller, *op. cit.*
58. This was mentioned as a possibility by the Reflection Group in its Report of 5 December 1995 (SN 520/95 (Reflex 21)) at Paragraph 54 thereof.
59. See "Adopting the European Union for the benefit of its peoples and preparing it for the future – a general outline for a draft revision of the treaties" (CONF 2500/96, Brussels, 5 December, 1996).
60. Article K.1 (7) additionally renders judicial cooperation in criminal matters a subject of common interest and Article K.1(9) does the same for police cooperation for the purposes of preventing and combating, *inter alia*, unlawful drug trafficking.
61. Article K.1(6) of the TEU as it now stands specifies as a matter of common interest only judicial cooperation in civil matters.
62. See generally the suggested new Article K.1 as found in the draft Treaty proposal, *op. cit.*, at p. 30 thereof.
63. See here the suggested new Article K.1 as found in the Irish Presidency's draft Treaty proposal, *op. cit.*, at p. 30 thereof.
64. Anderson, den Boer and Miller, *op. cit.*, pp. 115-116.
65. See for some useful criticisms here, D. O'Keeffe, "Recasting the Third Pillar", *loc. cit.*
66. A point made in, e.g. the Council Report of 6 April, 1995 on the Operation of the Treaty on European Union (5082/95) at p. 30.
67. J. Fortescue, "First experiences with the implementation of Third Pillar provisions" in Bieber and Monar, *op. cit.*, at p. 27.
68. It has been pointed out that in determining matters of "common interest", member states did not want to take a position with regard to the definition of competences of the EC, since Article K.1 specifies that matters of common interest are "without prejudice to the powers of the European Community". See A. Epiney, "Switzerland and the Third Pillar: implications and perspectives" in Bieber and Monar, *op. cit.*, at p. 338.
69. A. Achermann, "Asylum and immigration policies: from cooperation to harmonization" in Bieber and Monar, *op. cit.*, at pp. 129-130. Achermann observes that in 1993, Ireland had only 65 asylum seekers, while in the same year Germany had 320,000.
70. See "Adapting the European Union for the benefit of its peoples and preparing it for the future", *op. cit.*, at pp. 18-36.
71. Effect is given to the requirement of unanimity by Article K.4 which stipulates that the Council shall act unanimously, except on matters of procedure and in certain other limited circumstances – viz., (i) where the Council decides that measures implementing joint action are to be adopted by a qualified majority (see Article K.3(2)(b) and (ii) in implementing conventions, which, unless thy provide otherwise, are to be adopted within the Council by a majority of two-thirds of the contracting parties (see Article K.3(2)(c)).

72. See Article K.3(2)(c) and cf. D. O'Keeffe, "Recasting the Third Pillar", *loc. cit.,* at p. 898.
73. See Commission Report of 10 May, 1995 on the Operation of the Treaty on European Union at Paragraph 121 thereof.
74. Fortescue, *loc. cit.,* p. 26.
75. Dealing with respectively (a) immigration and asylum, (b) police and customs cooperation and (c) judicial cooperation in civil and criminal matters.
76. *Op. cit.,* at Paragraph 51.
77. Article K.3(2) of the TEU.
78. Writing in 1995, O'Keeffe suggested that, *de facto*, the Commission also shared its right of initiative with the Article K4 Committee (D. O'Keeffe, *loc. cit.,* at pp. 896 and pp. 902-903.
79. See here P. Myers, "The Commission's approach to the Third Pillar: political and organizational elements", in Bieber and Monar, *op. cit.,* at p. 286.
80. That is, the non-exclusive nature of the Commission's right of initiative and its relative lack of experience in this field.
81. Fortescue, *loc. cit.,* at p. 21.
82. Fortescue, *loc. cit.,* p. 24. The Commission has also simultaneously had the difficulty of having had to focus on the issue of its own initially rather unsuitable internal organization and of having to reconsider its own – originally unfavourable – attitude to the intergovernmentalised nature of cooperation in this area. See generally, Myers, *loc. cit.,* pp. 281-283 and p. 298.
83. Apart from the obligation placed on member states to defend them within international organisations and at international conferences (Article K.5 of the TEU). See D. O'Keeffe, *loc. cit.,* at p. 914.
84. *Loc. cit.,* at p. 35. The concepts of joint positions and joint actions are also found in (and indeed may have originated in) Articles J.2 and J.3 of Title V. Title V is entitled 'Provisions of the TEU on a Common Foreign and Security Policy'.
85. See D. O'Keeffe, *loc cit.,* at p. 914.
86. K. Hailbronner, "Migration law and policy within the Third Pillar of the Union Treaty" in Bieber and Monar, *op. cit.,* at p. 102.
87. See generally here, K. Groenendijk, "The European Court of Justice and the Third Pillar", Paper delivered to Conference on Political Union and The Agenda of the IGC, Irish Centre for European Law, 30 November, 1996.
88. *Op. cit.,* at pp. 34-35. See proposals for "specific decisions", "framework provisions" and the proposed reforms regarding the adoption of conventions.
89. See Hailbronner, *loc cit.,* at pp. 103 to 104.
90. D. Cullen *op. cit.,* p. 81.
91. In the case of the European Court of Justice (assuming the existence of the right of individual petition), recourse may be had to it by individuals only when domestic remedies have been exhausted, which may take a considerable period of time. The jurisdiction of the International Court of Justice is available only to resolve disputes between states and its application to the areas covered by Title VI is, in any case, unclear. (See O'Keeffe, *loc. cit.,* at p. 914.)
92. Article L of the TEU.
93. See Article K.3(2) and Article L of the TEU. A good examination of the Court's role is found in K. Groenendijk, *loc. cit.* Cf here also N. Neuwahl, "Judicial control in matters of justice and home affairs: what role for the Court of Justice?" in Bieber and Monar, *op. cit.,* at p. 301. O'Keeffe has pointed out that the Court also has a role in relation to the Community budget – but the practice until very recently has been to charge operational expenditure to the member states rather that to the Community budget, so that this jurisdiction has been effectively excluded. (See Article K.8 of the TEU and see O'Keeffe, *loc. cit.,* at p. 909).

94. Other arguments offered have been, e.g. the supposed adequacy of national courts, the availability of the European Court of Human Rights and the supposed lack of experience of the Court of Justice in such matters, although for a variety of reasons none of these reasons seems particularly convincing.
95. *Loc. cit.*, at p. 2.
96. Contrast Article 173 of the EC Treaty (as inserted by Article G(E)(53) of the TEU).
97. See Neuwahl, *loc. cit.*, p. 319.
98. See respectively Articles 169 (and in theory, at least, Article 170) and Article 177 of the EC Treaty (as substituted by Article G(E)(56) of the TEU).
99. A need raised in the Report of the Court of Justice in May 1995 on Certain Aspects of the Implementation of the Treaty on European Union at Paragraph 4.
100. See here, e.g. Curtin, *loc. cit.*, at p. 65.
101. See Article 2 of the Protocol Drawn up on the Basis of Article K.3 of the Treaty on European Union on the Interpretation, by Way of Preliminary Ruling, by the Court of Justice of the European Communities of the Convention on the Establishment of the European Police Force (P/CONV/EUROPOL/en1).
102. E. Esders, "The European Parliament's Committee on Civil Liberties and Internal Affairs – the committee responsible for justice and home affairs" in Bieber and Monar, *op. cit.*, at p. 259.
103. Article K.6. Apart from this, Parliament is entitled to ask questions of the Council and to make recommendations to it, although the form of response required to such questions or recommendations is not expressly stipulated.
104. Result of the Council meeting of 20 June 1994 as described by Esders, *loc. cit.*, at p. 268.
105. *Ibid*, p. 270.
106. J. Monar, "Democratic control of justice and home affairs: The European Parliament and the national parliaments" in Bieber and Monar, *op. cit.*, at p. 247.
107. D. O'Keeffe, *loc. cit.*, at p. 903. Logically, it would seem implicit in the provision that Parliament receive a certain minimum amount of advance information from the Council on what activities the Council proposes to undertake – otherwise how can the views of Parliament be said to have been taken into consideration in anything that is done? (Cf. Curtin and Meijers, *loc. cit.*, at p. 439).
108. J. Monar, "The evolving role of the Union institutions in the framework of the Third Pillar" in Monar and Morgan, *op. cit.*, at p. 77.
109. See here, e.g. Monar, "Democratic control of justice and home affairs: the framework of the Third Pillar" in Morgan and Monar, *op. cit.*, at p. 79 and Monar "Democratic control of justice and home affairs" – the European Parliament and the national parliaments" in Bieber and Morgan, *op. cit.*, at p. 249.
110. O'Keeffe, *loc. cit.*, p. 904.
111. See here, e.g. Report of the Committee on Civil Liberties and International Affairs on Cooperation in the Fields of Justice and Home Affairs under the Treaty on European Union (Title VI and Other Provisions) (EP Doc N. A3-0215/93) (1 July, 1993) The Robles Piquer Report at paragraph 1 thereof.
112. Esders, *loc. cit.*, at pp. 270-275.
113. A point reflected in the rather tentative way in which the subject is broached in the Irish Presidency's draft proposals (*op. cit.*, p. 26).
114. *Loc. cit.*, in Morgan and Monar, *op. cit.*, at p. 250.
115. *Ibid*, p. 250. Cf. Working Papers from Meeting Between the Committee on Civil Liberties and Internal Affairs and the Chairman of Related Committees of the Community of National Parliaments in Brussels, 18 and 19 March, 1993 (W-4, 1993). See pp. 35 and 36 for an account of the difficulties which are experienced by Irish Parliamentarians in attempting to secure details of treaties being negotiated. See the report of the *Guardian* of 8 December 1995 entitled "MPs denied their say on Europol law" outlining how the use of an obscure House of Commons procedure known as the Ponsonby Rules was used to stifle debate on the implementation of the Europol Convention into UK law.

116. Monar, *loc. cit.*, pp. 251-254. Monar has observed in addition the tendency of government ministers either to refuse to reveal their positions to national parliaments or to tell them that they must accept certain measures because to do otherwise would endanger the process of cooperation (*Ibid*, p. 246).

117. *Ibid*, pp. 254-256.

118. See Curtin and Meijers, *loc. cit.*, at p. 402.

119. J. Monar, "The evolving role of the Union Institutions in the framework of the Third Pillar" in Monar and Morgan, *op. cit.*, at p. 75. Monar has also cited the member states' concerns regarding efficiency – specifically anxiety about "paralysis by permanent parliamentary interference". (*Ibid*)

120. See Twenty-Eighth Report of the House of Lords Select Committee on the European Communities (November, 1993) at p. 71 referring to memorandum submitted to it by Liberty (quoted in Monar, *loc. cit.*, p. 50 at footnote 3 of Monar and Morgan, *op. cit.*)

121. J. Monar, *loc. cit.*, in Bieber and Monar, *op. cit.*, at p. 245.

122. Curtin and Meijers, *loc. cit.*, at p. 442.

123. *Loc. cit.*, at p. 394.

124. D. Curtin, "The constitutional structure of the Union: a Europe of bits and pieces" (1993) *30 CML Rev. 17.*

125. Curtin and Meijers, *loc. cit.*, at p. 439.

126. See Report of the Council of Ministers of 6 April 1995 on the Operation of the Treaty on European Union, at Paragraph 18 thereof. See G. de Búrca, "The quest for legitimacy in the European Union" (1996) *59 MLR 349.* Laffan has observed that "for some member states, notably the UK and Denmark, democracy is bounded by the territorial nation state and assured by national parliaments. According to this concept of democracy, any strengthening of the Union as a political space dilutes and undermines representative democracy. Therefore these member states oppose any direct democratisation of the Union." B. Laffan, in B. Laffan (ed.) *Constitution-Building in the European Union* (1996, Institute of European Affairs) at p. 203.

127. See further text above.

128. See Curtin and Meijers, *loc. cit.*, pp. 391-392.

129. The difficulties encountered by the European Parliament in securing for itself the provision of adequate information in this policy area have been noted in the text above. See in relation to the difficulties experienced by individual citizens here *Carvel and Guardian Newspapers Ltd v. Council of the European Union* (Case T-194/94, Decision of the Court of First Instance of the European Communities, 19 October, 1995). Cf. K. A. Armstrong, "Citizenship of the Union? Lessons from Carvel and *The Guardian*" [1996] *MLR* and see generally, Curtin and Meijers, *loc. cit.* Some slight room for optimism regarding a change in approach was perhaps given by the decision by the Council to publish a number of acts adopted under Title VI in the Official Journal in the latter half of 1996. (See *Official Journal* C 274, Volume 39, 19 September, 1996.)

130. See Part Two of the EC Treaty and here Anderson, den Boer and Miller, *loc. cit.*, esp. at pp. 107-109. For an analysis of the concept of citizenship under the EC Treaty (as amended by the TEU), see N. Hyland, C. Loftus and A. Whelan, *Citizenship of the European Union* (Occasional Paper, Institute of European Affairs, 1995).

131. See here, e.g., Resolution of the European Parliament of 17 May, 1995 on the Operation of the Treaty on European Union with a View to the 1996 Intergovernmental Conference at Paragraph 7 thereof.

132. G. de Búrca, "The quest for legitimacy in the European Union" [1996] *MLR* 349 at p. 361. Note that the Legal Affairs Committee of the European Parliament in an opinion annexed to the 1988 Report of the Committee on Youth, Culture, Education, Information and Sport expressed the view that the right to be informed should be recognised in Community law as one of the basic rights of citizens. The 1995 accession of Sweden, in particular, to the European Union can be said to have brought an increased concern for transparency in the Union. See, e.g. the proposals put forward by Sweden on 3 and 4 September, 1996 concerning access to documents (CONF 3899/96) and explanatory memorandum thereto by the Swedish Ministry for Justice (Ju95/4186) (17 September, 1996). Cf. the Danish proposal for Treaty amendments concerning transparency (CONF 3905/96).

133. D. O'Keeffe, "Recasting the Third Pillar" (1995) *CML Rev. 893*.

134. To adapt Curtin and Meijers, Title VI "concerns the legal position of individuals and in this area in particular, secret law, secret law-making and secrecy of documents should be reserved to authoritarian regimes." These comments were originally made in relation to the Schengen system, but are, it is submitted, readily applicable to Title VI (Curtin and Meijers, *loc. cit.*, p. 415).

135. M. Jessurum d'Oliveira, "Refugee and asylum policy within the European Community and European efforts in the field of asylum" (1991) *Migrantenrecht 76* at 81. Cf. here Achermann, *loc. cit.*, and chapter 10 by B. Shipsey in the present volume. De Búrca has also pointed out that "in the search for ways of enhancing the legitimacy of the European Union and of addressing the loss of public support for its institutions and policies, the danger of concession to the self-protective and less altruistic side of popular sentiments, as expressed, for example, in strong nationalistic and xenophobic movements, is very real."

136. See regarding the existing Council Code of Conduct, de Búrca, *loc. cit.*, at pp. 369-371 and see Curtin and Meijers, *loc. cit.*, at pp. 442-437 for an examination of the Commission and Council's approach here. A policy of openness may be very gradually evolving in both institutions – but it is a slow process, and the maintenance of pressure to continue along this route has necessitated European level case-law such as the *Guardian* case referred to above and the earlier pre-TEU Zwarfield case (Case C-2/88, [1990] ECR I-3365. Curtin and Meijers, however, have argued that what is needed is a "mentality revolution". *Loc. cit.*, p. 395.

137. De Búrca, *loc. cit.*, p. 375.

138. See for this argument in a different context, G. Soros, "Can Europe work? A plan to rescue the Union", 75 *Foreign Affairs,* Sept.-Oct. 1996.

139. Translation of address to European Parliament, 8 March 1994. Cited in de Lobkowicz, *loc. cit.*, at p. 122.

CHAPTER 2
THE POLITICS OF JUSTICE

BEN TONRA

INTRODUCTION

Perhaps the first question to be addressed is, "Why is a political scientist making a contribution to a volume in which many of the chapters address issues which seem to be first and foremost of concern to lawyers?" Such a query might be expected from many quarters but there are several bases upon which an avowedly political appraisal of European cooperation in the field of justice and home affairs might be deemed useful.

In the first instance, just as there is no politics – in the modern sense – without law, so also might it be said that there is no law without politics. Contemporary systems of liberal democratic government represent balances struck between the rights of individual citizens and the coercive capacity of states. In this respect, law, and the democratic political systems which underpin it, provides a restraint against the exercise of untrammelled executive power.

This balance also establishes law as a normative political value. It sets agreed standards in human conduct and, once acknowledged, operates as an external check upon the will of any actor within the political system. It is important to underline the normative nature of this external validation. It represents not an objective reality but the sum of a polity's expectations of itself. It is this which establishes the separation of powers as a key concept in political theory. In Montesquieu's words "... there is no liberty if the judicial power be not separated from the legislative and executive ..."

The second basis upon which a political scientist might validly peruse the field of the Third Pillar is as a consequence of its roots in European integration. Integration was designed as an incremental process which would lead to an "ever closer union" among European peoples. In the political theory which informed the earliest analyses of integration, this was to occur through two processes of "spillover".[1]

The concept of "functional spillover" was the expectation that integration in one socio-economic sphere would lead to pressure for integration in associated areas. Just as the integration of European coal and steel markets in 1952 steered the member states towards the creation of a common market in 1957, so might it be assumed that the abolition of internal border controls promised under the 1987 Single European Act (SEA) would necessitate co-operation in establishing common standards at Europe's external borders.

Perhaps the most intriguing aspect of cooperation in the area of justice and home affairs, however, is to be found in the expectation of "political spillover". Part of the assumption here is that the development – over time – of individual rights and obligations arising from European Community law would establish popular identification with the process of integration. Rights arising from a European citizenship would thus strengthen bonds between citizens and the common European institutions which vindicated those rights.

Political spillover might, however, have even more far-reaching implications in the creation of what might be called a European political space. For example, by establishing collective legal boundaries between European citizens and non-citizens European integration might also serve to demarcate the boundaries of collective identity and belonging.[2] This is achieved by setting common rules on asylum, refugee status, immigration and visa policy. In this way the "others" who rest among us are collectively identified and their rights regulated vis-à-vis those of European citizens.

The definition of borders and the control of these borders also have major implications for the member states themselves. Part of the social contract which has been identified as a basic foundation stone of contemporary democratic systems is that states undertake to protect their citizens from the threat of anarchy within and attack from without. The admission that states are incapable of fulfilling that function in isolation should not be underestimated. Indeed, a state's agreement to allow its functions in this regard be influenced or even determined by a legal regime which is outside of its direct control is of huge significance for the concept of the sovereign independence of states. For that reason it is also an issue of enormous sensitivity for the political leadership of member state governments.

Judicial cooperation in the criminal field may also have very significant political consequences. Some writers have gone so far as to suggest that by developing a common set of perceived threats (and associated collective efforts at control), in terms of criminality, illegal immigration, terrorism, narco-trafficking, cross-border paedophilia, fraud, etc., we are engaged in culture and identity-building.[3] This places what might at first glance be seen as a limited process of pragmatic and intergovernmental cooperation into a highly politicised realm. It may even be seen as part of a process of state-building or at least the definition of a distinct polity.

In sum, the political consequences of building a transnational legal system – regardless of how conservative its construction – are very significant indeed. In the European context, moreover, that construction is linked to an avowedly political aim, i.e. an as yet undefined political union. It is hardly surprising therefore that this legal effort is fraught with political pitfalls and that the political implications, whether explicit or implicit, will always play an important role.

THE POLITICS OF EARLY COOPERATION

In the early years of European construction, issues which might today be seen as part of the Third Pillar simply did not figure. These were areas of national responsibility which did not impinge upon the political or economic agenda of the European Communities.[4] Indeed, the first consideration of them did not begin until the mid-1970s when several member state governments were faced with the violence of politically-inspired terrorist groups such as the Red Brigades in Italy and the Baader Meinhof group and Red Army Faction in Germany.

Initially, cooperation was entirely *ad hoc*. The first meeting of the member states' justice ministers only took place in December 1975 while the second meeting was not to occur for ten years thereafter. The informal agenda in 1975 was to discuss ways in which member states might cooperate to fight international terrorism by sharing certain types of information and considering ways in which they might assist one another in the apprehension and prosecution of terrorist suspects.

An informal framework was established through which this cooperation might be pursued. The Trevi Group or Process (The name 'Trevi' supposedly had its origins in the venue for the first ministerial meeting and was subsequently said to be an acronym for terrorism, radicalism, extremism, and international violence) brought together officials of member state justice ministries, senior police officers and intelligence personnel. Its operations were entirely outside the framework of the Communities; it operated on a wholly intergovernmental and confidential basis and was responsible solely to national ministers. Three working groups subsequently evolved. These dealt with: police liaison on terrorism; issues of public order (football hooligans, inter-police communications, sharing of fingerprint data, etc.) and combating organised crime, drug-running, international money-laundering and art theft. A fourth working group was subsequently added in 1986 which looked at the implications of the 1992 single market programme. Any agreements which were arrived at through this process were established as intergovernmental accords, administrative understandings or, most formally, as international conventions and treaties.

It was the single market programme which brought the politics of co-operation in justice and home affairs issues closer to the top of the political agenda. In 1986 member state justice ministers met to discuss a sudden upsurge in Middle East-inspired terrorism throughout Europe and the consequent implications for free movement which had been agreed in principle with the Single European Act (SEA). With the Commission present to discuss the implications of its 1992 programme, the ministers sought ways in which they could ensure that free movement did not become a license for terrorists.

The ministers faced the challenge that the principle of free movement of persons could not discriminate. What was designed to be of benefit to Europe's citizens was also a boon to its criminals. Indeed, this came to frustrate the efforts of a minority of member states who, dissatisfied with the very slow pace of agreement on free movement in the EC, had moved to establish a truly border-free Europe among themselves.

The Schengen Agreement had its roots in a bilateral Franco-German accord, the Saarbrücken Agreement of 1984, which sought to liberalise travel between those two countries. Along with the Benelux states and Italy these member states set about eliminating internal border controls among themselves as common external controls were agreed. It was also established as a founding principle that their cooperation should be seen as a model or precursor of EC-level agreement rather than a substitute for it. The first Schengen Agreement, signed in 1985, was supplemented by an Implementation Agreement in 1990.

The ambitions of the Schengen countries have been frustrated by several elements. First, there have been significant logistical and technical difficulties in the establishment of the Schengen Information System (SIS) which is designed to provide a bedrock for inter-police communication and information exchange. However, more significant political difficulties also arose. Germany, for instance, insisted upon the right of hot-pursuit across its national border. For its part, the French government demurred, insisting that only French police officers could operate on French soil – although they might in limited circumstances be accompanied by officers from other member states. Most recently, the French government delayed the implementation of key aspects of the Schengen Agreement in an ongoing dispute with the Netherlands over Dutch narcotics policy. The French government insists that Dutch policy – which sees the abuse of drugs more as a health issue than as a criminal one and which also draws a distinction between soft and hard drugs – undermines the collective struggle against international drug trafficking. In consequence, it is argued, the French border cannot be left undefended against the drug menace.

These two examples serve simply to show that the politics of cooperation in the area of justice and home affairs remains one of the very greatest political sensitivity, even among those states whose level of commitment to collective action and joint standards is highest. It is this fact which traditionally made cooperation in the area of justice and home affairs so problematic and why the only very limited action which did occur took place within parallel, non-Community structures such as the Trevi Group and the Schengen agreements.

The Treaty on European Union signed at Maastricht in December 1991 represented an attempt to tie the rather ragged ends of this cooperation together into a coherent thread of policy. This was then related to the broader process of European construction by its inclusion as the third "pillar" – alongside the Community pillar and the foreign policy pillar – in the new European Union.

THE POLITICS OF MAASTRICHT

Providing a treaty base for cooperation in the field of justice and home affairs proved to be one of the more problematic areas for agreement in the Maastricht negotiations despite principled support from several member state governments. The UK government, for instance, argued for a more determined collective stand against international terrorism. British efforts to track down and extradite terrorist suspects in several European countries were frustrated in the mid to late 1980s and UK ministers pressed for a greater level of counter-terrorist cooperation. The German government's interest was motivated in part by a fear that its own national policies on asylum and migration could not cope with the threat of mass migration from Central and Eastern Europe which was being envisaged during the collapse of the Soviet Union and the Eastern bloc. This prompted their demand for a collective asylum and migration policy. For the Benelux states, free movement was seen as an intrinsic part of the single market programme and a potentially visible and popular illustration of the Community's utility to its citizens.

Another political motivation which underpinned some demands for institutionalising cooperation in this area was a concern for civil rights. The Trevi Group, and to a lesser extent the Schengen agreements, were seeking to establish a control and monitoring regime over European citizens. Moreover, this regime was being constructed as a parallel part of the European Community's political agenda but without even the very limited democratic checks and balances normally associated with that agenda. It was argued, therefore, that the process had to be brought together and had to be integrated into the institutional and legal framework of the Community.

Set against these aspirations, however, were several countervailing pressures. For several member states the extradition of nationals to another jurisdiction or the operation of non-national police forces posed significant constitutional and/or political difficulties. The French and Irish governments, for example, reacted negatively to suggestions that German or UK police forces might pursue suspects across their respective land borders. Similarly, establishing collective norms on issues such as migration, asylum and refugee status was not without its political ramifications. Immigration was a very sensitive political issue in Germany, France, Belgium, and the United Kingdom. In Germany and France, physical and political attacks against minorities had raised the spectre of racial politics and a growth in xenophobic nationalism. Finally, for the United Kingdom, the political psychology of eliminating border controls was such that the government insisted upon its right to maintain any and all controls deemed necessary to its national security. For all of these reasons, member states were determined to ensure that any cooperation in these areas remained firmly under their, i.e. intergovernmental, control.

In the event, Title VI of the Treaty on European Union reflected a security dilemma.[5] Governments sought to cooperate to meet a series of perceived threats arising from their ambition to establish a "border-free Europe". In so far, however, as that cooperation entailed a diminution of their own sovereignty and a consequent loss of control over their own internal security policies, their sense of insecurity only grew. This meant that while appropriate policy areas were identified for policy action, the member states could not agree on any decision-making mechanism which delimited their ability to define that action – resulting in a decision-making stalemate.

The justice and home affairs provisions of the Maastricht Treaty also reflected the reality of divergent interests among the member states – particularly in view of the fact that their exposure to potential threats was very different. Germany's geographic position at the cross-roads of Europe and its potential sensitivity to any significant migratory flows made its concerns for cooperation quite different to those of the United Kingdom, which lay at the western edge of Europe and which rejoiced in its relatively isolated island geography.

A political analysis of Title VI reveals three issues. First, it must be seen as a first tentative step towards what might potentially become a common policy. All of the variegated elements of justice and home affairs were indeed drawn together and set in relation to one another. Their linkage to pre-existing Community policy decisions, on the single market for example, was also formally conceded. More importantly, it was clear that these issues had their own functional logic – their own potential for further "spillover". In sum, Title VI might thus be seen as having been yet another victory for the integrating logic of the Community "method".

That victory, however, must be set in context. Many of the areas identified for further cooperation in the Maastricht Treaty were and are of a high level of domestic political sensitivity. In some cases they strike at the heart of national sovereignty and the associated ability of the state to control its own borders. For these reasons an attempt was made, structurally, to quarantine this area of cooperation from the Community's existing institutional and legal framework. This, however, created additional problems of confusion over competence, with the parentage of visa and drugs policies both coming into dispute. The security dilemma faced by the states was resolved by an attempt to drive a common policy with twelve pairs of hands at the wheel – and twelve feet on the brake.

Finally, a political analysis of Title VI would suggest that insofar as it had sought to establish an effective policy framework, it has failed. The aims and objectives of the Third Pillar are largely unfulfilled, its policy tools – such as joint actions and common positions – are under-utilised and its decision-making mechanisms are judged to have been less than effective. Overall, the Third Pillar was identified, in the run-up to the 1996 review of the Union's founding treaties, as a candidate for major reform. According to the interim report of the intergovernmental Reflection Group the provisions of Title VI were judged by a large majority of the member state representatives to be "inappropriate" and in its operation to be "... clearly defective".[6]

THE POLITICS OF AMSTERDAM

In their respective reports on the working of the Maastricht Treaty the Council of Ministers, the European Parliament and the Commission were all critical of the lack of progress made on Third Pillar issues. In considering amendments to the treaties, attention was focused upon clarifying the objectives of this policy area, providing it with the tools to arrive at those objectives and modifying the institutional and decision-making structures so that agreement upon those tools would be forthcoming. The most radical approach was to propose the communitarisation of the entire policy field'– a position which was endorsed in principle by seven member states and wholeheartedly opposed by four others.[7]

In the event, it soon became clear that a radical approach would not gather the necessary unanimity from among the member states. As the IGC Working Group, under the initial chairpersonship of Noel Dorr, began its "successive approximation" of national positions, an alternative strategy emerged. This suggested that instead of importing Pillar Three into the Community (First Pillar) domain, it might instead be possible to import significant elements of the First Pillar into the Third.

An additional political element in this debate eventually also surfaced. In its Presidency priorities, the Irish government had identified strengthened cooperation in the fight against drugs as one its three central goals. This was seen, in part, as a means whereby the Union might be made more relevant to its citizens and contribute in a meaningful way to improving the lives of European citizens. A European "fight against crime" was quickly seen as possessing some public resonance. Tragic events in Belgium in the autumn of 1996 – centred around the discovery of an extensive paedophile ring with trans-European connections – underscored this point.

Through various back channels, the Irish Presidency worked closely with several like-minded administrations – and in particular the German government – to draft a treaty text which reflected this political dynamic. The draft treaty which the Irish Presidency had been mandated to produce at the end of 1996 thus contained, in its very first section, provisions for the establishment of "An Area of Freedom, Security and Justice".

While not taking on board the more ambitious targets of those who had sought to wholly communitarise cooperation in the field of justice and home affairs, the text provided by the Irish Presidency did entail very significant reform. New tasks were appended to Pillar Three, new policy tools were proposed which mirrored those already in existence in Pillar One, some existing Third Pillar responsibilities were nominated for transfer to the First Pillar and provision was suggested for the introduction of Qualified Majority Voting.[8] These proposals were accepted as the basis for negotiations leading to a final treaty at the Amsterdam Summit in June 1997.

CONCLUSION

In many ways cooperation in justice and home affairs was both born of fear and imprisoned by fear. It was born as a result of insecurity on the part of member states. They were threatened by forces over which they had little or no control – terrorism and illegal immigration – and which they thought might be more effectively tackled through collective action. Soon, however, this initial agenda of fear was augmented by decisions taken in another context and the establishment of a single internal market. Free movement of persons threatened to worsen existing insecurities and again only collective action was deemed capable of meeting this new challenge.

Fear, however, also undermined these collective efforts. Member states, differentiated by administrative interests, by historical experience, by legal tradition and by political psychology, sought to maintain national control over any collective policy. They feared a loss of control over an area of public policy which in part defined them as independent states. This dynamic – or dialectic – guaranteed immobility and stagnation.

There is, as yet, no agreement to decisively break out of this immobile dynamic. An attempt is, however, being made to re-balance it. Greater weight is being thrown into an institutional and decision-making structure which will just marginally favour collective action over individual vetoes. Certain Third Pillar policy areas may yet emerge onto the Community agenda, institutional modifications will bring the Commission more to the centre of policy making, the employment of QMV remains up for discussion and the range of policy tools has been broadened.

A central question remains unanswered. To what extent is there a political identification among European citizens that they do indeed "share" problems which require collective resolution? On the other hand, to what extent are other member states and their citizens seen as part of the problem? It is the answer to these two questions which determines the strength or relative weakness of political spillover in the area of justice and home affairs. The stronger it is the greater may be the prospect for decisive movement towards a collective policy and *vice versa*.

One element which is left out of this particular equation is the status of non-citizens in this potentially new "judicial and political space". What rights pertain to persons who are not to be safeguarded and cosseted in this improved Union – especially those who are, as either refugees or migrants, defined as part of the problem to be solved or part of the threat to be met? How are the rights of such persons to be vindicated if the Union establishes the policies of internal security, but is not held – either by itself or under international law – to the human rights standards demanded of democratic states? This is perhaps the next great challenge to be faced by the part-formed polity known as the European Union.

NOTES

1. D. Muttimer, "1992 and the political integration of Europe: neofunctionalism reconsidered", *Journal of European Integration*, vol.13, 1989.
2. Brigid Laffan, "The politics of identity and political order in Europe", *Journal of Common Market Studies*, vol. 34, no.1, March 1996.
3. Soledad Garcia, "Europe's fragmented identities and the frontiers of citizenship", Discussion Paper No.45, Royal Institute of International Affairs, 1993.
4. The European Coal and Steel Community (ECSC) established by the Treaty of Paris in 1952 and the European Economic Community (EEC) and European Atomic Energy Community (Euratom) both of which were established under the Treaties of Rome in 1957.
5. This is explored by Malcolm Anderson, Monica den Boer and Gary Millar, "European citizenship and cooperation in justice and home affairs" in Andrew Duff, John Pinder and Roy Pryce (eds.), *Maastricht and Beyond: Building the European Union*, Routledge, 1994.
6. Progress Report from the Chairman of the Reflection Group on the 1996 Intergovernmental Conference, SN/509/1/95 (Reflex 10) Rev 1, Madrid, 1 September 1995, p.24.
7. Istituto Affari Internazionali (ed.), *Revision of Maastricht: Implementation and proposals for reform; a survey of national views*, Third Bulletin, Winter-Spring 1994, pp. 42-46.
8. Conference of the Representatives of the Governments of the Member States, "The European Union today and tomorrow: adapting the European Union for the benefit of its peoples and preparing it for the future – a general outline for a draft revision of the treaties", Conf 2500/96 CAB, Brussels, 5 December 1996, pp.9-36.

Part 2

Cooperation in Justice matters in the European Union and the Criminal Law Field

CHAPTER 3
CRIMINAL LAW AND PROCEDURE IN THE
EUROPEAN UNION

EAMONN BARNES

No political entity could long survive without laws and an effective law enforcement system. In considering this proposition in relation to the European Union, it can be argued that the Union is not in this context an entity but rather a combination of fifteen entities, each with its own laws and law enforcement systems, and that that arrangement is a perfectly adequate and acceptable one which can be maintained indefinitely. The purpose of this chapter is to examine whether or not the present situation throughout the Union regarding penal laws and law enforcement is indeed adequate, acceptable and maintainable and to suggest a way forward if, as I believe to be the case, the answer to the question is negative. While my particular viewpoint is that of a public prosecutor, I approach the question from a wider perspective. I also approach it from a minimalist position regarding post-Maastricht political unification, though such a position would not necessarily represent my personal views.

Irrespective of whether one thinks of the European Union as a very loose non-evolutionary association of sovereign states or as a supra-national unitary entity, I believe that it could only profit by the introduction of a much greater degree of cohesion and compatibility between the systems of criminal law and criminal procedure which are operated in the fifteen constituent states. For reasons touched upon later, I believe that such a development is both essential and inevitable. However, like so much else in the evolution of the Community and of the Union, it is an area which has to be approached slowly and with great care and patience. It is nearly true to say that it has to happen rather than be achieved.

The main obstacle is not that of the enormity of the work which would have to be done to achieve uniformity in penal law and procedure, though I do not underestimate that task. Rather is it the determined resistance to the whole idea which can confidently be expected from many, if not all, of the states within the Union. Legal establishments are notoriously resistant to change. When you add nationalism to that factor, you get an exceptionally potent brew. One's own legal system is always the best yet devised and it is so fair and so superior to all others that the prospect of any change, and particularly of a change tilted even slightly in the direction of another and, by definition, inferior system would be quite unthinkable. Inspired by the lawyers but enthusiastically adopted by those legislators and other functionaries suspicious of everything foreign, the inevitable opposition to any proposal for penal harmonisation is a factor which must be realistically faced by anyone seriously concerned by the necessity for movement in this area.

I say necessity because I believe change is indeed necessary, and for two main reasons. The first has to do with the nature, thrust and objectives of the Communities as they developed since the Treaty of Rome, and with the expectations thereby generated in the nationals of the constituent states who are now, of course, also citizens of the Union. For their benefit, standards and protections in very great numbers and detail are defined and devised and are enforced civilly over a very wide range of activity throughout the fifteen states. Rights and duties are created and regulated in profusion. A huge corpus of positive law has thereby been created. I mean no disrespect to the labours of those concerned when I say that many of the matters involved are of a relatively unimportant nature when perceived from the perspective of the average citizen. It is no doubt important that I can purchase a tomato anywhere in the Union secure in the knowledge that it conforms to certain standards. It would seem of much greater importance that I could travel throughout the Union secure in the knowledge that what is lawful in one country is lawful in all the others and that infringements of the law will throughout have similar if not identical consequences, both in penal procedure and in penalty range. In the area of criminality, where the citizens and indeed the institutions of the Union are at such risk, whether as victim, suspect, taxpayer or funding agency, it must seem anomalous to any moderately inquisitive Martian or other non-European that no attempt whatever has so far been made to achieve uniformity and cohesion in the penal area when so much has been done in all the other areas of activity.

This anomaly carries practical consequences for the citizen traveller in Europe. A minor but important example which touches the experience of many is the very considerable desirability of having a bail bond before driving into Spain, without which serious consequences may ensue in the event of an accident or suspected infringement of the traffic code. A point somewhat higher up the scale was exemplified last year by the troubles of the owner and the driver of a long-distance haulage truck who in France became liable to very severe penalties, including confiscation of the truck and its cargo, on summary trial for an offence which, judging from the newspaper account, would in Ireland have been a minor breach of the road traffic laws. At the top end of the scale would be the examples of travellers languishing in Continental jails for lengthy periods of time while suspected offences, not always of the most serious variety, were being investigated and thereafter processed through the courts. In Ireland they could not have been imprisoned at all before evidence sufficient to charge them was available, and thereafter they would have been on bail, apart from very exceptional cases, until completion of their trial. I mention these examples not to point up the relative virtues of the Irish or indeed any other criminal justice system, but to indicate that such divergencies of law and procedure – and there are very many – fit uneasily into the framework of a Union in which equality, and uniformity of high standards and of public policies, are so assiduously and rightly pursued. They are also, it seems to me, inconsistent with the development of any sense of common citizenship within the Union and with the support for its commercial and social activities which criminal sanctions provide, and are intended to provide, in individual countries.

The second reason why I believe that some beginning towards harmonisation of penal law, procedure and sanctions is necessary is a purely practical one. It has to do with the effectiveness of law enforcement in each of the states of the Union, with the quality of criminal justice throughout the Union, with inter-state cooperation in criminal matters and, using a slightly different focus, with the protection of the financial interests of the Community. In a short chapter it is not possible to address these matters adequately. A few points must suffice. When so much serious crime is transnational, any shortfall in international cooperation in criminal matters reduces the effectiveness of law enforcement in each individual state. The same consideration obviously applies to the quality of criminal justice viewed from a 'Union-wide perspective. What is perhaps rather more important in this context however is the widespread concern regarding efficiency and fairness in the delivery of criminal justice which is certainly not mitigated by the recognition or perception of disparities in matters such as speedy justice, access to legal aid, pre-trial custody and the vindication of human rights. Impatience with less than perfect interstate cooperation in criminal matters will I believe produce its own impetus towards some form of harmonisation, as will concern regarding fraud on Union funds.

I should state at this juncture that I do not think that the differences in substantive criminal law between the states present the greatest problem or that they would be particularly difficult to address. While there are significant textual differences in the formulation of specific offences from state to state – the non-textualised common law offences in the United Kingdom and Ireland presenting particular problems – the conceptual bases for nearly all the major crimes known throughout the Union are remarkably similar. Should it ever be decided to embark upon the project, harmonisation of them would for that reason not be a particularly daunting task, though no doubt much nationalist blood would boil in determining the relative merits of murder and *meurtre* or theft and *vol*.

However, one significant law enforcement problem arising from differences in substantive law lies in the area of extradition. Given the almost total adherence up to now to the principle of territoriality in criminal law and procedure, extradition remains the most effective weapon available in aid of cooperation between states in criminal law enforcement. That cooperation was never more necessary and important than it is now. Ease of movement has made evasion of justice a simple matter, and crime itself knows no boundaries. Many serious offences – fraud and drugs being notable examples – are essentially transnational in character. Unfortunately, the principle of mutuality – the principle which requires that there must be a precise correspondence of the ingredients of the offence as between requesting and requested state and which will remain unaffected by the coming into force of the Convention on Simplified Extradition – has several times been applied to frustrate extradition because of technical differences in the ingredients of the offence in each state. This is a matter which however could and should be rectified by modification of international extradition law without the necessity of harmonising the laws of each state. The real problems for law enforcement and cooperation lie in the area of criminal procedure.

With few exceptions, judicial criminal competence is governed by the territoriality principle. I make below some observations on possible modifications of that principle in the context of the European Union. For the present, it means that in most cases prosecutions must be conducted in the jurisdiction in which the offence was alleged to have been committed. Very often, however, much of the relevant evidence is to be found or has to be sought elsewhere. Many serious offences – fraud and drugs again being notable examples – involve transactions taking place in several jurisdictions. The task of assembling the necessary body of evidence for a presentation in just one venue can be and often is a nightmare. The procedures are cumbersome and slow and, in jurisdictions such as Ireland where expeditious trial is regarded as a fundamental right, can be self-defeating.

The main problems stem from the fundamentally differing structures for the investigation and prosecution of offences in the various states and from the equally fundamental differences in juridical procedure. The strict lines of division in the United Kingdom and Ireland between the investigative, prosecutorial and judicial functions, and between the legal powers deemed appropriate to each, are not observed to the same extent in any of the Civil Law countries and are quite unknown in many of them. This in itself presents considerable problems for inter-state cooperation in criminal matters and specifically in evidence gathering, an area in which the common and civil law systems differ fundamentally. This is greatly exacerbated by the differences in criminal procedure generally as between those two systems. The French Procureur de la Republique or Juge d'Instruction compiling a dossier has some difficulty in understanding the requirements of an Irish Court, whether in examining a witness for purposes of a prosecution in France or in seeking to obtain the *viva voce* evidence of a French witness for the purposes of a prosecution in Ireland. It is of course this last matter that presents the greatest single obstacle to international cooperation in criminal matters. The 1959 Council of Europe Convention on Mutual Assistance in Criminal Matters was a laudable first step in this area which provided some assistance to the hard-pressed prosecutor seeking to assemble the building blocks of his case. So did the 1990 Convention relating to the proceeds of crime. It is too early yet to evaluate the effectiveness of these Conventions in Ireland, the relevant enabling legislation being recent and not yet fully operational. One obvious deficiency stands out clearly, however. It is the inability to compel or ensure the attendance of a foreign-based witness to give *viva voce* evidence where that is required in a particular court. While various devices can be tried to circumvent this problem, such as that contained in Section 52 of the Irish Criminal Justice Act of 1994 (which provides for the taking of evidence outside the state for use inside the state), it seems to me that this is a major practical difficulty in international criminal law enforcement which will remain, as far as the Union is concerned, as long as its constituent states maintain unaltered the differences which at present exist between them in criminal matters.

In my view, accordingly, the two main obstacles to progress in improving international criminal law enforcement are the principle of territoriality and the differences in criminal procedure. Some modification of each, however modest, is required before progress can be made. This can, I believe, be successfully addressed. As to the principle of territoriality, two exceptions have long been recognised by international law, both of which are especially apt in the context of the European Union. They are the exceptions of nationality and of mutual consent. It has always been accepted that a state can take jurisdiction over the actions of its own nationals wherever performed. It is also accepted that states can consent to the mutual exercise of extraterritorial jurisdiction. There would be no obstacle in international law accordingly to the states of the European Union agreeing to each having jurisdiction over specified offences committed anywhere in the Union, and in view of the creation of European citizenship the nationality principle would reinforce the legitimacy of such a course of action.

The jurisprudential approach adopted by the United Kingdom and Irish legislatures in 1975/6 could serve as a useful precedent. Their mutual legislation at that time enabled the courts north of the political border in Ireland to take jurisdiction over offences physically committed south of it and *vice versa*. The underlying idea was that, in the circumstances then obtaining in the entire island, certain offences offended the body politic in both jurisdictions irrespective of where in the island they were committed. It has indeed been argued, correctly in my view, that this mutual legislation did not create extraterritorial jurisdiction at all but instead created by consent certain offences under and against the domestic law of each of the two jurisdictions involved. The relevant statutes created of course a very wide range of such offences. I am not suggesting, particularly at this embryonic stage of the idea, that a similarly extensive range of Union-wide offences should now be created. Two, mentioned twice already in this chapter, stand out for consideration – fraud and drugs. For purposes of what I propose below, I would narrow them down to fraud against the financial interests of the Union.

Regarding the second obstacle of disparities in criminal procedure, there are two options for change. One is to adopt one of the existing systems of criminal procedure and make it applicable throughout the Union. This is neither realistic nor desirable. I have long realised that each of the various systems of criminal procedure in Europe contains ideas of considerable value for law enforcement and the search for truth which are worthy of consideration by all. Equally, of course, each contains deficiencies and disadvantages. This is true of systems of criminal procedure elsewhere in the world also. It seems to me that a second and better option would be to identify what is best in each and to seek to construct from those elements a system, informed by the centuries of experience in the operation of those other systems which have evolved up to now, which would be designed to achieve efficiency, effectiveness, expedition and, insofar as it is ever possible in human affairs, certainty in criminal justice. Again the possible detail of any such new design is well outside the scope of this chapter. However, I could suggest a direction for one possible model by stating that I consider that the common law systems could benefit greatly from a much more inquisitorial approach to criminal investigation – there is already a hint of this in Scottish criminal procedure – and that the civil law systems would be greatly enhanced by adopting, at a later stage in the process, a more accusatorial procedure and by allowing a greater and more pro-active or adversarial role for the defence. Certainly the common law systems would be enriched by the introduction to it of some form of institutionalised role or status for the victim of crime such as has long existed in Continental Europe. Equally the civil law systems could benefit from the principle of liberty until after conviction which is practised in varying degrees in the common law countries.

These and very many other ideas, derived from a study of what is best in the two main traditions of criminal procedure, could, through a sort of induced osmosis, produce a system of criminal procedure worthy of the new Union. It could, and I believe should, be done on an experimental basis. There would be, as I have indicated, great suspicion regarding any attempt to introduce one extra-national system which would involve supplementing and abandoning existing ones. That suspicion would lessen if a new system was seen to work well transnationally or internationally in a very restricted field. I would accordingly propose for consideration the creation by convention of specific offences of fraud against the financial interests of the Community, that the ingredients and textual formulation of those offences be uniform in each state, that they be justiciable throughout the Union wherever within it committed and that they be investigated and prosecuted in accordance with a code of criminal investigation and juridical procedure drafted specifically for those offences alone which would be applicable throughout the Union. Fraud is notoriously one of the most difficult crimes to investigate and prosecute successfully. If the suggested new system were seen to be effective for it, it could then be more easily, and objectively, evaluated as a possible model criminal justice system for Europe in the future.

I firmly believe, as I indicated at the beginning of this necessarily brief chapter, that an evolution of a truly European system of criminal justice is essential to the development of the European Union, whatever form that development may take, and that it should be actively encouraged by the member states. I have suggested that the principal obstacles to such evolution are rigid adherence to the territoriality principle and to differing procedures which inhibit effective law enforcement throughout the Union and which in many cases are no longer effective when judged even from a purely national perspective. I have proposed a very limited but from the European Union viewpoint very important operational area, fraud on the finances of the Union itself, in which a specifically European system of substantive law and of procedure could be tried and tested. I would confidently anticipate that such a system, carefully designed, would be seen to be effective and fair, to pose no threat to our liberties, ancient or modern, and to constitute a suitable model for a more general system which would permit the European citizen of the future to live and to travel anywhere within the Union secure in the knowledge that his or her rights, liberties and liabilities are determined by one clear and universal code of law.

CHAPTER 4
INTERNATIONAL/EU CRIMINAL LAW

MICHAEL FORDE

The originally proposed title for this chapter was "An Assessment of Progress to Date" in cooperation within the EU in the criminal law field. Alas, solid "hard law" progress to date has been in relatively short supply (and where it is not, the progress achieved is the subject of another chapter in the present work). Thus, for example, the Convention on Simplified Extradition Procedure between the Member States of the European Union[1] relates only to persons who consent to their own extradition (although it must be noted that there is now also a more extensive and far-reaching draft Convention on the Improvement of Extradition Between the Member States).

Other limits on progress achieved to date include the fact that the Europol Drugs Unit has no executive authority and it has proved possible to provide Europol with a treaty basis acceptable to all member states only after the most protracted of political wrangling.[2] The main achievements in relation to Europol, customs and combating fraud are however examined elsewhere in this volume. Rather therefore than examining the otherwise somewhat limited progress achieved to date in the area of criminal law cooperation, a more fruitful exercise might be to examine the question of what can be expected in the *future* in this particular field of cooperation in justice and home affairs.

Until the procedures under Title VI of the Maastricht Treaty (the "Third Pillar") are substantially amended, it is unlikely that there will be bold innovations. At present significant advances in the criminal law field require unanimous approval from the member states and anything radical is bound to be controversial, attracting objections from at least one recalcitrant. This is not to say that notable initiatives are entirely out of the question; even if the "Third Pillar" were recast to allow for some form of majority voting, it is unlikely that somewhat controversial measures would be adopted against the wishes of an outvoted minority of states. We also need only look to the Council of Europe; its measures rely on consensus and yet it has been responsible for several remarkable measures in the field of international criminal law, most notably perhaps its Convention on Extradition of 1957.

Several of the topics in Article K.1 of the Maastricht Treaty do not easily fit the description of the "criminal law field" and will be disregarded here, viz.

crossing and controls on external borders, immigration and third-countries' nationals, judicial cooperation in civil matters and customs cooperation. There therefore remains in Article K.1

- combating drug addiction

- combating fraud on an international scale

- judicial cooperation in criminal matters

- police cooperation for the purposes of preventing and combating terrorism, unlawful drug trafficking and other serious forms of international crime ... in connection with the organisation of a Union-wide system for exchanging information within a European Police Office (Europol).

DEFINING CRIME

The substantive criminal laws of all the EU states are broadly similar in objective; they strike at common forms of anti-social conduct – offences against the person (e.g. murder, manslaughter), offences against property (e.g. larceny, embezzlement), offences against public order (e.g. disclosing official secrets, obstructing the highways). However, there are some striking differences between what is criminal in some countries and not in others. For instance, certain sexual activities and the use of soft drugs are serious offences in some countries but not in others. Divergences in social attitudes of this nature are bound to remain for decades if not longer.

Another source of divergence is the general attitude to the criminal law as an instrument of policy, i.e. where legislatures want to achieve certain objectives but differ about the use of criminal sanctions (as opposed to civil liability or regulatory means) in order to secure those objectives. For some years in Germany, many of what we would regard as road traffic offences have been de-criminalised; persons who for example park their cars in the wrong places are no longer prosecuted in the criminal courts for road traffic offences. Recently in Ireland we have an interesting example of the "criminalisation" option being adopted by the Oireachtas, in the shape of the Competition (Amendment) Act, 1996. Under the original Competition Act, 1991, anti-competitive acts were made civil wrongs, could be the subject matter of injunctions and could attract damages awards up to three times the loss actually suffered by a plaintiff. One of the main features of the new Act has been to criminalise cartels and abuses of monopoly powers, in the belief that criminalisation will provide encouragement for more ethical practices in the marketplace. Yet criminalisation may achieve the very opposite effect; it is quite likely that the courts will adopt a more strict construction of the Acts' substantive requirements, a higher degree of proof may be required and persons being questioned about their actions in the market place may be entitled to refuse answering, under their privilege against self-incrimination.

Another source of divergence in criminal laws is legislative inertia. In some countries considerable effort is put into keeping the criminal law entirely up to date and in line with current social and economic circumstances. In others, age-old laws remain neglected, but yet in force on the statute book, and activities that cry out for legislative intervention, although often deplored, are disregarded. Ireland tends to fall into the latter category.

There is a further divergence in criminal laws from the point of overall organisation and drafting techniques. Continental European countries have their criminal codes, in which the entire corpus of their criminal laws are compiled in one book and arranged in a systematic manner. It is relatively simple for individuals on the Continent who have no training in law to ascertain what is and is not prohibited by their criminal law; all they need is to consult their *Code Penal*. By contrast, the unfortunate Irish man and woman, or their brothers and sisters in the UK, still have to rummage through an entire library of statutes, repealed Acts and regulations; without legal training or access to a good textbook on the subject, it is virtually impossible for them to ascertain what their criminal law strikes at.

Finally, in the Continental European countries individual criminal offences tend to be defined in a broader or more general or abstract manner than in the United Kingdom and Ireland. Perhaps the best example is in the area of fraud, where the law in Ireland exemplifies the furthest extreme of particularity in legislative draftsmanship. We do not have an overarching offence of fraud; instead there is a wide variety of particular frauds such as obtaining by false pretences, embezzlement, etc. These are supplemented by the unsatisfactory catch-all offence of conspiracy to defraud, the precise ambit of which in Irish law is a matter for some debate. It is now almost thirty years since the United Kingdom filled gaps in the legislative scheme for fraud by enacting the Theft Act, 1968, which contains more expansive definitions of the conduct being proscribed.

As well as being objects of intense curiosity among comparative lawyers, the above differences in approach to the ambit of the criminal laws and to the very definition of particular crimes in the laws is of fundamental importance in at least one area of international cooperation in this field, viz. extradition.

To date all or virtually all extradition arrangements are based on the principle of "dual criminality", "double criminality", or "correspondence of offence". That is to say, practically every extradition arrangement is founded on the principle that the requested state will only extradite a person where the alleged offence for which that person is wanted abroad would also constitute an offence under its law. Thus, persons will not be extradited from the Netherlands to face certain drugs-related charges, nor from Germany to face certain road traffic charges, because the alleged wrong-doing would not constitute a criminal offence in those countries. Similarly, until the Competition (Amendment) Act became law in Ireland, persons could not be extradited from the Republic to face trial on competition or anti-trust charges; Ireland was thus a safe haven for fugitive monopolists and abusers of dominant positions.

CRIMINAL PROCEDURE

The differences in criminal procedure between Ireland and England on the one hand and Continental Europe on the other are far greater than in their approaches to defining criminal conduct; Scotland is something of a hybrid in this regard. The present system in Ireland and England evolved piecemeal from the medieval jury trial; the accused person's lawyers and the prosecution's lawyers each put their version of events to a jury of lay people, who then decide which version is the more credible. On the Continent, the criminal procedure systems are descended from the medieval inquisitions, in which the trained judge lawyer investigated the allegations, compiled his dossier of proofs and then concluded whether the accused was guilty or innocent. But few if any of the Continental systems remain truly inquisitorial; over the past 150 years the trend has been to make criminal trials more adversarial occasions. A full-blooded inquisitorial system would now contravene the European Convention on Human Rights.

Differences in approaches to criminal procedure impinges on international cooperation in at least two respects. One is at what perhaps is the very apex of such cooperation, the international criminal court. If Europe ever gets to that stage, it will have to be decided what mixture of common law and civilian procedures will be adopted. Will there be a *juge d'instruction* and/or a jury and, if a jury, how will it be comprised? Several decades most likely will elapse before those and related questions must be faced up to. Account no doubt will be taken of the provisions of the International Law Commission's draft statute for an International Criminal Court of 1993, which *inter alia* envisages trials by chambers of five judges but without a jury.

The above differences affect extradition to a far lesser extent than divergences in the ambit of criminal laws. Extradition arrangements are based on the premise that the state-parties to the arrangements in question ordinarily give persons a fair trial; if one state's criminal procedures were intrinsically unfair, other states would refuse to conclude extradition arrangements with it, due to an understandable reluctance to send their citizens for trial before some kangaroo-type court. Accordingly, when persons' extradition are being contested in the courts, the plea that they will get an unfair trial if extradited generally gets short shrift. As was observed in a recent English case:

> The law of extradition proceeds upon the fundamental assumptions that the requesting state is acting in good faith and that the fugitive will receive a fair trial in the courts of the requesting state. If it were otherwise, one may assume that our government would not bind itself by treaty to such process ... Our courts have consistently resisted attempts to import the requirements of domestic criminal procedure into extradition proceedings.[3]

Thus, for example, in the 1980s the courts in the Republic extradited persons to face trial in the so-called "Diplock Courts" in Northern Ireland. Even if it could be shown that the Oireachtas would never sanction a system of *juge unique* for trials of serious crimes, that is no reason for refusing extradition to a state which had such a system.[4] However, most extradition arrangements contain two exceptions to this principle, in respect of "military offences" and, more importantly, in respect of persons who had been convicted *in absentia*.

EXTRATERRITORIAL OFFENCES

Criminal law is territorial in the sense that, except where it is expressly provided otherwise, a state's criminal law applies only to what occurs within its own borders; it does not apply extraterritorially. With people travelling more and more abroad on business and for pleasure, criminal laws have become increasingly extraterritorial as well. One of the earliest such measures, which remains on the statute book in Britain, is the Criminal Jurisdiction Act, 1802, which in its preamblé describes itself as "An Act for trying and punishing in Great Britain persons holding public employments for offences committed abroad".[5] Under this, British civil servants who were serving aboard and who committed any crime or misdemeanour there could be tried and convicted in England in respect of that offence. If there had been an equivalent law in force in the Republic, it would not have been necessary in 1990 to extradite the Irish civil servant Kevin McDonald to be tried in England for unlawfully selling Irish passports from the Irish embassy in London;[6] instead, he could have been tried in Dublin.

Today, many states' laws on terrorism, on international drug trafficking and on money-laundering have an extensive extraterritorial reach. Thus, in Ireland the 1st Schedule to the Extradition (Amendment) Act, 1994, contains a long catalogue of what may be termed "terrorist" offences which apply extraterritorially. Section 20 of the Misuse of Drugs Act, 1977, is even more sweeping in this regard; under it:

- Any person who aids, abets, counsels or induces the commission in a place outside the state of an offence punishable under a corresponding law in force in that place shall be guilty of an offence.

- In this section "a corresponding law" means a law stated in a certificate purporting to be issued by or on behalf of the government of a country outside the state to be a law providing for the control or regulation in that country of the manufacture, production, supply, use, exportation or importation of dangerous or otherwise harmful drugs in pursuance of any treaty, convention, protocol or other agreement between states and prepared or implemented by, or under the auspices of, the League of Nations or the United Nations Organisation and which for the time being is in force.

A somewhat complicated area of extradition law is the application of the "dual criminality" requirement to extraterritorial offences. In the 1989 Act in the United Kingdom, which replaced the Extradition Act, 1870, Parliament set out in detail in s.2(1)(b), (2)-(4) precisely how such offences are to meet the "dual criminality" test. Many of the modern multilateral treaties that contain provisions on extradition also provide for this matter, for instance the 1988 Convention on the Illicit Trafficking in Narcotic Drugs and Psychotropic Substances.

The European Convention on Extradition of 1957, or any variant of it that may be adopted at some stage by the European Union, may require modification in this regard. According to Article 7, which is headed "Place of Commission":

- The requested Party may refuse to extradite a person claimed for an offence which is regarded by its law as having been committed in whole or in part in its territory or in a place treated as its territory.

- When the offence for which extradition is requested has been committed outside the territory of the requesting Party, extradition may only be refused if the law of the requested Party does not allow prosecution for the same category of offence when committed outside the latter Party's territory or does not allow extradition for the offence concerned.

What the first paragraph above precisely means is that where the crime, for which a person's extradition is sought, is also an offence under the law of the requested state (either as having been committed there or an extraterritorial offence under its law), that state may refuse to grant extradition. Obviously that state can be expected to try the accused before its own courts. The second paragraph, however, is somewhat opaque and does not seem to have received detailed consideration in the case law.

Article 7 of the above 1957 Convention has been translated into Irish case law in a most curious fashion – in s.15 of the Extradition Act, 1965, which states that:

> Extradition shall not be granted where the offence [in question] is regarded under the law of the state as having been committed in the state.

This section does not seem to have been authoritatively interpreted[7] but would appear to mean that any acts that would constitute an offence under Irish law, including any extraterritorial offences, "shall not be" the subject of extradition. If this is indeed what s.15 means, an amendment is called for because it has the effect of making a great number of serious offences non-extraditable.

In Continental Europe, extraterritorial offences have a special significance with regard to extradition in that many states there refuse to extradite their own nationals – for instance Germany and France. In these countries, however, where one of their nationals cannot be extradited, he instead will be tried before his national courts for the offence in question. This arrangement may be satisfactory in many instances but serious practical difficulties can arise in getting the necessary evidence from the place abroad where the offence in question was allegedly committed.

EXTRATERRITORIAL EVIDENCE

Especially in relation to the type of crime designated in Article K1 of the Maastricht Treaty, such as international fraud, drug-trafficking and terrorism, in order to secure a conviction it often is necessary to obtain evidence and secure the attendance of witnesses from abroad. This is even more so the case when the court is trying an extraterritorial offence, where all or almost all of the conduct in question would have occurred abroad. Until the enactment of the Criminal Justice Act, 1994, the question of the international transmission of evidence and witnesses for criminal cases has received scant attention. Section 51 of this Act authorises the Minister for Justice to institute proceedings in the District Court for the purpose of taking evidence to be used in the prosecution of an offence abroad. In this manner, depositions can be taken in Ireland to be used in foreign prosecutions. Section 52 of this Act provides that, in the course of prosecuting a criminal charge in Ireland, an application can be made to authorities abroad to take evidence for use in the Irish proceedings. However, especially in jury trials where the witness has key evidence to give, and much turns on his credibility, it is far preferable that he be present in court than merely reading to the jury a transcript of what he said when being examined elsewhere.

Within the United States of America this problem is resolved by arrangements which enable witnesses to be subpoenaed from one state to another – the Uniform Law to Secure Attendance of Witnesses from Within or Without a State in Criminal Proceedings, which was formulated in 1936 and has been adopted in most if not all states of the Union. In 1958 the US Supreme Court rejected a challenge to the constitutionality of this measure. It was also contended that, under the US Constitution, extradition and inter-state rendition are entirely federal matters and, accordingly, the individual states of the Union cannot encroach on these questions. That argument was rejected in terms that echo the principle of "subsidiarity" in the Maastricht Treaty:

> To hold that these and other arrangements are beyond the power of the states and the federal government because there is no specific empowering provision in the United States Constitution would be to take an unwarrantedly constricted view of state and national powers and would hobble the effective functioning of our federalism. Diffusion of power has its corollary of diffusion of responsibilities, with it stimulus to cooperative effort in devising ways and means for making the federal system work. That is not a mechanical structure. It is an interplay of living forces of government to meet the evolving needs of a complex society.

> The Constitution of the United States does not preclude resourcefulness of relationships between states on matters as to which there is no grant of power to Congress and as to which the range of authority restricted

within an individual state is inadequate. By reciprocal, voluntary legislation the states have invented methods to accomplish fruitful and unprohibited ends ... Comity among states, an end particularly to be cherished when the object is enforcement of internal criminal laws, is not to be defeated by an *a priori* restrictive view of state power.[8]

EXTRADITION

Unless major steps are taken to secure the attendance of witnesses from abroad and the international transmission of evidence, extradition will play a pivotal role in the battle against international crime. When considering extradition in respect of such crimes, in respect of which many states will have extraterritorial jurisdiction to conduct the trial and enter a conviction, the question often will be not simply whether the requesting state has jurisdiction under its own laws to try the accused but whether that state is the most appropriate place for the trial – a kind of criminal *forum conveniens* question. It will be in the state where most of the prosecution witnesses are present or where their presence can be compelled that a conviction is most likely to be obtained.

For extraditions being sought under the European Convention on Extradition or in the EU states with legislation modelled on this convention, this question will arise under Articles 7 and 17; the former, which has been mentioned briefly above, deals with where the offence in question is also an offence under the law of the requested state, the latter deals with where two or more states make concurrent or conflicting requests for a person's extradition. Any new convention or measure would need to pay more attention to this problem, which would have rarely occurred in the mid-1950s when the European Convention on Extradition was being drafted.

CONCLUSION

To date comparatively little has been achieved (at least outside the fields of police and customs cooperation and the fight against fraud) under Article K.1 of the Maastricht treaty in terms of hard law initiatives directed at combating international crime and, before the European Union adopts significant initiatives in the international criminal law field, it may be that the procedures for decision-making under the "Third Pillar" will have to be altered to remove the veto of any single member state or to facilitate lesser numbers of states in forging ahead with closer cooperation between themselves. One way or another, the agenda for potential initiatives will be large and it will be interesting to see which topics are given precedence in the concerted effort to combat the rising tide of transnational crime.

NOTES

1. See OJ No.C 78, 30 March, 1995.
2. See in this regard the Presidency Conclusions of the Florence European Council of 21 and 22 June 1996 (SN 300/96).
3. *R.* v. *Governor of Pentonville Prison, ex p. Lee* [1993], 1 W.L.R. 1294 at p.1300.
4. *Shannon* v. *Ireland* [1984] I.R. 548.
5. 42 Geo. III. c. 85.
6. Cf. *McDonald* v. *McMahon* (Barrington J. 13 May 1988).
7. Cf. *Aamand* v. *Smithwick* [1995] 1 I.L.R.M. 61.
8. *New York* v. *O'Neill*, 359 U.S. 1 (1958) at pp.11-12.

CHAPTER 5
EUROPOL – A WATERSHED IN EU
LAW ENFORCEMENT COOPERATION?

VAL FLYNN[1]

"THE MOST EFFECTIVE WEAPON AGAINST ALL FORMS OF CRIME IS
COOPERATION"[2]

INTRODUCTION[3]

This chapter focuses on one relatively modest, but vitally important initiative by European Union (EU) member states to create a European Police Office (Europol). It includes a brief overview of how law enforcement is organised within different member states, and alludes to some of the different inter-governmental fora dedicated to advancing law enforcement cooperation within the Union.[4] This is followed by a critical appraisal of the role of the Irish government with regard to the development of Europol during its six-month Presidency of the European Council.[5] Finally, it recalls the origins of Europol and traces the initial development and planning stages of its establishment to date. First, to illustrate the need for creating a form of dedicated agency like Europol to improve EU law enforcement cooperation, it is appropriate to take a look at the current and future threats to the security of the EU citizen from all aspects of organised crime.

INTERNAL SECURITY THREATS AND CHALLENGES

Transnational criminals and terrorists have been very quick to realise and seize upon new opportunities in what is for them a new world disorder. Crime has become a global industry using the latest commercially available technologies and sophisticated networking methods. Organised crime groups frequently pose a threat to the integrity of national financial and commercial institutions in Europe and throughout the world. Although the patterns may vary, all EU member states including Ireland are confronted with serious problems arising from the use, smuggling and production of illegal drugs and associated money-laundering activities.[6] While the majority of illicit drugs consumed in member states originate outside the Union, illegal drug use is expanding both geographically and in terms of products.

The EU member states are viewed by drug cartels and transnational organised crime groups as cash-rich societies where they can readily market their illegal drugs.

While closer European integration has undoubtedly brought substantial economic and social benefits to the overwhelming majority of its citizens, it has also created small pockets of social exclusion, which occasionally become a breeding ground for extremist groups and radical single issue groups. Over the past few years a number of EU member states have experienced an upsurge in racism, xenophobia and anti-Semitism. In particular France, Germany and Austria have witnessed a substantial increase in the number of racist and anti-Semitic incidents which have involved shocking acts of violence.

The collapse of the former Soviet Union and the emergence of new democratic market-economies in Central and Eastern European Countries (CEEC) have created exciting new business and investment opportunities and challenges for everybody.[7] However, the social and political changes needed for the transition phase have brought about unwelcome by-products such as high levels of violent organised crime, widespread corruption and sporadic ethnic conflicts. Crime organisations have infiltrated the banking industry in most of these countries and their economies are being strangled by bribery, extortion and corruption. The changes in the nature of political-ly-motivated violence, and the acceleration in the growth of organised criminal activity within these countries add to the numerous other problems associated with the transition to a free market economy in many CEEC countries. The rapid change to a market economy and the unparalleled rise in organised crime have resulted in a near total breakdown in law enforcement in many of these countries. It is inevitable that widespread corruption and organised crime will permeate into and affect the integrity of EU society as a whole.

Although the incidents of terrorist-related acts of violence in the Union have declined since the 1980s, terrorism continues to be a threat to civil society in a number of member states.[8] The ideologically motivated terrorism of the 1970s and 1980s, as depicted by Germany's Red Army Faction (RAF) and Italy's Red Brigades (RB), may have rescinded for the time being; nevertheless there are still groups like the Greek *quasi* Marxist-Leninist group, the Revolutionary Organisation 17 November (17 Nov.), which continue to target state interests like the police, military and business community. Moreover, certain members states like Ireland, the United Kingdom and Spain are still confronted by separatist/nationalist groups such as the Provisional Irish Republican Army and the Basque Fatherland and

Liberty (ETA). The risk of political violence from the ethnic, cultural and religious stress on the opposite side of the Mediterranean Basin and in some parts of Eastern Europe is also a very real one. France is currently affected from time to time by spillover from extremist Islamic terrorist groups sponsored by certain North African and Middle East regimes.

Some authorities have recently pointed out that in addition to traditional forms of insecurity there is a need to pay particular attention to new and emerging forms of crime which are appearing on the scene, e.g. the smuggling of illegal nuclear, biological and chemical materials.[9] A number of seizures and arrests in 1994/5 by German law enforcement authorities highlighted the sobering possibility of nuclear materials falling into the hands of terrorists. The involvement of organised crime in the trafficking of women and sexual exploitation of children, and the illegal trafficking in body parts, proves once more that for organised crime, if the profits are high and the risks are low, then the nature of the commodity is more or less irrelevant. Moreover, the increased popularity of the Internet and the possibility of using the net to disseminate terrorist propaganda, racist, anti-Semitic and pornographic material has become a new and worrying feature on an already crowded internal security agenda. Already this year the Swiss government took action against an Internet server company for allowing the Basque separatist group to publish a home page using their service.[10] Cybercrime and the improper use of the Internet have become new forms of crime which raise a number of questions: should we police the net, can we police the net, and who should police the net?

The fear of many senior EU law enforcement officers is that in the global market-place of the twenty-first century, terrorists and organised crime groups will continue to undermine traditional methods of law enforcement. It is not surprising, therefore, that many senior police officers have openly stated that the establishment of a structured dedicated system of information-gathering and analysis like Europol would be a necessary and vital first step towards combating these internal security threats by strengthening EU law enforcement cooperation.

All the above-mentioned traditional and emerging crime areas are in a sense distinct. However, all have one common denominator in that they are a transnational/transfrontier phenomena. As a result, they should not be viewed as simply problems for individual member states to combat on their own, and from time to time within specialised but loose intergovernmental fora. There is a need to move progressively from the traditional internal security paradigm which is largely based on territorial integrity to one which is capable of handling the new and asymmetric vulnerabilities,[11] which have already begun to emerge. It is apparent that the first step to successfully combating and countering these security threats would be to create new institutionalised law enforcement mechanisms within the EU institutional structure, mechanisms which would be capable of giving a lucid as possible analysis of the internal security problems confronting the EU and the member states, as well as drawing up a strategic action plan which would provide for combating them.

The existing international fora for dealing with law enforcement cooperation are inadequate for dealing with these traditional and emerging law enforcement threats. A recent consensus has developed that a multinational response with multi-agency activity, to deal with EU law enforcement issues, is urgently needed.

THE NATURE OF LAW ENFORCEMENT IN EUROPE – POLICING

EU law enforcement[12] is extremely complex. Indeed the word "policing" and the term "law enforcement" have very different meanings in different EU member states. This lack of uniformity between member states is further complicated by the fact that there is no appropriate framework to compare and contrast the different systems. The organisational structure and operational duties of law enforcement agencies and judicial systems vary greatly between – and often within – EU member states. This is a reflection of the history, culture and traditions of each member state in question. There are approximately 121 separate police forces in the fifteen EU member states employing over 1.3 million police officers.[13] A number of member states, such as France and Belgium, have twin structures with a state police force and a *gendarmerie*. Others like the UK (which has 42 independent police forces) and The Netherlands have regionalised systems, while in countries like Denmark and Ireland, law enforcement is organised at national level. The criminal justice systems under which they operate are also different. These are, adversarial *or* inquisitorial systems, with either statute with case law, *or* systematic codes and regulations. The powers of law enforcement officers and the accountability of their agencies vary depending on the member state in question.

Reliable statistics about the incidents of transfrontier crime in the EU are scarce and those that do try to give a Euro-level picture are contentious. It is extremely difficult to give accurate crime statistics at a European level because of the differences in member states between the procedures and techniques for reporting and investigating crime.[14]

In general, law enforcement is a policy area which is much neglected in the past and characterised by large helpings of rhetoric and very little real political will. The level of priority or attention given to these issues by respective EU governments is low and appears to depend primarily upon what has often been called the politics of the latest outrage. With very few exceptions, law enforcement strategies tend to be reactive as opposed to proactive. Almost every endeavour or campaign to change or improve the way law enforcement works in member states is the direct result of public outcry or discord at some recent tragic event involving law enforcement issues. Ireland is no exception to this rule: we should consider such the organisational changes that were imposed upon the Irish police as a result of the spate of unsolved murders in the West of Ireland in 1995, the reinforcement of the various units responsible for combating illegal drugs and organised crime as a result of the recent murder of the crime reporter Veronica Guerin and the anti-drugs demonstrations in Dublin.

What is policing going to look like in the EU in the near future? Already in most member states, as has been the case in the United States some years now, those employed by private security companies outnumber those employed in the police force.[15] If this trend continues, the traditional image such as the Garda on the beat in Ireland will soon be a thing of the past. Policing in Ireland, as in the rest of Europe, will mean little more than a mobile, heavily armed gendarmerie moving from one flash point to another to maintain public order and quell social unrest. In recent years, there has been a trend in many EU member states away from the traditional decentralised law enforcement systems towards more centralised law enforcement systems which are supplemented by national specialist units.

There has been a general agreement among EU member states for some time that the myriad of existing organisations do not adequately address the realities of contemporary law enforcement issues in the Union. There are numerous intergovernmental consultative and cooperation bodies which were set up by governments or international organisations and which deal with international police cooperation among other matters, bodies such as ICPO/Interpol, GAFI (G15), CEPC and the Pompidou Group in the framework of the Council of Europe, the Co-ordinators' Group, TREVI, UCLAF, MAG, MAG '92, and the Ad Hoc Group on Immigration, the Benelux or Schengen countries, the police working group.[16] The quality and intensity of cooperation within and between these groups varies greatly. Their agreements and structures fall into two different categories: those which are similar in terms of their Crime area (drugs, terrorism, fraud, etc.) and those which are similar in their territorial remit (European Union, Council of Europe, UN, etc.) What these initiatives have in common is that they are predominantly intergovernmental in character and outside the traditional EC decision-making mechanism.[17]

Taking into account the above-mentioned internal security threats and the way law enforcement cooperation has been traditionally organised, it may be suggested that if the decision to create an effective European-level law enforcement agency had been a question solely for law enforcement practitioners then a body such as Europol might well have been the sort of entity which would have been established long before now. However, decisions and agreements needed to establish Europol are ones which are – and must be – formulated in a Community policy which is politically driven and politically accountable.

THE TABOO SUBJECT

When the founding fathers of European integration drafted the Treaty of Rome,[18] they decided in their wisdom to omit any specific reference to security cooperation (either internal or external) in a treaty which they hoped would be a blueprint for a peaceful and safer Europe. In fact, security in the context of the European Economic Community (EEC) remained largely a taboo subject and very much outside the legitimate remit of the civilian power image of the EEC. It was not until the mid-1970s and early-1980s, when a majority of the then member states began to experience a dramatic upsurge in indigenous and international terrorism, that certain aspects of internal security appeared on the fringes of the EEC agenda.[19] Realising that they all faced similar problems, which they could not solve individually, and recognising the problematic nature of the various international counter-terrorism conventions and the inadequacies of the existing multilateral fora (such as ICPO/Interpol, UN, WTO, Council of Europe, Trevi, etc.), member states decided to inject a degree of predictability and commonality into their known positions on terrorism.[20] Originally there was never any intention of developing a common policy to combat terrorism. However, it did give rise to the European Council creating the Trevi Group,[21] an intergovernmental system of consultation between senior justice and interior officials.[22]

Partly due to the divergence between the civil law states and the common law states, but mainly due to the wariness that many member states had about the incursion of EC law into the realm of issues of national sovereignty little, if any, institutional progress was made during the initial period. However, member states agreed to more common positions with regard to counter-terrorism. Furthermore, senior interior ministers came together regularly (every six months) to discuss common problems arising from terrorist attacks within certain member states or against their interests abroad. Cooperation during this period was *ad hoc* and piecemeal but it can however also be described as the first generation of EC law enforcement.

Nearly thirty years after the Treaty of Rome, the process of creating a Single European Market (SEM) by the end of 1992, which was introduced by the Signal European Act (SEA),[23] brought many issues relating to internal and external security firmly on to the EC agenda and led to a qualitative change in the status of EC law enforcement cooperation. The objective of the completion of the SEM and the abolition of all frontier controls between EC member states required that the external frontier controls be reinforced to compensate for any loss of security arising from terrorism, transnational crime, illegal immigration and asylum seekers. The idea of removing the internal frontiers raised alarm bells among many informed observers who forecast a rising tide of terrorism, increased transnational crime and a dramatic upsurge in illegal immigration.[24] This opinion was shared by many senior police officers in member states who urged their respective governments to undertake special measures to off-set the perceived threats.[25]

The 1988 Rhodes European Council set up a Group of Coordinators consisting of national representatives to work out the complexities of eliminating internal frontier controls. On 9 December 1988, an additional working group called Trevi '92 was added to the existing three Trevi working groups. The working group met regularly (nearly every month) and focused on law enforcement and security issues relating to the free movement of people and the measures needed to compensate for any resulting loss of security. In Dublin in 1990, this working group drafted the Trevi Programme of Action, which outlined specific areas and methods of cooperation between police and security services for the implementation of the SEM.[26]

The creation and development of the Trevi Group is of particular significance, both directly and indirectly, to the birth of Europol. While its initial objective was to provide a basis for greater cooperation among EC member states to combat terrorism, its remit was quickly widened to include other areas of law enforcement including illegal drug trafficking and organised crime. More importantly, it helped exorcise the taboo surrounding any form of cooperation between EC member states on law enforcement issues. In addition, it played a major psychological role in bringing together, on a regular basis, ministers and senior officials from the different interior ministries, who until then had very little, if any, experience in cooperating in a multilateral environment with their colleagues in other member states. This, in addition to Trevi's new role in organising the security measures judged essential to compensate for any loss of security as a result of the abolition of the internal frontier controls for the SEM, involved the European Commission for the first time (as an observer). It created a tangible (if weak) link between the efforts to complete the SEM and greater cooperation between EC law enforcement agencies.

The establishment of the SEM, on the other hand, created for the first time the concept of a European internal security continuum.[27] It lumped together issues like illegal immigration and asylum with traditional law enforcement issues like terrorism, organised crime and drug trafficking. It resulted in the widening and intensification of the activities of the Trevi Group. This marked a small but significant shift in EC judicial and law enforcement cooperation from one of loose *ad hoc* cooperation to one of continuous interaction.[28] While the EC member states had taken an extraordinarily long time to learn just to speak with one voice on these issues they now had to formulate together Community-wide measures to compensate for the abolition of the internal frontier controls which was an essential part of the completion of the internal market. During this period, a new and healthy level of cooperation was also established between the senior law enforcement officers and European Commission officials, who had primary responsibility for realising the completion of the SEM and a central role in initiating co-ordination policies in this area. It also led many of those closely involved in the process to start asking vital questions about where EU law enforcement cooperation should go from there. However, EU law enforcement cooperation remained non-treaty based and more importantly very non-transparent.

EUROPOL – THE IDEA

The idea of creating a dedicated European law enforcement structure is not as new as many may think. Its origins cannot be justifiably pin-pointed to any one particular political statement or declaration. The true origins of the Europol idea lie in many places.[29] Discussions about creating a Europol-type structure for enhancing police cooperation in Europe first came to the fore within the International Criminal Police Organisation (ICPO/Interpol) in the 1970s.[30] At an Interpol European Regional Conference in 1981, the German delegation proposed the setting up of a European Regional Bureau,[31] and created a special committee which met regularly to discuss the proposal. However, the idea was never realised despite "a long and varied discursive career".[32] In 1989 Sir Peter Imbert, a former UK Metropolitan Police Commissioner, noted that "The time is not right to consider a European Police Force – and those who are currently advocating it are perhaps expecting us to run before we have shown we can walk".[33]

However, the political origins of the current initiatives to establish Europol are often rightly linked to a number of statements made by Chancellor Kohl. In 1988, he spoke at a Franco-German conference of the immediate need to create a European FBI, to combat terrorism, drug-trafficking and major international organised crime. At that time not only was Germany, as ever, the front engine of the EU train trying to quicken the pace of European integration in a number of different political and economic policy areas. There were also underlying domestic factors. As a front-line state with former Soviet Union countries, Germany feared that they would be particularly vulnerable to any increases in transnational organised crime, illegal drug trafficking, illegal immigration or even illegal trafficking in nuclear materials. The idea of creating a European-style FBI to combat these perceived threats was highly popular with German voters.

In Edinburgh, in May 1991, with the full weight of the German government behind him, Chancellor Kohl declared to his fellow EU heads of state that greater cooperation between the various EU law enforcement agencies was not only essential for the completion of the SEM but a vital and overdue component of EU political union. He insisted on the creation of a European Police Force "that would be able to operate without let up or hindrance in all the Community countries in important matters such as the fight against drug barons or organised international crime".[34]

Later in the year at the European Council meeting in Luxembourg in June 1991,[35] Kohl made the first official proposal for a central European Criminal Investigation Office to be fully established and competent in the area before the end of 1993.[36] The European Criminal Investigation Office which Chancellor Kohl had in mind was proposed along the lines of the Bundeskriminalamt (BKA) which is similar in many ways to the more familiar US FBI federal model of law enforcement. The boldness of the proposal was greeted with a certain amount of astonishment by some heads of state and their ministers, but they agreed late at night to have a detailed feasibility study on the proposal, allegedly only after Chancellor Kohl threatened to re-negotiate everything that had been agreed over the previous two days. At this stage, the opposition was from a small minority of member states led by the Danish and United Kingdom governments, who feared that the proposal would lead to a supranational body being created which would eventually encroach on what they believed to be core areas of national sovereignty.

In August 1991, a special Ad Hoc Working Group on Europol (AHWGE) was established under Trevi. This group was given the responsibility of establishing a needs assessment report on Europol and reporting back to Trevi ministers. At a meeting in Maastricht in December 1991 the Trevi ministers adopted a *Report on the Development of Europol* and agreed to accelerate the process of its establishment.[37] The report recommended the establishment of Europol/EDU in a number of progressive stages. First, they agreed to establish a European Drugs Intelligence Unit (EDIU),[38] as a non-operational centralised system with responsibility for the exchange of information and experiences which would serve as a clearing house point for the different National Drugs Intelligence Units (NDIU) in each member state.[39] Secondly, entry and exit points or Liaison Centres were to be set up in each of the then twelve EC member states. The final stage would be the expansion of the first two stages into a mature non-operational Europol/EDU which would have as its core business and initial priority the strategic analysis of intelligence relating to the different aspects of illegal drugs trafficking and drugs related crime.

The choice of the fight against drugs as the focus of Europol's initial activities is not surprising given the scourge of drug addiction in Europe in recent years and the unwelcoming effect it was having on the social fabric of society throughout the Union.[40] It was also an area where greater and more effective cooperation between the different EC member states' law enforcement agencies was urgently required. At the time there was ongoing heated debate between the French interior ministry and The Netherlands ministry over the latter's soft line approach and flexible therapies towards curbing illegal drugs.[41]

THE EMBRYONIC STAGE

The European Council in Lisbon on 26-27 June 1992 decided that a draft Convention[42] should be prepared which would provide a legal basis for the fully developed Europol.[43] Also in the same month, the Trevi ministers decided at their meeting to create a Europol Project Team (EPT) accountable to the Ad Hoc Working Group on Europol (AHWGE)[44] for the planning and overseeing of the setting-up stage of Europol/EDU which was to be the precursor to a fully-fledged Europol. To lead this project team, which was to be the embryo of what was to become Europol, Jürgen Storbeck[45] was seconded from the German BKA. He wasted no time in establishing four sub-groups within the EPT in order to achieve their main task of creating a permanent structure for establishing Europol/EDU:

- International technical coordination

- Data processing

- Computer and telecommunications

- Logistics (personal finance, administration etc).

From the outset, the location of EPT was the subject of much discussion and sometimes unfair ridicule. The temporary accommodation in Strasbourg where the EPT was based from September 1992 until December 1993 was described by Lord Bethall as "this shabby hut outside Strasbourg".[47] The long and intense wrangling over the eventual permanent location of Europol is an excellent example of EC horse trading at its best. The various different proposals ranged from a German proposal for it to be located at or beside the BKA in Wiesbaden, a British one to have it housed in the Metropolitan Police HQ in London, to another suggestion that it be co-located with Interpol in Lyon in France.

Unfortunately, as with many other of the issues with regard to Europol/EDU the question of where to permanently locate Europol involved much more than the simple question of the optimum physical location. Instead, it became embroiled in the overall agreement by EC member states on the permanent sites for the main EC institutions.[47] The whole issue of the location of the EC Institutions (in particular the European Parliament, European Commission and European Central Bank) was subject to much heated debate not only between the EC member states, but also between EC member state governments and opposition parties especially at election times. However, the long list of possible permanent locations for Europol was eventually reduced to a choice between the two most viable locations: the newly-vacated HQ of the Dutch Criminal Investigations Department (CRI)[48] and an unspecified building close to the EP in Strasbourg.

At a JHA Council Meeting in Copenhagen in June 1993 a Ministerial Agreement[49] was signed, which set out for the first time the scope and remit of "European Drugs Unit Europol/EDU" as it was officially called. Restating the urgency of the need for greater EU-level law enforcement cooperation, the ministers set out the initial function of Europol/EDU which was to organise the exchange of information on narcotic drugs. The unit was to act as a non-operational team for the exchange and analysis of intelligence in relation to illicit drug trafficking to the criminal organisations involved and to associated money laundering activities affecting two or more member states. On 29 October 1993, the European Council decided at its meeting in Brussels that the Hague would be the permanent location for Europol/EDU.

The next major step in the development of Europol/EDU arrived with the signing of the Maastricht Treaty.

TREATY ON EUROPEAN UNION (TEU) – MAASTRICHT

As has been seen elsewhere in this book, the TEU established the Union as a three-pillar structure and introduced a major new policy field called Title VI Justice and Home Affairs (JHA).[50] Article K.1 of Title VI identified nine areas as matters of common interest including: "police cooperation for the purpose of preventing and combating terrorism, unlawful drug trafficking and other serious forms of international crime, including if necessary certain aspects of customs cooperation, in connection with the organisation of a Union-wide system for exchanging information within a European Police Office (Europol)".[51]

While for the first time the Maastricht Treaty brought the whole area of JHA cooperation much closer to the EC framework, it was, however, a disappointment to those who wanted to move forward from the traditional intergovernmental decision-making procedure to full communitarisation of JHA issues.[52] The new EU security continuum[53] mentioned in Article K.1 above bears a resemblance to the list which was cobbled together during the process of completing the SEM. It should be pointed out that it fails to incorporate all the existing and newly emerging internal security threats which face the citizens of the Union. However, this interesting subject is well beyond the scope of this particular chapter.

The inclusion of a European Police Office (Europol) under Art. K.1(9) and the Declaration on Police Cooperation[54] in the Final Act of the TEU was above all a confirmation of the discussions and agreements which had already taken place on the creation and establishment of Europol. The provisions on Europol in the TEU were far less extensive or ambitious than had originally been proposed by Chancellor Kohl, but it nonetheless established a solid treaty basis for future progress. Shortly before the French referendum on the Maastricht Treaty, President Mitterrand used the Europol/EDU idea to warn French citizens that "No to Maastricht would be a Yes to the Mafia."[55]

Title VI did, however, provide for much-needed structural changes in the workings of EU law enforcement cooperation. Importantly, it provided for the replacement of the outdated Trevi Group, with the creation of the new K.4 Committee and its three Steering Groups (see JHA Organisational Structure p.92). The work of setting up Europol/EDU and the preparation of the draft convention were transferred to the K.4 Steering Committee II, which was responsible for law enforcement issues (see Title VI Organisational Structure). A draft convention drawn up by the Steering Group II was presented to the European Council on 8 November 1993. The draft covered the following headings:

- the creation of EDU, its objectives and functions (not including terrorism)
- national units and their functions
- capacity of EDU to adopt its own rules of procedure
- creation of an Administrative Council
- principles behind the apportionment of a Director
- principles governing EDU's budget, and the auditing of accounts.

DRAFTING A CONVENTION

The process involved in concluding a draft convention for Europol/EDU was slow and cumbersome and the problems were manifold.[56] First, there was, as we have already seen, very little tradition of activity in this area at EC level. There was a strong underlying belief held by a majority of EU member states that anything to do with law enforcement cooperation on an EU level meant an almost certain erosion of national sovereignty. Secondly, conventions as legal instruments under Title VI are cumbersome legal instruments which require not only unanimity in the European Council, but also parliamentary ratification in all fifteen EU member states before they legally come into force. Thirdly, the five-level decision-making apparatus of the new JHA organisational structure (see following diagram), required unanimous approval by the JHA Council of Ministers and was thus ideal for slowing-down or even impeding the decision-making process. Furthermore, the German government, so long the political godfather of the Europol idea, seemed to go temporarily cold on the whole idea.[57]

The initial debate between member states on drafting the convention concerned the question whether or not Europol/EDU should be provided with executive and/or operational powers in order for its officials to be able to conduct law enforcement investigations in the member states. In the absence of a suitable EU criminal justice framework, it was generally agreed that this was not feasible in the near future.

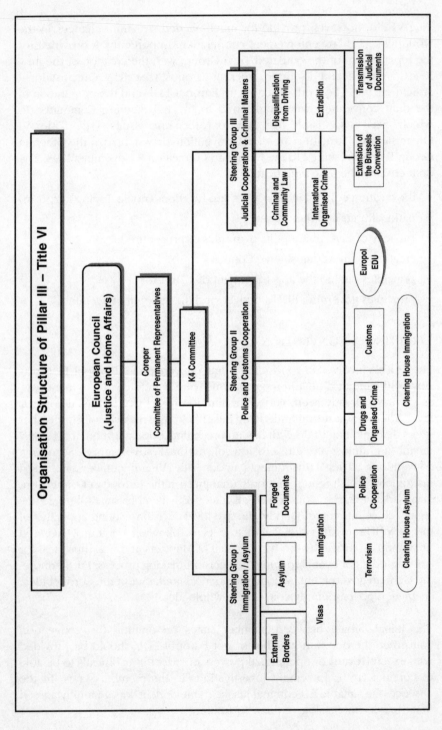

Organisation Structure of Pillar III – Title VI

Further delays and problems in drafting the convention were mainly related to Europol's objectives and remit. Attempts by Spain and Greece, with the support of many EU member states, to include counter-terrorism within the initial mandate of Europol provoked major disagreement.[58] The disagreement was eventually widened to involve a tit-for-tat filibustering between Spain and the UK over the Europol/EDU Convention and the External Borders Convention. This somehow became embroiled in the centuries-old dispute between Spain and the UK over the status of Gibraltar. In the end, it was agreed that terrorism would be included in the remit of Europol/EDU within two years at the latest following the entry into force of the Europol Convention.[59] Due to the controversial nature of terrorism and the absence of any agreed legal definition on terrorism, this arrangement seems reasonable.

In an effort to try to satisfy the apprehension of certain member states, AHWGE suggested that the list of functions of Europol/EDU should not be definitive. They advised that a pre-emptive clause should be included, which would allow other specific functions, within the limits specific in Art. K.1(9) to be bestowed on Europol as necessary in the future. This would have to be done by unanimous decision of the JHA Council of Ministers.

Additional issues which proved difficult to resolve at first were those involving accountability and data protection. Accountability and the question of "who guards the guards" have always been among the toughest conundrums of state craft, especially where law enforcement and human rights are involved.[60] The question was raised: What if a citizen wanted to register a complaint against Europol/EDU? Should they do so in their national courts or would they have to apply to the Dutch courts where Europol is based? Furthermore, the fact that Europol/EDU was to have the power to hold information (and intelligence) on people raised many questions about personal privacy concerns. As a result the provisions in the convention had to be elaborate in order to comply with the different data protection laws in EU member states.

The longest and most contentious deadlock was over the issue of whether or not the European Court of Justice (ECJ) in Luxembourg should have the power to settle disputes arising from the interpretation of the rules establishing Europol.[61] Again, the vast majority of member states supported a role for the ECJ but the UK government steadfastly opposed it saying that their opposition to any role for the Court was simply a legal matter.[62] They insisted that under the provisions of the TEU only the member states could be the final arbitrators. The UK Home Office refused to be moved saying that the JHA is and will remain fundamentally intergovernmental in nature and that precludes any role for the ECJ including the right to make preliminary rulings on cases arising from the operations of Europol/EDU.

At the Essen European Council in December 1994, despite intensive action by the German Presidency,[63] there was no political agreement on the final text of the draft Convention. However, the Council did decide to enlarge Europol/EDU's remit to include motor vehicle crime, crime connected with nuclear and radioactive substances, illegal immigration smuggling and illegal money laundering.[64] The Cannes European Council in June 1995 agreed to settle the question of the possible role and jurisdiction of the ECJ with regard to the Convention at its June 1996 meeting. On 26 July 1995, the Europol Convention was signed by the fifteen governments of the EU without resolving the dispute over the ECJ. Later in the year, an effort by the Spanish Presidency to negotiate a compromise in time for the European Council in Madrid in December 1995 failed.

Just as an agreement was being reached by all member states on the remaining issues, the process became embroiled in the British Beef Crisis which resulted in the UK government withholding agreement to any formal EU decisions, including any agreement on the Europol/EDU Convention.[65] It was not until the Florence European Council in June 1996 that the outstanding problem was solved concerning the establishment of Europol/EDU, enabling the ECJ to give a preliminary ruling on the interpretation of the Europol Convention.[66] At a conference of representatives of the member state governments in July 1996, the Committee of Permanent Representatives (COREPER) signed the Protocol to the Europol Convention on behalf of their respective governments.

This event now makes way for the signed Convention and Protocol to be ratified by the fifteen EU national parliaments before it can come into operation. A voluntary Protocol was established giving the ECJ juristiction over preliminary judgments only in those member states which wanted it. National parliaments can only agree the Convention as a whole; they cannot amend or change it in any way. There were at least ten draft texts of the Europol/EDU Convention, the most significant ones being: November 1993, October 1994, November 1994 and April 1995.[67] The European Council had on three occasions set deadlines for the completion and signing of the Convention.

As requested by the Essen European Council and in anticipation of the Europol Convention, a Joint Action[68] was signed on the basis of Article K 3 of the TEU by the fifteen EU member states on 20 March 1995 to allow Europol/EDU to operate. This Joint Action replaced the Copenhagen

Ministerial Agreement of June 1993 on the establishment of the Europol/EDU in addition to encompassing three new member states (Austria, Finland and Sweden); it also extended the mandate of Europol/EDU to support EU-wide information exchange on:

- illicit drug trafficking

- illicit trafficking in radioactive and nuclear substances

- crimes involving clandestine immigration networks

- illicit vehicle trafficking

together with criminal organisations involved and associated with money-laundering activities.

ADDED VALUE OR DUPLICATION ?

While the negotiations to draft a Convention progressed cautiously, the question of duplication between existing initiatives or organisations and the likelihood of inter-agency rivalry between Europol and Interpol was the focus of much discussion in EU law enforcement circles. Fortunately, the debate moved quickly into a more mature phase and as one senior Europol/EDU official observed, the reality is that the Euro-crime market is big enough to accommodate one more organisation or structure.

In fact, not only do Europol and Interpol differ greatly in geographical coverage (one being regional and the other being international), but they also differ greatly in intensity of activities with Europol operating at a much closer level to EU member states' law enforcement agencies than is possible for an organisation like Interpol with a membership of 176 countries. Unlike Europol/EDU, Interpol operates without government involvement. Critics of Interpol, mostly US police chiefs, have often unfairly described it as an elaborate and expensive electronic Post Box for simply transferring messages from one national police HQ to another. In this, Europol/EDU will have added value over Interpol in many respects – notably in the fact that it is very much a multi-law enforcement agency which includes the police and customs, and is responsible for the strategic analysis of the information it receives. Speaking to Police Officers in Sunne in Sweden in August 1995, EC Commissioner Anita Gradin pointed out that the Europol Convention specifically provided for Europol/EDU to cooperate with other law enforcement organisations and she hoped that when the Europol/EDU

Convention came into force cooperation with Interpol would be quickly formalised.[69]

Europol/EDU activities will be very different from those of Interpol. Unlike Interpol, it is not a straightforward police organisation, since its works will involve customs officials and analysts. Analysis will be one of Europol/EDU's principal assignments; this will involve both trend analysis and operational analysis. Europol will also work on developing methods of combating crime as well as helping national police and customs authorities to coordinate their preliminary investigations in cases affecting more than one EU member state. Shortly, Europol/EDU's two large databases are expected to be more comprehensive and detailed than those of Interpol.

During the long and difficult period of political wrangling and bickering over the final text of the draft Convention, it was not surprising that fresh doubts emerged over the project. Some members of the Swedish parliament questioned if the same effort and the 5 million ECU required to set up Europol/EDU would not have been better spent on trying to improve and re-engineer existing fora like Interpol or even the UN. Other suggestions concerned the enlargement of the Council of Europe over the past few years to incorporate all the CEEC, and more recently Russia, to make a European House of thirty-nine member states. A number of observers questioned whether or not Europol or an equivalent law enforcement agency would be better suited under the aegis of the Council of Europe than the EU. It is the view of the author that the answer to these questions will only become apparent in the fullness of time.

ROLE OF THE EUROPEAN PARLIAMENT AND COMMISSION

From the outset, the European Parliament's Committee on Civil Liberties and Internal Affairs which deals with JHA issues played a leading role in promoting and supporting the Europol idea. It was very active in guaranteeing that the questions about accountability and transparency of Europol/EDU were adequately addressed. They were highly incensed when they were not consulted under Article K.6 of the TEU at any stage during the negotiations. This, many MEPs believed, was reminiscent of the pre-TEU days when negotiations were carried out by a small group of bureaucratic elites in secrecy behind closed doors. The Cooney Report[70] in 1992 on the Spread of Organised Crime linked to Drug Trafficking in the EU, marked the beginning of an important commitment by a number of Irish MEPs in helping to forge an important role for the EP in a wide range of JHA matters and in particular the establishment of Europol/EDU.

The Limerick-based MEP J. Cushnahan, a former member of the influential EP Committee on Institutional Affairs and a long-time advocate of greater EU law enforcement cooperation, including the establishment of Europol,[71] believes that the role of the EP in supplementing and enhancing the proposed scrutiny by national parliaments is indispensable. Furthermore, he would like to see the EP being regularly consulted in advance about the Europol budget (article K.6) and the appointment of the Europol coordinator (article K.8). He believes that Europol is but the tip of the iceberg when it comes to what could and should be achieved in the field of EU law enforcement cooperation. He also foresees the creation of a European Coastal Guard Service to follow closely in the wake of a fully functioning Europol. Maritime crime is not the stuff of Blackbeard, he says, but a forgotten area of EU law enforcement which also needs to be tackled at the earliest opportunity. He refers to the recent drugs haul of cocaine made off the south west cost of Ireland, estimated to be worth in the region of £200 million, as a triumph for the new multi-agency approach which is being adopted in Ireland in the fight against drugs.[72]

Mary Banotti MEP has campaigned relentlessly in recent years for tougher action to combat the illegal trafficking of women and sexual exploitation of children. She recently received strong support from the EP and a number of senior EU law enforcement officers for her proposal on the creation of a EU-wide Register on Missing Children and the widening of the Europol/EDU mandate to enable it to create such a database.

In January 1993 Pádraig Flynn was appointed the first European Commissioner with responsibility for JHA. Right from the outset Commissioner Flynn, a former justice minister, set out to explore how the Commission could use its very limited role in matters of JHA to speed up the process of establishing Europol/EDU. He has steadfastly pointed to the serious dangers facing EU citizens from drugs, terrorism and organised crime. In a final speech to the EP and the Justice and Home Affairs Council in December 1994, he was critical of the lack of concrete achievements under the Third Pillar as a whole, taking into consideration its relatively short existence. Commissioner Flynn expressed the view that the lack of progress on Europol/EDU was especially worrying and that the EU was doing nothing different to pre-Maastricht days when it was running scared of anything which might contain a real commitment to initiatives like Europol/EDU. Responsibility at Commission level for cooperation in justice then passed to the new Swedish Commissioner, Anita Gradin, who immediately took up the challenge and made the establishment of Europol/EDU one of her top priorities. She has been frank and outspoken in her assessment of the apparent lack of political commitment by EU member states on JHA and their half-hearted commitment to complete remaining legal procedures for ratification and entry into force of the Convention. She has supported calls for the widening of the Europol/EDU mandate to include trafficking in human beings, and questions concerning the sex trade with women and children.

Notwithstanding the on-going EU political battle over the Convention, Jürgen Storbeck (Coordinator of Europol/EDU) and his team continued with the day-to-day business of developing a Europol/EDU infrastructure which could tackle the law enforcement challenges facing the Union. From their high-tech, state of the art HQ in the heart of the Dutch capital, the Hague, progress is being made in leaps and bounds. All the national liaison officers have taken up their positions and the initial technical teething problems with communications have been speedily resolved. Storbeck's two-pronged approach for establishing Europol could be regarded as a microcosm study in European integration. While Storbeck plays the role of the ever-attentive courtier at the European Council of Ministers where political showdowns take place in the *realpolitik* fashion away from public scrutiny, he also maximises the functionalism bottom-up evolutionary approach to EU cooperation within agencies.

Already, within a short period of time and without the benefit of any formal agreement, Europol has proved its usefulness by helping various EU law enforcement agencies in a number of drugs-related crime and associated money laundering operations. It was able to provide expert advice on certain complicated technical investigations and strategic intelligence which allowed law enforcement agencies to maximise their over-stretched resources. It has already contributed to several successful law enforcement operations which have mostly been in drugs seizures. In early 1994, tactical intelligence supplied by Europol/EDU assisted Greek, Belgian and French law enforcement officers to successfully execute a major European illegal drugs operation. It also played a significant role in helping Spanish, Irish and UK agencies to smash an alleged Irish-based drugs running cartel.[73]

Acting as a non-operational team, it claims to provide added value to EU law enforcement agencies by:[74]

• exchanging information and intelligence

• supporting law enforcement agencies

- providing direct analysis support

- safeguarding confidentiality for EU member states' cross border cooperation and crime analysis

- developing expertise

- offering judicial insight

- bridging cultural, linguistic and judicial differences

- establishing bilateral and multilateral contacts.

STRUCTURE AND MANAGEMENT OF THE ORGANISATION

On Monday 3 January 1994, Europol/EDU commenced its activities in the former building of the Dutch Criminal Intelligence Service (CRI). A schematic outline of the structure is produced in the diagram on p. 103. From this it can be seen that the Unit has a management team which is headed by a coordinator.[75] He is assisted in his day-to-day running of the Unit by two assistant coordinators and two other members of the management team who report directly to him. The management team is supported by a staff unit, planning and development unit and a representative of the host state (The Netherlands). At present the 110 personnel employed include 35 liaison officers and assistants seconded to the liaison bureaux for the fifteen EU member states and 55 other staff members from member states.[76] Under the Europol Convention, each EU member state must establish a national unit to be the only liaison body between Europol and the competent national authorities.[77] There is provision for EU member states to have additional personnel (at their own expense) for multilateral coordination, planning and development.

The Convention also set out how the budget is drawn up and how the annual audit is carried out.[78] Being an intergovernmental Convention, the cost of running Europol is financed by member states. Contributions are determined according to a standard formula which takes into consideration the GNP of each member state. In March each year, the coordinator has to draw up a draft budget and draft establishment plan for the following financial year. After examination by the financial committee, they are then submitted to the management board for adoption in accordance with the procedure laid down in Title VI of the TEU.

IRELAND'S CONTRIBUTIONS TO THE EUROPOL/EDU BUDGET				
	1994	1995	1996	1997
Provisional contribution, IRL (year n), ECU	12,390	21,259	31,390	32,418
Estimated GNP, IRL (year -1), 1%, MECU	348,600	406,900	409,300	452,400
Estimated GNP percentage, IRL (year -1), %	0,600	0,600	0,600	0,700
Total budget EDU (excl. The Europol Computer System), MECU	2,065	3,918	5,002	5,602

(Source: Europol/EDU, The Hague)

By the end of May each year, the co-ordinator has to submit a report on the annual accounts of the previous year to be audited by a joint audit committee composed of three members, appointed by the Court of Auditors of the Communities, on a proposal from its president. The rules for performing this audit are laid down in the financial regulations. The establishment and maintenance costs for Europol/EDU are covered according to the above-mentioned scale. The maintenance costs of the liaison officers sent to the unit by member state ministries are covered by the respective ministries.

In June 1995, the Council adopted the final report on the 1994 budget and approved that the unspent budget be used to reduce member states' contributions to the 1995 budget.[79] The reason for this considerable surplus is mainly due to the fact that it was the first annual budget and it was very difficult to accurately foresee the real budgetary needs of the unit. It was also affected by the fact that the activities of the unit were considerably restricted by the continuing problems over its Convention. The 1995 budget was amended to a total amount of 3,918,000 ECU in June of 1995 in order to take into consideration the accession of the new EU member states (Austria, Finland and Sweden), as well as the unit's new tasks. The 1996 common budget of 4,997,000 ECU was approved in June 1995.[80] A recent proposal for an outline procurement strategy for the development of a Europol computer system has been approved and a small project team has been appointed to produce a cost statement of requirements at the end of 1996.

ACTIVITIES

The primary activity of Europol/EDU is currently the exchange of information and intelligence between Europol liaison officers (ELOs) and

Europol national units in respective law enforcement agencies of member states (police, gendarmerie, customs). An operational support room within Europol/EDU HQ ensures an expert round-the-clock multi-lingual service on investigations and analytical activities related to criminal activities of criminal groups active on an international basis.

Every day the number of bilateral and multilateral information requests from originating countries and enquiries handled through the ELO network is increasing.

The enquiries handled by the ELOs in 1995 can be broken down into working fields. The majority of enquiries are related to support of sensitive investigations, i.e. checking names, telephone numbers, vehicle licence plates, etc. The second largest working field relates to special expertise, i.e. concerning particular phenomena, e.g. "Crack", precursor chemicals, ethnic criminal groups, etc. or related to legal and technical or tactical questions. The remaining enquiries concern ongoing support for special law enforcement operations, i.e. controlled deliveries, etc.

NUMBER OF REQUESTS HANDLED BY EUROPOL/EDU – 1994/1995

Liaison Bureau	1994		1995	
	Sent	Received	Sent	Received
Austria	*	*	4	84
Belgium	104	72	112	263
Denmark	9	45	7	131
Finland	*	*	8	73
France	66	102	127	280
Germany	104	93	378	252
Greece	12	56	45	144
Ireland	15	45	83	125
Italy	27	116	115	257
Luxembourg	10	50	18	134
Portugal	22	34	124	137
Spain	8	106	34	351
Sweden	*	*	17	85
Netherlands	25	215	71	681
United Kingdom	62	97	281	251
TOTAL	**462**	**1,036**	**1,404**	**3,248**

(*Figures for Austria, Finland and Sweden are only from March 1995)
(Source: Europol/EDU, The Hague)

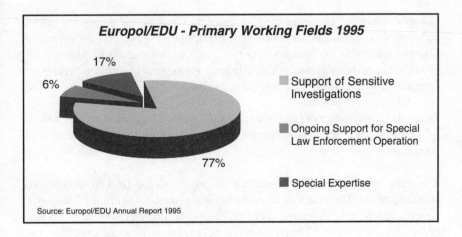

Europol/EDU - Primary Working Fields 1995

17%

6%

- Support of Sensitive Investigations

- Ongoing Support for Special Law Enforcement Operation

77%

- Special Expertise

Source: Europol/EDU Annual Report 1995

These enquiries can also be broken down by subject. The majority of requests relate to the ever-growing drugs problem, with the remainder divided between requests for exchange of information and intelligence on money laundering, illegal immigration networks and stolen vehicle trafficking. Europol/EDU hosts expert meetings to develop common EU strategies on controlled deliveries and trans-border surveillance operations. With regard to its three new areas of activity – radioactive and nuclear substances, clandestine immigration networks and vehicle trafficking – Europol/EDU has been meeting with different bodies and experts from member states in order to identify the issues, define the role of the unit in the particular field, create project teams and plan multi-annual work programmes and activities.

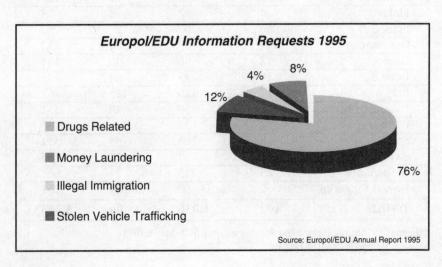

Europol/EDU Information Requests 1995

4%   8%

12%

- Drugs Related

- Money Laundering

- Illegal Immigration

- Stolen Vehicle Trafficking

76%

Source: Europol/EDU Annual Report 1995

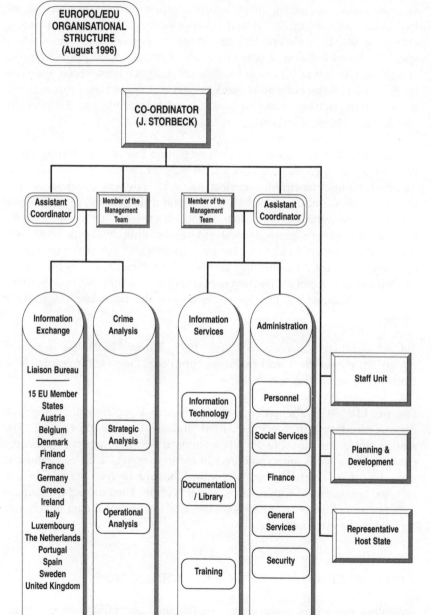

Despite its relatively short existence, the analytical department of Europol/EDU, with a staff of seven,[81] has produced a number of valuable strategic reports including an EU situation report on drug production and trafficking and the threats posed by specific organised criminal groups within the EU. They also provide assistance in operational enquiries where specialist knowledge and assistance are required to support complex enquiries. The first EU Criminal Intelligence Analysts' Conference organised by Europol/EDU recently at its headquarters highlighted the need for more work in standardising crime analysis throughout the EU and the need for developing analytical guidelines on technical analysis.

The unit also has an exceptional documentation bureau which they like to describe as an open sources information support service. It has formal and informal on-line electronic connections with law enforcement agency documentation centres, official EU institutions and agencies, world criminal justice library networks, the United Nations criminal justice information network, and various governmental and non-governmental organisations in the law enforcement field. Selective participation and use of the Internet as an open-source information support service is proving to be a useful support tool for law enforcement. The unit uses two electronic bulletin boards which serve as a permanent forum for discussion on the latest law enforcement issues.

Since the official opening in March 1995, Europol/EDU has organised twenty-six conferences and major meetings and over 3,000 visitors have been welcomed at the new facilities.

Europol/EDU is in the process of developing a sophisticated three-part computerised system for information and intelligence processing. The system will eventually contain data relating to persons suspected of having committed, or who are considered likely to commit, a crime (including accounts of a targeted person's criminal history or membership of any criminal organisation) within Europol/EDU's remit. The Europol Convention imposes a number of restrictions on the kinds of personal data which may be held in the system.[82]

READY-MADE MECHANISM FOR EU-WIDE ACTION

Following the recent tragic events in Belgium and other member states involving the sexual abuse and murder of children and the conclusions of the Vienna and Stockholm conferences on trafficking in women and the sexual exploitation of children respectively, the narrow scope of the

Europol/EDU mandate came up on the EU political agenda. At an informal meeting of JHA ministers held in Dublin Castle on 26 and 27 September 1996, at the initiative of the Irish Presidency, the Minister for Justice Nora Owen, TD put forward a motion to extend the mandate of Europol/EDU to cover all forms of trafficking in human beings and questions concerning the sex trade of women and children were accepted. Unlike the past, when such issues resulted in nothing more than political soundbites, this time the ministers of justice had an EU-wide law enforcement mechanism in the form of Europol/EDU which they could call upon to take a decisive role in this work. The meeting made significant progress and agreed on the following:

- that the mandate of Europol/EDU should be expanded to deal with trafficking in children
- that within the Europol/EDU a directory of expertise in EU member states in combating drug trafficking and trafficking in women and children be set up and maintained
- that a training and exchange programme on these issues be established.

Following the approval of the JHA Councils on 29 November, 16 December and 17 December 1996, a new Joint Action based on Article K.3 of the TEU was adopted to extend the existing mandate of Europol to include work to combat trafficking in human beings. The task of creating and maintaining a new EU-wide directory of specialised competences, skills and expertise in the fight against international organised crime was also entrusted to Europol/EDU.[83] Initially their work will centre on establishing the directory in the area of drug trafficking and trade in human beings.

THE EU PRESIDENCY AND THE IGC

When Ireland took over the six-month Presidency of the EU Council in July 1996, it set out a number of key priorities for its presidency:[84] secure jobs, safer streets, sound money and a peaceful Europe. It stated that its overriding objective would be to contribute to further EU integration in a manner which corresponds to the legitimate aspirations and concerns of its 370 million citizens and pointed to the necessity for the EU to take measures in the fight against all forms of organised crime.[85] It promised to make the most efficient use of the existing instruments available under the Third Pillar to achieve real progress in the area of EU law enforcement cooperation. It pledged to work for the speedy ratification of the Europol Covention by saying that it was the most appropriate place for EU action on the containment of drug trafficking and associated crimes. It also called for member states to ratify the Europol Convention by the end of 1997. It is ironic, given its objection to accept preliminary judgments by the ECJ, that the UK became the first, and so far only, EU parliament to ratify the Europol Convention.[86]

With Ireland continuing to experience increasingly high levels of illegal drugs use and drug-related crimes with violence, Justice Minister Nora Owen presided over the JHA Council of Ministers, which produced a six-point work programme on a series of Union-wide initiatives to enhance EU law enforcement cooperation under the Third Pillar. It included a plan to foster and enhance greater cooperation between national forensic science laboratories, customs administrations, trade bodies and companies, as well as a review of national practices in the fight against drugs smuggling.[87]

During the Presidency Ireland also had the responsibility for chairing the work of the IGC Special Representatives in their efforts to prepare a draft revision of the EU treaties. As part of a broader plan to enhance the popular appeal of the EU and to improve on the shortcomings of the Maastricht Treaty, the negotiations focused on a small number of issues, including those affecting JHA. The general outline for a draft revision of the EU treaties, submitted by the Irish Presidency to the European Council in Dublin on 13 and 14 December 1996, was welcomed by the Council as a good basis for the final phase of the IGC. The Irish Presidency document gives particular importance to strengthening EU capacity for action in many areas of JHA and reaffirms the commitment to maintain and develop the Union as an area of Freedom, Security and Justice (FSJ).

With regard to Europol in particular, the Presidency document recommends that Europol should be given, after a yet to be specified number of years following the entry into force of the Treaty, "operative powers" as opposed to "operational powers", which would allow it to request police forces in member states to conduct investigations in specific cases. This formula, proposed by the Irish Presidency, is sensitive to the views of the majority of member states which support a stronger and more effective role for Europol and the minority of member states which have an aversion to bestowing the EU with what the latter see as supranational JHA capabilities.

As we enter the final phase of the IGC, there has been a change of heart by some governments on internal security and a clear consensus is emerging that changing the existing decision-making process of JHA should be a priority at the IGC Conference when it concludes at Amsterdam in June 1997. A number of diplomats who are party to the IGC negotiations believe that Europol's current remit is not adequate to tackle contemporary international organised crime. They also believe that Europol should be allowed to support and, in certain instances, coordinate criminal investigations by national law enforcement agencies.

CONCLUSION

The EU is currently faced with many opportunities and challenges, e.g. fighting unemployment, coping with enlargement, preventing environmental degradation, developing a coherent common foreign and security policy and providing an area of freedom and security for its citizens. Irish citizens, as well as other citizens of the Union, feel threatened by a wide range of law enforcement issues: organised crime, drugs trafficking and terrorism. They appreciate that these problems cannot be effectively combated by any member state acting in isolation. It is clearly evident that this task demands comprehensive modern security analysis and corresponding criminal justice and law enforcement structures and instruments.

We have also seen that the nature of policing and in its wider definition, law enforcement, is a complicated and much misunderstood public policy area. In Ireland and most other EU member states intragovernmental law enforcement also urgently requires reorganisation and modernisation. It is now accepted that no single law enforcement agency can pretend to cope with contemporary transfrontier criminality. An EU law enforcement mechanism like Europol is both desirable and necessary. We have also seen that the delays and problems in establishing Europol and the improvement of EU law enforcement cooperation are very much subject to the broader political questions and issues over the future direction of greater EU integration which continually dominate policy-making.

Already Europol has shown that it can provide a suitable working platform for enhancing EU-level law enforcement cooperation. The substantial increased use of Europol by various EU law enforcement agencies is itself a testament to the contribution and added value the professionals believe it offers in combating contemporary criminality.

The IGC and the review of the Maastricht Treaty provides an opportunity for the governments of EU member states to demonstrate to all citizens of the Union that they have the political will to tackle the issues which worry them most, issues like drug abuse and organised crime which are the scourges of modern society. The IGC provides the governments of the EU with a unique opportunity to build upon the early achievements of Europol and help strengthen and deepen the effectiveness of the Third Pillar.

In conclusion, it is important to remember that the solutions to most contemporary law enforcement issues are not always to be found in legislation. More often than not they can be found in the development of concrete and concerted action within a comprehensive and strategic framework. Within only two years of its existence, Europol/EDU has developed into a potent mechanism for good which has no parallel in the world of law enforcement cooperation. When compared with pre-existing initiatives, structures and frameworks Europol does without doubt mark a crucial watershed in EU law enforcement cooperation.

NOTES

1. The opinions expressed in this chapter are solely the author's and should not be interpreted in any way as representing the official views or policies of the EU institution for which he works.
2. Eight-inch high carved bronze inscription from J. Edgar Hoover on the Ground Floor of the Federal Bureau of Investigation (FBI) Building in Pennsylvania Avenue, New York – Ronald Kessler, The FBI, Pocket Books, New York (1993).
3. The author would like to acknowledge the help and cooperation he received from the Coordinator of Europol/EDU Jürgen Storbeck, Emanuele Marotta, Member of the Management Team and Frans-Jan Mulschlegel, Head of Documentation.
4. Title I of the Maastricht Treaty on European Union (TEU) establishes the notion of a Union and the concept of citizenship of that Union.
5. This is the fifth time since accession that Ireland has had the honour of holding the Presidency of the European Council.
6. Recent estimates suggest that approximately 45 million people world-wide are addicted to illegal drugs and that the annual turnover from illicit sales is in the region of 400 billion ECU (Source: European Voice 9-14 May 1996).
7. Ten of the CEEC countries are candidates to join the EU during the next enlargement phase.
8. Statistics on terrorism and organised crime vary from one member state to another. Even within member states the interpretation of these statistics differs depending on the agency providing the data.
9. For an overview of EU measures to combat the illicit trade in nuclear material see "clamping down on the nuclear smugglers", by J. Lodge & V. Flynn in European Brief, December 1994.
10. Recently an American University was unknowingly the site for a similar type of home page about IRA propaganda.
11. For an assessment of the security-related events around the world see "The International Institute for Strategic Studies 1994/5", published by Oxford Press 1995.
12. The term "law enforcement" is used to describe one or all of the various agencies involved in combating crime, e.g. customs services, immigration services and police.
13. For a detailed analysis of policing in the EU see Benyon, J. (1993), Police Co-operation in Europe: An Investigation, and Police Forces in the new European Union: A Conspectus, Leicester: Centre for the Study of Public Order.
14. Informed observers often point to the unhealthy relationship between the latest crime statistics and the way police performance is appraised.
15. In an increasing number of EU member states, private security firms supplement the police in a wide range of non-core policing activities. Group 4, the private security company, recently won a £49 million contract to ferry inmates to court in the UK. The seven-year contract is expected to save the taxpayer £2.4 million a year (Times, London 22/10/96).

16. EP Report on the Setting up of Europol. 26 November 1992 (PE 202.364/fin.)
17. See Anderson, M. and den Boer, M. (eds.), *Policing Across National Boundaries* (London, 1994).
18. Signed in March 1957 by the governments of Belgium, France, Italy, Luxembourg, The Netherlands and West Germany.
19. Indigenous in this context refers to groups like the Italian Red Brigades (Brigate Rosse), German Red Army Faction (RAF) and the Spanish ETA (Euzkadi Ta Azkatasuna). International terrorism refers to groups originating outside the EC and acting against them, their subjects, or organisations and individuals on their territory.
20. J. Lodge, "Terrorism and the European Community: towards 1992" in *Terrorism and Political Violence,* Vol. 1, 1986, Frank Cass, London.
21. Trevi was established following the European Council Meeting in Rome 1975 and a meeting in June 1996 of ministers of justice and internal affairs in Luxembourg.
22. While there is contention about the origins of the name TREVI, the acronym is generally accepted to mean Terrorism, Radicalism, Extremism and International Violence. Some argue that the name derives from a pun on the names of the chairperson of the first meeting Mr Fonteijn and the famous Trevi fountain in Rome.
23. The Single European Act came into force on 1 July 1987.
24. This forecast did not seem to take into consideration the fact that existing internal frontier controls posed little, if anything more than, a minor inconvenience to hardened terrorist and major crime groups.
25. At the same time a core group of like-minded EC member states (Belgium, The Netherlands, Germany, France and Luxembourg) who wanted deeper and more rapid integration in order to remove the internal frontier controls, created the Schengen group. The Schengen Agreement was signed on 14 June 1985.
26. Trevi (1990) Programme of Action relating to the Reinforcement of Police Cooperation and the Endeavours to Combat Terrorism or other forms of Organised Crime.
27. Bigo, D., "The European internal security field: stakes and rivalries in a newly developing area of police intervention", in *Policing Across National Boundaries.* M. Anderson & M. den Boer (eds.) (London, 1994).
28. J. Lodge (ed.), *The Threat of Terrorism.* (Brighton, 1988).
29. R. Woodward, "The establishment of Europol: a critique", Paper presented to the Cyprus Police Academy International Seminar, Nicosia, Cyprus April 1993.
30. M. Anderson, "Agenda for police co-operation", in M. Anderson & M. den Boer (eds.), *Policing Across National Boundaries,* (London, 1994).
31. The origins and destinations of the "message traffic" passing through Interpol HQ in Lyon have always been predominantly European.
32. M. den Boer & N. Walker, "European policing after 1992", in the *Journal of Common Market Studies* 31 (1) pp. 3-28.
33. Sir Peter Imbert, former Metropolitan Police Commissioner, quoted in *The Job,* July 1989, p.6.
34. H. Kohl, *Our Future in Europe,* Konrad Adenauer Stiftung and Europa Institute Edinburgh, p.16. (1991).
35. See Agence Europe, 30 June 1991.
36. See Agence Europe, 30 June 1991.
37. At the same meeting they also decided upon a 1992 Programme of Action on the removal of internal EC frontier controls for the completion of the SEM on 1 January 1993.
38. The name was later to change to European Drugs Unit (EDU). As den Boer points out the semantic career of "Europol" is a good illustration of issue-transformation in the area of European police cooperation. The concept has undergone several name

changes from the original "European Drugs Intelligence Unit" to European Drugs Unit which does not suggest that its remit was only confined to the exchange of information and intelligence. The official name has also changed from the term use at the time of the Luxembourg Summit in June 1991 of "European Criminal Investigation Office" to as it stands in the final text of the TEU "European Police Office".

39. In 1989 the idea of having National Central Drugs Units in member states (at the time, not all member states had a unit of this kind) which would serve as a basis for a European Drugs Intelligence Unit (EDIU) had been moved by Trevi.[40]

40. According to a new study from the European Monitoring Centre for Drugs and Drug Addiction in Lisbon, up to one in six of EU adults has tried illegal drugs. European Monitoring Centre for Drugs and Drug Addiction Annual Report 1995.

41. The 1995 Annual Report by the European Union's Drugs Monitoring centre, the European Drugs Observatory, concludes that there was "little relationship" between tough anti-drugs policies and reduction in the number of offences committed.

42. Conventions are provided for under Article K.3(2)(c) of the TEU.

43. EC Bull. 6-1992, at 13.

44 A special Ad Hoc Working Group on Europol was established under Trevi in August 1991. It was later entrusted with the job of preparing an agreed text for a draft convention on establishing Europol/EDU.

45. Jürgen Storbeck's credentials for the post were impeccable, having a legal background and wide-ranging professional experience (over 20 years) in the German BKA. He also worked as a legal advisor at ICPO Interpol HQ in Lyon where he became very familiar with the ins-and-outs of international law enforcement cooperation.

46. Lord Bethall, *Police,* November 1992, p.52.

47. It must be remembered that the seats of the European Institutions remained temporary ones for over twenty five-years.

48. Centrale Recherche Informatiedienst.

49. The Agreement was a basis of understanding between ministers and did not have the legal weight of a convention.

50. The TEU introduced the separate Pillars under one institutional framework. The First Pillar deals with traditional EC matters, the two new Pillars deal with common foreign and security policy (CFSP) and justice and home affairs (JHA) respectively.

51. The functions of Europol were further specified in an additional Declaration on Police Cooperation which was included in the annex to the TEU.

52. For an analysis of EU attempts at communitarisation in the fields of JHA see "European Community cooperation in the fields of justice and home affairs", research dissertation by V. Flynn, St. Andrews University Sep. 1993.

53. See D. Bigo, 1991.

54. The Declaration on Police Cooperation, in the Final Act of the TEU, delineates Europol/EDU's activities and functions:
    • support for national criminal investigation and security authorities, in particular in the coordination of investigations and search operations
    • creation of databases
    • central analysis and assessment of information in order to take stock of the situation and identify investigative approaches
    • collection and analysis of national prevention programmes for forwarding to member states and for drawing up Europe-wide prevention strategies
    • measures relating to further training, research, forensic matters and criminal records departments.

55. *Financial Times,* 11 September, 1992.

56. F. Boschi Orlandini, "Europol and the European Drugs Unit: a cooperation structure in the making", in *The Third Pillar of the European Union*, J. Monar & R. Morgan (eds.) College of Europe 1995.

57. Germany did not experience the expected very high levels of illegal immigration, asylum seekers and organised crime which were first predicted when Germany was reunited after the collapse of the Berlin Wall. Their Federal police, the BKA, were very successful in negotiating and establishing bilateral law enforcement cooperation with Central and Eastern European States.

58. Spain and Greece were in favour of including terrorism in the mandate of Europol/EDU because of the 17 November Group and the ETA terrorist groups.

59. Article 2.(2) Europol Convention.

60. *Police Accountability; Principles, Patterns & Practices.* R. Reiner & S. Spencer (eds.) (1993).

61. European Parliament Briefing, Feb. 1996 (Strasbourg).

62. While the UK government and the Home Office were widely viewed as the "bête noire" the HM Customs and in particular the Metropolitan Police were staunch supporters of Europol from the outset. They have supplied invaluable technical, logistical and managerial support throughout the process. As one senior Met Police Officer said, they had nearly dug the Channel Tunnel themselves with the amount of toing and froing to attend endless meetings on Europol.

63. 28 days of meeting over the six-month period.

64. German police authorities had reported a six-fold increase in the number of cases of suspected crimes involving nuclear material. *New Scientist,* 20 August 1994, "Germans issue nuclear smuggling alert".

65. *Le Figaro,* 5 June 1996.

66. Bull. EU 6-1996.

67. Tony Bunyan, *The Europol Convention* (London, December 1995).

68. Joint Action of 10 March 1995 Adopted by the Council on the Basis of Art. K.3 of the TEU Concerning the Europol/EDU.

69. EC Spokesman's Service note, 30 August 1995.

70. Cooney Report (1992). Report on the Spread of Organised Crime linked to Drugs Trafficking in Member States of the European Community, European Parliament Session Documents, A3-0358/91, 23 April.

71. Among its many other responsibilities, the Institutional Affairs Committee is responsible for coordinating the EP response for the IGC'96 while the Civil Liberties Committee is directly responsible for coordinating EP activities which come under Title VI of the TEU.

72. Interview with the author in September 1996.

73. *Daily Telegraph,* 11 July 1995.

74. Europol Annual Report 1995, the Hague.

75. Appointed by the JHA ministers on 20/12 June 1994.

76. Europol Annual Report for 1995, Europol Drugs Unit, the Hague.

77. Article 3. of the Europol Convention.

78. Articles 35 & 36 of the Europol Convetion.

79. Only 1,397,751 ECU of the Common Budget of 2,065,000 ECU was spent.

80. Europol Annual Report 1995, the Hague.

81. Increased from four to seven in July 1996.

82. F. Monaco, *Europol: The Culmination of the European Union's International Police Cooperation Efforts.*

83. *Official Journal* L 342, 31 December 1996.

84. Presidency of the European Union: *Priorities for the Irish Presidency of the Council of the European Union.*

85. A survey published in December 1996 showed that 66% (71% Irl) of EU citizens fear an increase in drugs trafficking and international organised crime. When asked what priority policy objectives the EU should set itself over the next ten years, 87% (92% Irl) said fighting organised crime and 86% (95% Irl) said fighting drug trafficking (*Source:* Euro-barometer No. 45, December 1996).
86. Article in *European Voice,* 12 December 1996.
87. European Voice 1-7 August 1996.

Chronology

(Key dates in the establishment of Europol)

28-29 June 1991	Council of Ministers (CoM) in Luxembourg agree to set up Europol
4 December 1991	Trevi Ministers agree to set up Europol Drugs Unit (EDU) as precursor to Europol
9-10 December 1991	CoM sign the TEU (Maastricht Treaty) which includes the creation of Europol in Title VI
26-27 June 1992	Lisbon CoM agrees to draw up a draft Convention for the creation of Europol
18 September 1992	Trevi Ministers announce that EDU will start covering illegal drug trafficking (and associated money laundering) from 1 January 1993
2 June 1993	Copenhagen Trevi Ministers sign Ministerial Agreement on setting up EDU
30 October 1993	Ministerial Agreement setting up EDU comes into effect
1 November 1993	TEU comes into effect: setting up Council of Justice and Home Affairs Ministers and K4 Committee (which replaces Trevi)
16 February 1994	Europol/EDU's HQ in the Hague, The Netherlands is officially opened
December 1994	Essen EU Summit increases the remit of Europol/EDU to include: illegal trade in radioactive and nuclear waste, traffic in humans and motor vehicle theft
10 March 1995	Brussels CoM agree to a Joint Action on Europol/EDU extending its mandate to three new crime areas
26 July 1995	Europol Convention signed by COREPER
23 November 1995	CoM fail to agree on the role of European Court of Justice (ECJ) with regard to the Europol Convention
July 1996	COREPER sign the Protocol to the Europol Convention regarding the role of the ECJ and making way for full ratification

Selected Bibliography

Anderson, M. (1989). *Policing the World. Interpol and the Politics of the International Police Co-operation* (Oxford).
Anderson M., M. den Boer, P. Cullen, W. Gilmore, C. Raab and N. Walker (ed.) *Policing The European Union: Theory, Law, and Practice.* Oxford (1994).
Anderson, M. (1994). "The Agenda for Police cooperation", in M. Anderson and M. den Boer (eds.), (1994) pp. 3-21.

Anderson, M. and den Boer, M. (1994) (eds). *Policing Across National Boundaries* (London).

Benyon, J., Davies, P. and Willis, P. (1990). *Police Cooperation in Europe: A Preliminary Report* (Leicester).

Benyon, J., Turnbull, L., Willis, A., Woodward, R. and Beck, A. (1993). *Police Cooperation in Europe: An Investigation* (Leicester).

Boer, M. den (1992). "Police Cooperation after Maastricht", Research Paper No 2/92, European Community Research Unit (Hull).

Boer, M. den (1994a). "Europe and the Art of International Police Co-operation: Free Fall or Measured Scenario?", in D. O'Keeffe, and P. Twomey (eds.), (1994) pp. 279-91.

Tony Bunyan (ed.), *"The Europol Convention"*, A Statewatch Publication, December 1995.

Clutterbuck, R. (1990). *Terrorism, Drugs and Crime in Europe after 1992* (London).

Cooney Report (1992). *Report on the Spread of Organized Crime linked to Drugs Trafficking in Member States of the European Community*, European Parliament Session Documents, A3-0358/91, 23 April.

House of Lords (1993). "Scrutiny of the Intergovernmental Pillars of the European Union, Select Committee on the European Communities, Session 1992-93", 28th Report, HL Paper 124.

Presidency Conclusions, Dublin European Council, 13–14 December 1996.

Project Team Europol (1993). "The Position of Europol within the Framework of European Cooperation. Member State Institutions, European Information Systems, International Organizations and Agencies".

Robles Piquer, C. (1993). "Cooperation in the field of justice and internal affairs under the treaty on European Union (Title VI and other provisions)". Committee on Civil Liberties and Internal Affairs of the European Parliament (Brussels).

Salisch, H. and Speroni, F. (1994). *Report of the Committee on Civil Liberties and Internal Affairs on criminal activities in Europe*, A3-0033/94, (Brusssels).

Walker, N., "The accountability of European Police Institutions". *European Journal on Criminal Policy and Research*, vol 1.

"Practical Police Cooperation in the European Community". *Seventh Report from the Home Affairs Committee Session 1989-90* HC 363-I.

Woodward, R., "Establishing Europol", Rachel Woodward. *European Journal on Criminal Policy and Research* 1993.

CHAPTER 6
CUSTOMS COOPERATION IN THE THIRD PILLAR

DERMOT GILROY

ROLE OF CUSTOMS IN THE CONTEXT OF THE SINGLE MARKET

The introduction of the single market on 1 January 1993 brought with it some fundamental changes in the way customs go about their work. With the removal of internal borders between member states, the emphasis from a customs point of view moved towards the external frontier of the Union. In the context of the single market, commercial trade, once it gains access to the market through any of the fifteen member states can, for the most part, then circulate freely to any of the other member states as a result of the abolition of internal borders; the previous regime of systematic checks at internal union frontiers can no longer be used to control the onward movement of third country goods which enter a member state via another member state. In order, therefore, to compensate for the removal of these internal borders, customs services throughout the Union have been endeavouring to strengthen controls at the external frontier, and this has become a major objective of the Union both in the First Pillar (European Community) area and in the Third Pillar (i.e. the more intergovernmental cooperation carried out under Title VI of the Treaty on European Union) area.

As regards the First Pillar area, the tasks of customs at the external frontier include:

- collecting EU customs duties and agricultural levies on goods coming from third countries
- collecting national excise duties and VAT on imports from third countries
- applying EU and national licensing and quota regimes
- enforcing EU animal and plant health standards
- collecting statistics on international trade and applying restrictions on exports.

Customs tasks falling within the Third Pillar area of operations would include enforcing a wide variety of import prohibitions and restrictions on items such as drugs, arms, explosives, nuclear materials, hazardous waste, etc.

In addition to carrying out checks at the external frontier to protect against the smuggling of such goods, customs can also carry out selective checks at internal borders for drugs, and a number of other prohibited goods where these are suspected of being smuggled from other member states.

Customs has, therefore, the primary responsibility for prevention of the smuggling of drugs whether from outside the European Union or from another member state; police services normally have primary responsibility for drug law enforcement within member states.

PRE-MAASTRICHT: INTERGOVERNMENTAL COOPERATION IN THE CUSTOMS FIELD

Prior to the Maastricht Treaty there was already a high level of inter-governmental cooperation in the field of customs. This had its origins in the Naples Convention on Mutual Assistance between Customs Administrations, so-called because it was signed in Naples in 1967. A Mutual Assistance Group (commonly known as MAG) was set up to facilitate cooperation between the customs administrations under the Convention and to deal with any matters concerning interpretation of the Convention such as monitoring of the application of the Convention and smoothing out any problems arising. A parallel group, the Mutual Assistance Group '92 (known as MAG '92) was set up during the lead-in to the introduction of the single market on 1 January, 1993; the purpose of MAG '92 was to examine the implications of the advent of the single market insofar as intergovernmental cooperation in the field of customs is concerned and to make preparations accordingly for a smooth transition to the single market situation. Both the MAG and MAG '92 operated solely within the sphere of customs and were not involved in the wider area of police-customs cooperation.

Two of the main items being considered by MAG '92 in the run-up to the single market were the revision and updating of the 1967 Naples Convention (which by that time was more than twenty years old) and the strengthening of the Community's external frontier in the light of the abolition of customs controls at internal borders between member states in the new single market situation; on-going examination of both of these issues has been carried over into the new Title VI structures of the Maastricht Treaty and now falls within the remit of the Customs Cooperation Working Party.

While both the MAG and the MAG '92 were intergovernmental in nature, the EU Commission played an active role in both groups. It provided meeting rooms for the groups, reimbursed travel expenses for member state delegates and also provided document translation facilities as well as secretarial assistance and interpretation services during meetings; in addition, the Commission was permitted to be present at the meetings in an observer capacity and was involved in providing administrative assistance to the groups from time to time, at their request. Meetings of both groups were attended by customs delegates from all the member states. The chairing of both the MAG and MAG '92 was carried out by member states but it did not follow the same rotational practice as for the presidency; the chairmanship was taken on a voluntary basis and was retained by the holder for a few years at a time; Spain held the presidency of the MAG group in the years leading up to the single market, while the UK held the presidency of MAG '92. Matters requiring high-level decisions went through a three-tier decision-making process, viz. initial examination by MAG or MAG '92, then submission to the deputies group (deputy heads of customs) and finally to the heads of customs for decision.

In addition to providing facilities for MAG and MAG '92 meetings, which dealt mainly with the development of policy matters in the customs field, in the pre-Maastricht situation, the Commission also provided similar facilities (including meeting rooms, reimbursement of travel expenses, etc.) to enable operational experts in the field of drugs to meet on a regular basis as a working group of the main MAG group, thus enabling these experts in the field to exchange experiences and ideas, to develop good personal contacts and to organise joint annual air/sea exercises together.

POST-MAASTRICHT: INTERGOVERNMENTAL COOPERATION IN THE CUSTOMS FIELD

Since the entry into force of the Treaty on European Union in November 1993, intergovernmental cooperation in the field of customs is one of the matters of common interest governed by Article K.1 of the Treaty.

Under Article K.3 of the Treaty, the right of initiative in the customs cooperation area, as well as in the areas of preventing and combating terrorism, unlawful drug trafficking or any other serious forms of international crime, rests with the member states, i.e. the Commission has no powers of initiative in relation to these issues. In summary, Title VI of the TEU lays down a statutory obligation on member states to cooperate in police, customs and judicial matters which are of common interest to the member states of the Union and in those areas the latter have an exclusive right of initiative. (This situation may change as a result of the deliberations of the intergovernmental conference, which is currently looking at possible powers of initiative for the Commission in some Title VI areas.)

Following the entry into force of the Treaty, intergovernmental cooperation in the field of customs which was previously carried out in the Mutual Assistance Group (MAG) and the Mutual Assistance Group '92 (MAG '92), has been subsumed into the new institutional arrangements set up under the TEU, and the Customs Cooperation Working Party is now carrying this work forward (the MAG and MAG '92 groups having been wound up).

The Customs Cooperation Working Party, like other Council working groups, is serviced by delegations from each of the member states, with meetings being chaired on a six-monthly rotating basis by the Presidency country; the president/chairman of the meeting is assisted secretarially by an official from the Council secretariat. Member state delegations are for the most part serviced by customs delegates although one or two member states often have representatives present from other services (police, guardia di finanza, justice ministry, etc.). The EU Commission is also represented at all meetings of the working party. Under the Treaty, the Commission is entitled to participate in the work of Title VI (Article K.4 of the Treaty states that "the Commission shall be fully associated with the work in the areas referred to in this Title"); however, it has no powers of initiative in the intergovernmental area in relation to customs cooperation; it therefore sits in at meetings of the Customs Cooperation Working Party largely in an observer capacity.

WORK AGENDA SET BY THE COUNCIL

At its first meeting under the TEU in November, 1993, the Justice and Home Affairs Council laid down a series of tasks to be undertaken by the new structures with a view to ensuring, *inter alia,* better protection of society against threats from terrorism, organised crime and illegal drugs. In addition to the then impending start-up of the European Monitoring Centre for Drugs and Drug Addiction, the Council agreed on the development of a global strategy to combat drug trafficking, to reduce demand and to act against producer and transit third countries, focusing on the strengthening of controls at external frontiers and on measures to counter "drug" tourism. (Drug tourism refers to the practice of drug addicts/drug traffickers travelling to other member states to shop around for lowest price drugs with a view to bringing them back home for consumption in their own member state.) The Council drew up a 1994 action plan in late 1993 (Council Doc. 10655/93 - JAI 11 refers) covering, *inter alia*, "Police and Customs Cooperation". Under this action plan all forms of police and customs cooperation were to be developed in order to attain the common objective of greater security for the Union's citizens. The Council also drew up at that time a work programme of priority actions (Council Doc. 10684/93 - JAI 12 refers) which were to be implemented in the shorter term. Based on the Council's 1994 action plan and work programme, the Customs Cooperation Working Party has dealt with the following issues over the past three years or so since the TEU came into operation:

- Finalising the CIS Convention (Customs Information System).
- Defining an action plan to implement the recommendations of the Report of the External Frontiers Strategy, which was endorsed by the Directors-General of Customs Administrations in May 1993.
- Contributing to the development of a strategic Union plan to combat customs fraud in the internal market.
- Organising joint customs surveillance operations (intensive surveillance on an EU-wide basis of, e.g. air and sea freight/passenger traffic) by all the customs services of the member states cooperating together during specified periods of the year.
- Reviewing and updating the 1967 Naples Convention in order to strengthen and modernise the legal basis for mutual assistance between member state customs authorities.
- Developing cooperation links between the Union and its member states on the one hand, and third countries on the other, in the field of drugs.
- Discussing the customs role in relation to the following items of joint interest to both customs and police, viz.
  - smuggling of counterfeit goods
  - smuggling of works of art
  - smuggling of nuclear materials.
- Cooperating with police (via the Drugs and Organised Crime Group) in the development of a European Union strategy to combat illicit drug trafficking; this included drafting of the customs input into the:
  - European Union's Action Plan to Combat Drugs 1995-1999
  - Report of the Expert Group on Drugs which was presented to the Madrid European Council Meeting in December 1995
  - European Drugs Manual.

Other measures contained in the Council's 1994 action plan/work programme but which have not yet been taken up by the Customs Cooperation Working Party to any great extent include the following:

- Extending, as part of the Matthaeus Programme, the arrangements for the exchange/training of customs officials (in the Third Pillar area).
- Training members of law enforcement agencies (this would include both police and customs where it forms part of their work) in the field of money laundering.

- Exchanging police and customs information in the money laundering area, in particular by means of rapid, effective cooperation between central contact points in member states.
- Developing, in accordance with the Council's work programme, close collaboration between customs and police for the implementation of action in areas of common interest to both services. The work programme emphasises that such collaboration is particularly essential in the following areas:
  - training programmes of common interest
  - border controls, including border security, combating all kinds of traffic, in particular in relation to drug trafficking, money laundering, the safety of means of transport, environmental crime, vehicles, works of art, forgery and illegal immigration.
- Developing cooperation with police in the re-inforcement of external border controls to combat drug trafficking and in the taking of measures to counter "drug tourism".
- Ensuring complementarity of measures taken by customs and police in the fight against drugs, including money laundering.

During the Irish Presidency (July-December, 1996), the work programmes of the various working groups in the justice and home affairs area were largely driven by the recommendations contained in the Report of the Expert Group on Drugs to the Madrid European Council Meeting in December, 1995. A total of sixty-six action points were identified in this report, some of which relate to the First and Second Pillars but about a third of which relate to the Third Pillar. In the customs area, significant progress was achieved on a number of these action points under the Irish Presidency, viz. a joint action was approved by the Council on the greater use of memoranda of understanding between customs and trade interests in relation to the fight against drugs; a resolution on police-customs cooperation was agreed by the Council; the Council have also approved a joint action which involves the EU contributing funding to a strategic operation on drugs planned by the World Customs Organisation along the Balkan route. Considerable progress was also made on a number of other topics arising from the Madrid Report, viz. external frontier controls, container traffic, mobile search squads at the external frontier and targeting criteria for detecting drugs shipments.

CUSTOMS INVOLVEMENT WITH OTHER THIRD PILLAR GROUPS

Within the Third Pillar, the hierarchical decision-making structure works as follows: at the lower level there are six working groups, viz. the Customs Cooperation Working Party, the Drugs and Organised Crime Group, the Europol Group, the Police Cooperation Group, the International Organised Crime Group and the Working Group on Terrorism.

The Customs Cooperation Working Party deals with items of specific customs interest, although in some cases the issues involved may have a joint customs/police dimension. As its title implies, the main area of customs interest under the Third Pillar rests with the Customs Cooperation Working Party but customs may also have an interest in the work of two other groups in the Third Pillar area, which are mainly of a justice/police nature, viz. the Drugs and Organised Crime Group and the Europol Working Party. These two groups sometimes deal with issues which are of joint concern to both police and customs, such as cross-border movements of drugs, stolen works of art, nuclear materials, hazardous waste, etc.; and customs delegates may, therefore, attend meetings of these two groups as appropriate.

The six working groups in the Third Pillar all report to Steering Group II. The main purpose of this steering group is to direct the work of the working groups and to refer the results of their work to the next level of the hierarchical structure, viz. the K4 Committee.

The K.4 Committee is a high level body which coordinates the work within the Third Pillar and prepares it for presentation to the Council of Ministers (normally the Justice and Home Affairs Council). Matters for decision by Council would normally be channelled from the K4 Committee through Coreper (the Committee of Permanent Representatives, at which member states are represented by their ambassador or deputy ambassador to the European Union).

INSTITUTIONAL ARRANGEMENTS FOR POLICE-CUSTOMS COOPERATION

Police and customs cooperation arrangements within the Third Pillar are governed by Article K.1(9) of the Treaty, viz.

For the purposes of achieving the objectives of the Union, in particular the free movement of persons, and without prejudice to the powers of the European Community, member states shall regard the following areas as matters of common interest:

—   Customs cooperation
—   Police cooperation for the purposes of preventing and combating terrorism, unlawful drug trafficking and other serious forms of international crime, including if necessary certain aspects of customs cooperation, in connection with the organisation of a Union-wide system for exchanging information within a European Police Office (Europol).

The Justice and Home Affairs Council in drawing up its first action plan and a separate priority work programme for 1994 on the entry into force of the TEU in November 1993 also identified police and customs cooperation as an area in which action needs to be taken to achieve the objectives of the Treaty insofar as the Third Pillar is concerned.

The following are among the more important references to police and customs cooperation in the Council's 1994 action plan/work programme.

- All forms of police and customs cooperation must be developed in order to attain the common objective of greater security for the Union's citizens (action plan).
- To strengthen police and customs cooperation, a strategy to combat illicit drug trafficking needs to be set up, including the extension of checks at external frontiers as well as measures against "drugs tourism" (action plan).
- Council reaffirms the importance of exchanging police and customs information in the area of money laundering, in particular by means of rapid, effective cooperation between central points in member states (action plan).
- Close collaboration should be developed between the police and customs in relation to, *inter alia,* training programmes of common interest, border controls, and combating all kinds of illicit traffic (work programme).
- Efforts shall be made to ensure the complementarity of measures taken by the police and customs in the fight against drugs (work programme).

Since the above action plan and work programme were first drawn up in November 1993, the need for ensuring the complementarity of measures taken by police and customs in the fight against drugs has been reiterated in the European Union's Action Plan to Combat Drugs (1995-1999) presented to the Cannes European Council in June 1995 and in the Report of the Group of Experts on Drugs presented to the Madrid European Council in December, 1995.

The Madrid Drug Experts Report proposes that the EU's strategy on the reduction of illicit trafficking of drugs should, *inter alia,* aim to maximise the input of police and customs services at both national and international level in the fight against drugs by improving practical cooperation and greater complementarity of action between these services and by improved sharing of intelligence between them. In the context of strengthening the EU's external borders, the Report states that special attention should be paid to the effectiveness of controls at external borders and to the development of practical cooperation between police and customs authorities. In the sphere of intra-EU actions, the Report proposes that priority consideration be given, *inter alia,* to common actions to fight internationally-operating criminal organisations involved in the drugs trade at the borders as well as within member states (in this context, the report suggests that consideration be given to the creation of joint task forces of police and customs officers to avoid duplication of effort and to optimise the use of their complementary skills, manpower and resources). The report also urges greater police-customs cooperation in the field of joint training, control of container traffic, controlled deliveries of drugs, international surveillance and enforcement measures against the diversion of precursors.

CURRENT ORGANISATIONAL ARRANGEMENTS UNDER TITLE VI

One of the most striking features of the new post-Maastricht arrangements in Title VI of the TEU when compared with the pre-Maastricht arrangements previously in force is the cumbersome decision-making procedure of the new arrangements as compared to the old ones, viz. a five-tier decision-making structure as compared to the previous three-tier structure. This is not just a feature of the customs arrangements but appears to be common to all areas of Title VI and is commented on more extensively elsewhere in this volume. (The Irish Presidency addressed this issue in the justice and home affairs area during the latter half of 1996 by reducing the number of Steering Group II meetings to one for the six-month period in question.)

Generally speaking, organisational arrangements for intergovernmental activities under the Third Pillar leave a lot to be desired. The Council Secretariat and the interpretation/translation services are still grappling with the explosion of work and activities which has arisen under the post-Maastricht situation and there is some ground to be made up to cope with the eighteen or so new committees which were created under the new TEU arrangements.

A major advantage which the First Pillar has over the Third Pillar is the Commission and its proven capacity and resources to prepare draft documents, proposals, regulations, etc. and to generally move things forward between meetings at Commission level. This Commission right of initiative does not exist under the Third Pillar. Under the First Pillar arrangements there is a degree of continuity provided as a result of the active involvement of the Commission in the on-going activities. While some of these drawbacks can be addressed to a certain extent by the introduction of multi-annual programmes spread over three or four presidencies, Third Pillar activities will continue to be at a disadvantage compared to the First Pillar for as long as there is an absence of an active permanent secretariat which can progress issues on an on-going basis. A streamlining of decision-making procedures in some areas would also be desirable.

LACK OF SUITABLE FORUM

A drawback of the Third Pillar arrangements from a customs perspective is the absence of a forum for discussing issues at an operational/technical level. The only customs forum under the Third Pillar is the Customs Co-operation Working Party; this is more a high level group suitable for discussing policy issues and for drawing up strategic plans, rather than a group dealing with issues at operational/technical level. This is in contrast to the First Pillar where there is a separate technical working group or committee organised by the Commission for each of a whole range of customs subjects.

Prior to the Maastricht Treaty, when intergovernmental cooperation in the customs area was under the MAG (Mutual Assistance Group), the MAG group dealt with the higher level issues while operational/technical matters were dealt with by a sub-group of the main MAG group, serviced by technical representatives from all the member states (with the meeting rooms, the secretarial services, the interpretation and translation services and the reimbursement of travel expenses being provided by the Commission out of Community funds). If genuine progress is to be made, it is essential that a suitable forum is provided where member states' operational experts on, say, anti-drugs measures, can meet and discuss common problems at a technical level. The need for such a forum is even more evident when one compares the situation with the organisational arrangements for police cooperation under the Third Pillar where there are five different groups for dealing with police issues, some of which are higher level groups and some of which are of an operational/technical nature. The Irish Presidency of the Customs Cooperation Working Party addressed this issue to some extent during the latter half of 1996 by devoting two of its meetings to operational matters; it also got a commitment that for the future, at least one meeting of the Customs Cooperation Working Party during each presidency will be devoted to operational/technical matters.

POLICE-CUSTOMS COOPERATION: HOW IS IT WORKING IN PRACTICE?

In the initial stages of the TEU, discussions within the Third Pillar on drugs issues tended to be predominantly police-orientated and the customs role was very often overlooked. However, the situation is gradually changing and justice/police groups in the Third Pillar area are becoming more and more conscious of the fact that many of the issues under consideration have a joint police/customs interest.

There is a fair degree of commitment within the Council to the need for improving cooperation in this area, particularly in relation to the fight against drugs. This is borne out by the number of references to the need for police-customs co-operation contained in the Council's action plan/work programme drawn up in late 1993, in the European Union's Action Plan to Combat Drugs (1995-1999) presented to the Cannes European Council in June 1995 and in the Report of the Group of Experts on Drugs presented to the Madrid European Council in December 1995. Unfortunately, many of these references have largely remained aspirational up to now and have not yet translated into practical cooperation at the operational level.

One area where police and customs are cooperating with each other at a practical level as a result of Third Pillar actions under the TEU is the operation of the Europol Drugs Unit (EDU) where some member states have seconded both police and customs liaison officers to serve alongside each other with a view to providing a drugs intelligence information service to both police and customs services in the member states; reports indicate that the level of cooperation between police and customs liaison officers working together in the EDU centre in the Hague is very good.

There is scope for further improvement in cooperation generally between police and customs at committee/working group level within the Council's Third Pillar structures. In areas of joint interest to both police and customs (e.g. drugs), some member states provide a fair degree of cross-fertilisation as between the two services by including both police and customs representatives on their national delegations attending meetings in Brussels; in other member states there is close pre-coordination between police and customs prior to meetings in Brussels; again the level of this varies from member state to member state and depends to a large extent on how good relations are between the police and customs in individual member states.

There is also scope for improvement in the level of practical cooperation between Justice/police and customs in the Third Pillar area. In several member states there appears to be a strong commitment to the concept while in others the idea of closer police-customs cooperation is only in its infancy and needs to be nurtured and developed over the coming years. The level of cooperation between Justice/gardaí and the customs service in Ireland is now very good. This is evident not only in the growing level of coordination and cooperation between both sides in relation to meetings within the Third Pillar area but also in relation to improvements in the degree of cooperation and sharing of intelligence data at the operational level between the gardaí and the customs service. The situation has been helped enormously by the joint "Memorandum concerning Proposals to improve Law Enforcement in relation to the Drugs Problem and Related Matters" which was drawn up by Justice and the Gardaí on the one hand and the Revenue Commissioners on the other, and which was presented to Government in July 1995 and subsequently accepted by them. This report recommended a series of actions which will lead to the setting up of joint structures to oversee the whole area of cooperation between the gardaí and customs in the fight against drugs, all of which will be further underpinned by a Memorandum of Understanding which was signed on 12 January 1996 by the Chairman of the Revenue Commissioners and the Commissioner of the Gardaí and which was endorsed by the Ministers for Finance and Justice.

FUTURE POLICE-CUSTOMS COOPERATION

Following on the practical steps which had been taken here in the area of improvement of police-customs cooperation, Ireland indicated at the start of its recent six-months Presidency that it intended to take a lead in relation to seeking improvements in the field of police-customs cooperation. This initiative was spearheaded by the Department of Justice, with the support of both the gardaí and the customs service here. As a first step, Ireland hosted a very successful joint seminar on police-customs cooperation in the opening days of the Irish Presidency (3/4 July, 1996).

Ireland followed this up by successfully piloting through a Council Resolution on police-customs cooperation during its Presidency. Again, under the Irish Presidency, a joint meeting of the Drugs and Organised Crime Group (mainly a Justice/police group) and the Customs Cooperation Working Party was held for the first time to discuss matters of mutual concern to both police and customs.

Notwithstanding the very positive progress made in the area of police-customs cooperation during the Irish Presidency, if there are to be on-going improvements in the level of such cooperation at both national and international levels within the Union, it may be necessary to look closer at the existing Committee structures to see whether they are adequate for the purposes of achieving a greater degree of cooperation in this area. The potential for greater improvement in the area of police-customs cooperation might be helped somewhat if Council were to lay down that instead of police and customs discussing issues of joint interest in separate fora, a proper joint police-customs forum should be established for discussing such issues and where both sides would be equally represented; to maintain a balance between both sides, the chairing of such meetings could rotate between police and customs for each alternate meeting. In this way, a proper partnership approach between police and customs could be developed in relation to the fight against drugs, without either side having the feeling of being dominated by the other.

A good foundation for improved police-customs cooperation has been laid by Ireland during its Presidency; this can be enhanced further by police and customs jointly attending meetings together, participating in joint training courses and jointly sharing intelligence data on drugs, etc.; the Dutch Presidency have indicated that they are keen to continue the process initiated by Ireland and are particularly interested in developing police-customs cooperation at the practical level. Many of the action points set out in the Madrid Drugs Experts Report will involve police and customs working closely together in relation to particular issues and, therefore, offer an opportunity for real progress in practical cooperation between police and customs over the coming years.

◼ Chapter 7

The European Union – Ten Years of Action against Drug Abuse

Paul Gormley

Although large quantities of all kinds of illegal drugs circulate within the European Union, it is difficult to determine the exact size of the problem. Seizures by customs officers in the various member states give some idea of the quantities involved. In 1994 alone more than 200 tonnes of cannabis were seized by Spanish customs officers and as much by their Dutch colleagues. That same year more than 1.5 tonnes of heroin were seized in Germany, some 6.6 tonnes of cocaine in Italy and over 1.3 tonnes of amphetamines in the UK. The list does not stop there, of course, given that all EU countries are affected. Not surprisingly, therefore, this common threat has prompted attempts to identify jointly the elements of this scourge and to work together to attain shared objectives.

What was then the European Economic Community based its fight against drugs in the 1980s on the general provisions of the first European treaties. In the early 1990s, it adopted basic legal instruments dealing with precursors (chemicals used to make certain drugs), chemical substances and money laundering. From the coming into force of the Treaty of Maastricht on 1 November 1993 the European Union was created. The European Economic Community (rechristened the European Community) became just one pillar of the three-pillar structure comprised by the Union. Each pillar of the Union acquired specific powers in the area of drugs.

Pillar One

Under Article 129 of the European Community Treaty (as amended by the Treaty of Maastricht), the Community can help prevent drug addiction by promoting research into this phenomenon and providing health information and education. EU member states must coordinate their policies and programmes in this field, and the European Commission may help them. Moreover, the Community and its member states must foster cooperation with all other countries as well as with international organisations, and the United Nations in particular, which have a global strategy to fight drug trafficking.

Pillar Two

European Union heads of state or government have included drug abuse among the questions deserving of particular attention in the framework of the common foreign and security policy (CFSP), instituted under the Maastricht Treaty.

Pillar Three

Under Article K.1 of the Maastricht Treaty EU member states regard the fight against drug addiction as a matter of common interest. Other matters of common interest listed in Article K.1 include customs cooperation, and police cooperation for the purposes of preventing and combating, *inter alia,* unlawful drug trafficking, including, if necessary, certain aspects of customs cooperation, in connection with the organisation of a Union-wide system for exchanging information within a European Police Office (Europol). The member states alone can initiate legislation in matters of customs, police and criminal justice cooperation; however, they share this right with the European Commission in all other aspects of the fight against drugs.

Ten years of action at European level

The measures now being taken under the Maastricht Treaty provisions are the culmination of ten years of action at European level. This decade of cooperation involved the following steps, *inter alia.* In 1987, the European Economic Community (EEC) was a participant in the Vienna Conference on the illicit trade in narcotic drugs and psychotropic substances. It also made its first financial contribution to the international fight against drugs at this point.

A year later, the EEC was a signatory to the United Nations Convention against the illicit trade in narcotic drugs and psychotropic substances. At the initiative of the European Parliament, specific funds to combat drugs were allotted in the European budget.

In 1989, the European Committee to Combat Drugs (ECCD) was set up, bringing together the national coordinators from the EEC member states.

In 1990, Regulation EEC/3677/90 came into force. It dealt with the measures to be taken by the Community to prevent the diversion of certain chemicals for the illicit manufacture of narcotic drugs and psychotropic substances.

The European Council adopted the first European plan to combat drugs during its Rome session in this year.

A year later, Directive EEC/308/91, aimed at preventing the financial system from being used for money laundering, came into force, while in 1992 the Treaty on European Union, which refers to the fight against drug addiction, was signed in Maastricht. Also in 1992, the Directive on the manufacture and marketing of certain substances used in the illicit manufacture of narcotic drugs and psychotropic substances came into force (92/109/EEC).

In 1993, the European Monitoring Centre on Drugs and Drug Addiction (EMCDDA) was set up and in 1994, a new global European Union action plan to combat drugs (1995-2000) was agreed.

In 1995, the European Council, which met in Madrid, gave a fresh impetus to the European Union's fight against drugs. A conference on the policies on drugs was organised jointly by the European Parliament, the Presidency of the EU Council of Ministers and the European Commission.

Last year, the European Council opened the way, at its meeting in Florence, to the ratification of the European Police Office (Europol) Convention. The fight against drugs was one of the top priorities of the EU's Irish Presidency and the Presidency and the Commission cooperated in the holding of a Citizens' Hearing on combating the drugs problem in Dublin Castle on 5-6 November 1996.

A EUROPEAN ACTION PLAN

The European Commission submitted an action plan to combat drugs, covering the period 1995 to 1999, in June 1994. The plan was designed to enable the European Union to take advantage of the numerous possibilities offered by the Maastricht Treaty within the framework of a global strategy. It was adopted by the European Parliament in June 1995, and by the European Council at its meeting in Cannes the same month.

The action plan provides for simultaneous intervention on four main fronts:

- Action to reduce the demand for drugs. This involves both drug prevention and training, particularly of young people; a reduction of the risks for people on drugs and the reintegration of former addicts.
- The fight against drug trafficking. This includes the protection of the EU's external borders, the implementation of the regulations on money laundering and the diversion of chemical substances as well as police cooperation.

- Cooperation with other countries, whether through international organisations or in the framework of the relations the EU maintains with individual countries and groups of countries.
- The development of information flows and coordination between the fifteen member states as regards the drugs phenomenon, thanks to a European monitoring centre for drugs, a network of national centres, the use of information technology and scientific research.

The funds devoted by the European Union to combating the drugs problem have increased on a more or less continuous basis in recent years; from ECU 5.5 million in 1987 they rose to ECU 14.8 million in 1991, reaching the sum of ECU 27.9 million in 1995. The activities conducted within the Union itself account for 47 per cent of the total budget, with the remainder being allocated to projects in third countries.

ACTION PROGRAMME ON THE PREVENTION OF DRUG DEPENDENCY

As further evidence of the increasing efforts at EU level to respond to the scourge of drug abuse, the European Parliament and the Council, on 16 December 1996, adopted a Community action programme on the prevention of drug dependency.

The first element of the action programme is that Community activity for preventing drug addiction has as its top priority the supporting of the actions of the member states. Each government is free to set its own policy, its programmes, and the organisation of its prevention structures. In fact, the European Community Treaty (as amended at Maastricht) specifically rules out, in the domain of public health, any harmonisation of legislation in the member states. So the approach which governed the definition of the programme respects social and cultural diversity in the member states and, in the same way, respects the specific characteristics of the strategies and policies which are implemented at national level.

The programme is designed to encourage cooperation between member states, support their activities and promote the coordination of their policies and programmes. Generally speaking, the role of the Commission is therefore to encourage and promote exchanges of information, experience and examples of good practice. The Commission particularly provides a stimulus for implementing projects which are designed jointly by bodies in various member states, whether they be government organisations or non-government organisations, and, where necessary, the Commission may coordinate the activities at local level. In order to get maximum benefit from the relatively limited resources at its disposal, namely a budget of 27 million ECUs over a five-year period which corresponds roughly to IR£21 million, the Commission concentrates its Community support on projects which involve several, if not all, member states. Thus, in 1996, 50 per cent of the budget allocated for this was devoted to networks of bodies in the fifteen member states and 24 per cent of its budget was devoted to supporting projects involving five to nine member states. Member states have been slow to allocate large amounts of funding at European level which reflects to some extent different approaches to the problem in each member state and the pressure to be seen to be providing adequate resources at national level.

The Community prevention programme recognises that there are activities which are more prevalent in some member states than others, instruments for prevention which are more tried and tested in certain regions of Europe than in others, and most of all there are common needs where everybody is seeking to find a specific appropriate response. From the Commission point of view, this diversity of analyses and practice is a good thing because Europe in fact represents a laboratory, generating approaches and model references which may be useful to everybody involved in prevention.

In this differentiated context, one of the major merits of interlinking the bodies in member states is to substitute for partisan or emotional attitudes, a more professional approach, and scientific and technical analyses, rooted in the daily reality of addiction. More specifically, the programme provides for the prevention of dependency linked to the use of narcotic and psychotropic substances, and the use linked with other products for addictive purposes. This covers multi-addiction and the use of chemical products such as solvents used for addictive purposes.

The prevention of abuse of substances such as alcohol and tobacco, or the use of pharmaceuticals for purposes other than legitimate purposes, are covered by other Community policies in the public health domain, particularly the European programme for the prevention and promotion of public health, for combating cancer and AIDS.

The Drug Addiction Programme defines two types of specific objectives, and identifies a number of priority actions that have to be put into practice between now and the year 2000. The programme targets an improvement in knowledge of drugs and addiction, their repercussions, methods of prevention and risk reduction. In order to help achieve this objective the Commission will support actions targeting an improved knowledge of the factors linked with addiction. It will also support actions relating to women who are addicts, actions to reduce the risks involved in drug injection, actions to assess substitution programmes and, finally, programmes targeted on addicts in prison. With this programme, the Commission will also be in a position to support information and experience exchange on the whole question of the rehabilitation of addicts.

What type of project is the Commission in a position to support at Community level? One example is the International Network on Parenthood and Drug Usage. This is a network involving researchers in eight member states. It is focused on coordinating studies relating to pregnant drug addicts, those who are breast feeding, and the children of drug addict women, and the wide distribution of information on the existing methods of helping them, supporting them and taking responsibility for them. The second example is the European Network on Drugs and AIDS in the Prison Environment. This involves fifteen member states. It trains specialists in the area of prevention of addiction and AIDS in prison. It liaises with initiatives outside the prison environment. The network participates in evaluating pilot projects which are innovators in this field.

The programme supports general actions in assessing the effectiveness of information campaigns and public opinion polls and in organising new European Weeks for the Prevention of Addiction. In parallel with this it provides for targeted actions aimed at specific groups such as young people or groups which are particularly vulnerable. The European Networks or the Regional Cross-Border Networks are particularly well placed. They create a dynamic which means that over the whole of the member states covered, account can be taken of developments in consumption practices, developments in products being used, all aspects to do with addiction, and also the transfer of the best preventative action.

Another example of an initiative receiving support from the Commission is a foundation which is called the European Foundation for Telephone Helplines. This is a partnership between the SOS Drugs Lines in the fifteen member states. The partnership has made it possible to undertake a joint analysis of the problems involved in informing the public at large and young people to define specific training programmes for this activity and to produce reference documents to do with telephone helplines.

RESEARCH ON ILLICIT DRUGS

The Commission has given prominence to the field of illicit drugs by making this subject an important sub-area of several research programmes, especially within the so called Framework Programmes which are co-decided between the Council and the European Parliament.

The Life Sciences Programmes focus on Biomedicine and Health, Biotechnology and Agriculture and Fisheries Research. In these programmes, the Commission has been supporting a series of transnational research projects in the area of drug demand reduction. Research is conducted on the differences and respective role of national legislation, on the responsibility of individuals for their own health, and on the social framework in illicit drugs consumption.

The need for a biomedical approach to drug demand reduction was recognised during the preparation of the specific programme within biomedicine and health, Biomed 2, during the preparation of the Fourth Framework Programme (1994-1998). Within the biomedical programme, the sub-areas for research specifically on illicit drugs are: pharmaceutical aspects of illicit drug demand reduction (including doping in sports), illicit drugs in brain research, research in AIDS, tuberculosis and other infectious diseases, and, in particular, behavioural and socio-economic research and public health and health services research.[1]

In the Biotech Programme there is no specific mention of illicit drugs, but three areas of the programme are indirectly linked to the problem of illicit drugs.[2]

The Joint Research Centre (JRC) is another Community set of services with independent research facilities which can allow the detection of narcotics and drugs at border crossings and in luggage and living bodies.[3]

The Commission is now preparing its proposal for the Fifth Framework Programme (1998-2002) and a number of areas are being considered for future research. These encompass the problem of drug abuse in pregnancy, vulnerability to drug addiction, solvents abuse in adolescents, patterns of combination of drugs, immunological disturbances in drug abuse, mutagenic aspects of drug abuse, and the development of biosensors for drug detection.

EUROPEAN MONITORING CENTRE

The European Monitoring Centre on Drugs and Drug Addiction, one of the specialised agencies of the European Union, was established in 1993 in Lisbon, with the objective of providing reliable and comparable information at the European level on drugs, drug addiction[4] and their effects. The centre became operational in 1995, and in practice must undertake four different activities: (a) It must collect and analyse data; (b) It must improve the methods for rendering data from different countries comparable; (c) It is required to make information widely available and, finally, (d) It must cooperate with various European and international bodies, as well as with countries outside the European Union.

The REITOX network which was launched in the middle of 1995 links the European Monitoring Centre to fifteen contact points, in the shape of national monitoring centres, and to a sixteenth point, located in the offices of the European Commission in Brussels. This network constitutes the infrastructure for the collection and exchange of information and documents needed by the monitoring centre to carry out its mandate effectively. Once the network is fully computerised – a process which is underway – it should enjoy maximum security and efficiency.

TITLE VI AND THE COMBATING OF DRUG ADDICTION

The system of combating drug addiction found in the Third Pillar (Title VI) – as opposed to the Community Pillar – of the European Union is descended from the *ad hoc* intergovernmental cooperation which preceded the adoption of the Treaty on European Union. Among the steps taken at the old intergovernmental level a Coordinators' Group on Drugs was set up by decision of the European Council in 1989. Its objective was the coordination of Community drug-combating measures in the light of the activities of the member states in addition to the carrying out of activities such as the coordination of health measures, of money laundering prevention measures and of measures to monitor substances which can be used in drug production. It also aimed at the stepping up of cooperation with producer and processing countries.

The coming into force of Title VI led to the streamlining of the formerly *ad hoc* cooperation procedure. Henceforth cooperation effected at European Union level (insofar as it is carried on outside the first pillar of the Union, the Community) would be carried out under the Council of Justice and Home Affairs Ministers. A working group dealing solely with drugs and organised crime was set up in order to assist matters.

Much of the anti-drug cooperation carried out under Title VI is carried out in the framework of customs cooperation and police cooperation (more specifically the European Drugs Unit, or Europol), but there are separate chapters in the present volume dealing with cooperation under these headings. It should be added, however, that there are aspects to cooperation under Title VI which fall outside these two areas. In this regard, and others, the Irish Presidency Conclusions of December 1996 give a good idea of what the European Union is at present doing, and intends to do in the immediate future, in the area of combating drug addiction.

The Presidency Conclusions noted that the European Council welcomed as a concrete expression of a shared political will, the agreement which has been reached on a joint action on the approximation of the laws and practices of police, customs services and judicial authorities in the fight against drug addiction and illegal drug trafficking, and resolutions on sentencing for serious drug trafficking offences, on combating drug tourism and on drug production and cultivation.

The European Council stressed that this constituted a first step and that the momentum achieved must be maintained and further developed, in particular through:

- continued examination of further harmonisation of laws, insofar as an agreed need for it is identified, complemented by reinforced cooperation between the institutions and the member states. (The European Council noted that the dangers posed by synthetic drugs deserve special attention);
- continued review of further cooperation between law enforcement agencies to combat drug trafficking;
- full application of the Community's Directive on money laundering and its possible extension to those relevant professions and bodies outside the classical financial sector;
- development by the Council and the Commission of the contribution which research activities can make in addressing the medical, socio-economic and detection aspects of drug abuse;
- energetic implementation of the Community's action plan to combat drugs in the Caribbean, as well as the implementation of the agreed follow-up of the report by the expert mission to Latin America;
- further development of the structured dialogue with the associated countries of Central and Eastern Europe in regard to drugs issues; comparable cooperation with the Russian Federation, initiated during the current Presidency, should be pursued;
- examination of ways to assist Central Asian republics, utilising the TACIS programme, to fight transit in and production of drugs.

The European Council also noted that cooperation with transatlantic partners in these fields had also to be continued and, where appropriate, improved.

The European Council confirmed the priority it attached to sustained and coordinated action in the fight against drugs, making full and coherent use of all the instruments of the Union and invited the Council to draw up, by the end of 1997, a first assessment of measures undertaken, with a view to strengthening and supplementing them.

CONCLUSION

The fight against drug abuse is a multifaceted one. Through its action plans, its programme for prevention, its research activities and the work of the European Monitoring Centre, as well as through such measures as those anticipated in Presidency conclusions, it may fairly be said that the European Union is seeking to play a significant complementary role alongside the efforts of each member state.

NOTES

1. Four proposals that pertain to these objectives were funded through the first call of the biomedical and research programme. Two proposals focused on the study of brain receptors to dopamine and on their relation to drug addiction and withdrawal. Also, novel therapeutic strategies are studied. Another proposal looked at the delta opiod system in the brain and its role in pain control and drug addiction. The last proposal dealt with the problem of doping in sports, from the point of view of the abuse of growth hormone and related substances. The Commission believes that state-of-the-art technologies for brain imaging can now allow a better understanding of the effect of drugs on different parts of the brain and consequently, the building up of scientific knowledge in order to devise pharmacotherapeutic strategies. Moreover, it is nowadays possible to envisage a pharmacological treatment to prevent the effect of drugs and even a vaccine to block their effects.
2. These are cell communication in neurosciences (immunology and transdisease vaccinology including possible vaccines for treating drug addiction in humans) and structural biology, mainly in its nano-biotechnology aspects, including research on biosensors.
3. This is made possible by existing desk instruments such as ion mobility spectroscopy. Newer technologies such as the time-of-flight mass spectrometry, allowing analysis of samples within tens of microseconds, are about to be installed in one of the JRC institutes and will contribute significantly to the research on illicit drugs.
4. The Monitoring Centre gives priority in its work to several aspects of the drug problem. They are: the demand for drugs and reduction of the demand; national and European strategies and policies; the origin and transit of drugs; international cooperation; implications of the drugs phenomenon for different countries in the world.

CHAPTER 8
TITLE VI AND THE FIGHT AGAINST FRAUD

EILEEN BARRINGTON

INTRODUCTION

Title VI of the Treaty on European Union (TEU) sets out the provisions governing cooperation in the fields of justice and home affairs. Article K.1 of Title VI provides that:

> For the purposes of achieving the objectives of the Union, in particular the free movement of persons, and without prejudice to the powers of the European Community, member states regard the following areas as matters of common interest ...

This Article goes on to list certain matters, such as asylum policy, rules governing the crossing by persons of the external borders of the member states, and immigration policy. In fact, the wording of Article K.1 is a little misleading since the thrust of the Article is not so much to deal with the furtherance of the free movement of persons but rather with the problems which inevitably arise where an internal market allowing for such free movement of persons exists. Thus Article K.1(5) lists as one of the matters of common interest "combating fraud on an international scale insofar as this is not covered by 7 to 9". K.1(7) to K.1(9) deal respectively with judicial cooperation in criminal matters, customs cooperation and police cooperation for the purposes of preventing and combating terrorism, unlawful trafficking and other serious forms of international crime.

The inclusion of the combat against fraud in Title VI, and under its own heading separate from the general provision on judicial cooperation in criminal matters, illustrates the concern among the member states that action should be taken against what was perceived as the significant and increasing level of fraud within the Community. The primary objective appears to have been the combat against what has become known as "Euro-fraud" or fraud against the financial interests of the Community.

Over the past ten years, the issue of fraud against the Community's interests has been steadily moving centre-stage. It has been used by Euro-sceptics in certain member states to attempt to halt the development of the Community.

If for no other reason, it thus became essential that the Community should be seen to react to the problem.

In 1989 the British House of Lords Select Committee on the European Community, in its Report on Fraud against the Community, did not mince its words, concluding that:

> The huge sums which are being lost due to fraud and irregularity against the Community are losses borne by all the tax payers and traders of Europe. This strikes at the roots of democratic societies, based as they are on the rule of law and its enforcement, and is a public scandal.[1]

The report found that financial management within the Community was weak, that the failure both to detect fraud and to take action when it was detected allowed fraudsters to continue in business, and that for years there had been no political will to tackle the problem.

Thus the inclusion of fraud within Title VI illustrated the strengthening of the political will by the member states to combat this problem. The question which will be addressed in this article is whether or not this form of crystallisation of the political will in the TEU is capable of providing an adequate response to the problem.

In its 1994 Report on Financial Control and Fraud in the Community, the House of Lords Select Committee on the European Community took the view that there was "still a long way to go to achieve the sound financial management which Community tax payers have the right to expect".[2] The Report went on to identify the weaknesses of the present system of management of the financial interests by the Community, being in particular the "spending culture" which the report claimed to exist within the Community and the lack of accountability in the spending of Community funds. The report illustrates one of the problems encountered in this area which is that of the member states' tendency to cast blame for Community fraud on the Commission for its lack of management. The Commission reacts by pointing out that "the fact that 80 per cent of EU money is spent by the member states means we must deepen cooperation with them in order to get to grips with fraud for once and for all". While making this point it nonetheless acknowledges that "the fight against fraud has intensified in recent years, scoring some notable successes, but a lot remains to be done."[3]

In order to evaluate the adequacy of the political response to fraud, this article will briefly trace the developments in the fight against fraud, and will address certain problems already identified in the operation of Article K.1(5).

The general failings common to all the subjects covered in Title VI are examined in Chapter 1 of this book. The complexity of the institutional framework, the difficulty caused by the requirement of unanimity and the reluctance of the member states to avail of the new legal instruments provided by Title VI rather than availing of the classic non-binding instruments of intergovernmental policy and, lastly, the reduced roles of the Commission, the Parliament and the Court, are generally acknowledged to be factors which have made action taken to date under Title VI disappointing.

The combat against fraud is, however, also faced with a structural problem, which will be discussed at greater length below, since it is clear that certain aspects of the fight against fraud fall within the EC Pillar of the TEU. Thus there is debate as to which aspects of anti-fraud policy come within Title VI, the intergovernmental Third Pillar, and which aspects remain within the supra-national First or EC Pillar.

THE FIGHT AGAINST FRAUD BEFORE MAASTRICHT

It is perhaps useful, before tracing the extent of the Community's anti-fraud measures which pre-date Title VI, to outline the main contexts in which fraud occurs.[4] Frauds may be perpetrated in relation to both money that is collected for the Community and sums that are paid out to traders from the Community budget. Revenue frauds are prevalent in particular in the area of the Community's original own resources: agricultural levies and customs duties. These are levies collected by member states' customs authorities on imports into the Community. Here, in view of the complexity of the common customs tariff, a misdescription of the goods imported can be very profitable. The Community has not been so preoccupied with fraud in the other area of revenue which is VAT, since, while this is again collected by a member state's authorities, most of the revenue is destined for the national exchequer and any fraud is thus of as much concern to the member states as it is to the Community.

The second area of fraud is that of Community payments. Administration of the CAP through the European Agricultural Guidance & Guarantee Fund (EAGGF) accounts for approximately 50 per cent of the Community budget (approximately 76 billion ECU in 1995). The range of possible fraud in this area is very broad: from false declarations, to monetary compensatory amount frauds, to wrongful receipt of subsidies.[5] While the most significant fraud would appear to be in the agricultural sector, the structural funds, which now account for approximately 30 per cent of the total budget expenditure, are also targeted by fraudsters.

Since the Community had no fraud control procedures of its own, the responsibility for the investigation and prosecution of frauds and irregularities affecting the Community budget always lay with the member states. The attitude of the member states towards meeting this responsibility and the role of the Community in encouraging the member states evolved over time and has been usefully divided up by one commentator into three phases:[6] the first phase being that of "benign neglect", the second that of "control coordination" and the third, or active phase, that of "adminstration to punishment". The first of these phases, commencing from the setting up of the CAP in 1962, was characterised by a "climate of 'laisser aller' and uncertainty (which) must have felt, to some, like an invitation to defraud".[7] In the early years of the CAP, anti-fraud enforcement did not appear to be an urgent priority for the member states. In 1976 a draft Treaty for the Protection of the Financial Interest of the Community was rejected by the member states. Not until 1977 when the Court of Auditors was created to work alongside Parliament to improve budgetary control was there an institutional mechanism to advise on budgetary control or to review anti-fraud measures.

The establishment of the Court of Auditors, which is based in Luxembourg, was provided for under the terms of the Financial Provisions Treaty of 1975. The decision to set up this new body was linked with the decision set out in the 1975 Treaty to grant to the European Parliament the sole responsibility of discharging the Commission of its responsibility concerning the accounts of the Community. These new financial arrangements should, it was felt, be accompanied by an intensification of control and audit best achieved by the creation of a new body, such as the Court. The Court is charged with the responsibility of examining the accounts of all revenue and expenditure of the Community and of all bodies set up by the Community. It also has the task of examining financial management within the Community. The Court draws up an annual report after the close of each financial year. The institutions also have the right to seek the opinion of the Court on specific matters.

The second phase of "control coordination" commenced in the 1980s when divergences among the member states over the budget became more significant. The Commission became more active in supervising and detecting fraud in the agricultural sectors and certain sectoral regulations were adopted to deal with the problem.[8] UCLAF (L'Unite de Co-Ordination de la Lutte Anti-fraude) was set up in 1988 to coordinate the efforts both within the Commission and between the Commission and the member states in order to tackle fraud. Thus "the Community acquired limited power and personnel to oversee the control efforts of individual member states."[9]

In the third, or active phase, a major step in the development of fraud policy was taken by means of the case law of the European Court of Justice (ECJ). Technical measures on fraud control were adopted and institutional innovations were made, culminating in the adoption of a number of provisions in the TEU.

The first significant development in the fraud case law of the ECJ was in the *Greek Maize* case.[10] While the EC Treaty at this stage contained no provisions relating specifically to fraud, the ECJ nonetheless emphasised the legal consequences for member states who did not live up to their obligations to detect and prosecute fraud. The Court stated that inactivity on the part of a member state in the use of its criminal law or other disciplinary procedures to deal with such frauds against the financial interests of the Community amounted to a failure to fulfil the states' obligations of Community membership under Article 5 of the Treaty. In essence, this means that the principle of equivalence must apply as between breaches of national law and Community law.[11]

However, the most significant development in the case law of the ECJ, from the Commission's point of view, came in the case of *Germany-v-Commission*.[12] The judgment concerned the power of the Community in general, and the Commission in particular, to insert clauses in agricultural regulations specifying the penalties to be imposed by national authorities on farmers who committed irregularities when applying for financial aid.

The Court held that the Community was quite within its powers to impose this type of penalty. This judgment made it clear that the Community in general and the Commission in particular had the power to provide administrative penalties to be imposed on persons who had committed irregularities.[13]

Once the power of the Community to impose administrative penalties was recognised, the next question which arose was clearly that of whether or not the Community had power to lay down criminal penalties. While the member states seem to contest that the Community has competence in this area, the ECJ has not had to give its views on the matter as of yet and certain commentators argue that the view that the Community does not have any competence in the area is not free from doubt.[14]

THE INNOVATIONS OF THE TEU

In addition to the introduction of Title VI the TEU also amended the First-EC-Pillar in two ways in order to further the fight against fraud.

Firstly, Article 209(a) was inserted into the EC Treaty. This Article provides that:

> Member states shall take the same measures to counter fraud affecting the financial interests of the Community as they take to counter fraud affecting their own financial interests.

> Without prejudice to the other provisions of this Treaty, member states shall coordinate their action aimed at protecting the financial interests of the Community against fraud. To this end they shall organise, with the help of the Commission, close and regular cooperation between the competent departments of their administrations.

Article 209(a) thus provides an express legal basis for the principle of assimilation which had already been developed by the ECJ in the *Greek Maize* case.

Secondly, the TEU contains a number of provisions on budgetary and financial review. The Treaty raises budgetary discipline (Article 201(a)) and sound financial management (Article 205) to the status of principles. Likewise the Treaty strengthens the role of the Court of Auditors and raises it to full institution status (Article 4). This underlines the Union's desire to grant the Court of Auditors greater authority and to strengthen the role of financial management in Community life.

THE PROBLEM OF OVERLAP

The problem that immediately becomes apparent is that of the possible overlap between K.1(5) and the EC Pillar. Admittedly, Article K.1(5) is not expressly limited to fraud affecting the financial interests of the Community. However, the instruments adopted to date on the basis of K.1(5) have all related to this subject.

The examination of the two measures adopted recently for the protection of the financial interests of the Community sheds some light on the view the Commission and the member states appear to be taking of the respective areas of competence of the EC Pillar and Article K.1(5).

The first major measure was adopted within the framework of the Third Pillar. In July 1995, the member states adopted a Convention on the Protection of the European Community's Financial Interests.[15] This Convention states that "the member states regard the combating of fraud affecting the European Community's financial interests as a matter of common interest coming under the cooperation provided for in Title VI of the Treaty". The Convention goes on to provide for criminal penalties for such fraudulent activities.

A regulation[16] on the protection of the financial interests of the Community was also adopted within the framework of the EC Pillar. The legal basis invoked for this regulation is Article 235 of the EC Treaty, the general provision whereby the member states may take action to attain one of the objectives of the Community where the Treaty has not provided the requisite express powers. The Regulation states that "the effectiveness of the combating of fraud against the Community's financial interests calls for a common set of legal rules to be enacted for all areas covered by Community policies."[17]

The Regulation provides for the general rules relating to penalties for irregularities affecting the financial interests of the Community and is examined in more detail below.

Therefore, in general the member states appear to be taking the view that, as regards the protection of the financial interests of the Community and the legal enforcement of Community law, this is divided between the first, or EC Pillar (administrative law enforcement) and the Third Pillar (criminal law enforcement). Verwaele[18] has criticised this new development, stating that it will have a negative effect on European integration, since a coordinated enforcement of EC law is an essential part of the last phase of integration.

While the adopted versions of the Convention and Regulation were considerably watered down in comparison to the original proposals made, they nonetheless constitute a significant advance in the fight against fraud. The adoption of the Fraud Convention constitutes one of the few successes of Title VI, even though the choice of Title VI as its legal basis has been criticised.[19]

THE MEASURES ADOPTED

THE CONVENTION[20]

Article 1 of the Convention defines fraud affecting the European Community's Financial Interests as consisting of the following:

In respect of expenditure or revenue, any intentional act or omission relating to:

- the use or presentation of false, incorrect or incomplete statements or documents, which has as its effect the misappropriation or wrongful retention of funds from the general budget of the European Communities or budgets managed by, or on behalf of, the European Communities or the illegal diminution of same.

- The non-disclosure of information and violation of a specific obligation, with the same effect.

- The misapplication of a legally obtained benefit, with the same effect, or the misapplication of such funds for purposes other than those for which they were originally granted.

The Article goes on to provide that each member state shall take the necessary measures to transpose these offences into national criminal law. The member states must ensure that such offences are punishable by effective, proportionate and dissuasive criminal penalties including, at least in cases of serious fraud, penalties involving deprivation of liberty which can give rise to extradition. Member states are free to set a minimum threshold for serious fraud which may not be less than 50,000 ECU. The member states are also obliged to take measures to allow for criminal liability to be imposed on heads of business. In order to combat the international nature of most Euro fraud, the Convention obliges the member state to take necessary measures to establish jurisdiction over offences where (a) fraud is committed in whole or in part within its territory, or where (b) a person within its territory knowingly assists or induces the commission of such fraud within the territory of any other state or where the offender is a national of that member state concerned, provided the law of the member state may require the conduct to be punishable also in the country where it occurred.

In order to effectively combat Eurofraud, which is often international in nature, the Convention provides for changes in municipal law in relation to extradition and prosecution of the offences defined in Article 1. A member state may not refuse to extradite its own nationals for such offences nor refuse to extradite on the grounds that the offence relates to a tax or customs duty offence only.

Article 8 confers jurisdiction on the ECJ for disputes relating to the Convention. However, in view of British opposition to the ECJ being given jurisdiction, Article 8 copies the compromise provision in the Europol Convention. Thus disputes must firstly be sent to the Council and only if the latter fails to find a solution within six months, may the matter then be referred to the ECJ.

Ireland has signed but not yet ratified the Convention. Ireland appears to be taking the view that the conferral of jurisdiction on the ECJ will not require a constitutional amendment. However, national legislation will be required to incorporate this Convention into Irish law and to allow for certain changes which will have to be made to national law to enable Ireland to live up to the undertakings it has committed itself to under the Convention. The Department of Justice apparently envisages a bill next year for this purpose.

The Commission has adopted an additional Protocol to the Convention directed at acts of corruption on the part of national and European officials likely to damage the European Communities' financial interests. The draft provides that member states shall take the necessary measures to ensure that its law criminalises the conduct described in the Protocol. The Protocol is currently the subject of negotiations at Council level.[21] The Protocol would, of course, also have to be adopted by the member states in accordance with their respective constitutional requirements.

REGULATION 2988/95

Regulation 2988/95 on the protection of the financial interests of the Community is significant in that, based on Article 235, it does not relate to one EC fund only, as anti-fraud measures did in the past, but rather is a horizontal measure applicable to *all* EC funds (CAP funds, structural funds etc). The Regulation provides for a list of administrative measures and penalties for irregularities, which are defined as follows:

> Any infringement of a provision of Community law resulting from an act or omission by an economic operator, which has, or would have, the effect of prejudicing the general budget of the Communities or budgets managed by them either by reducing or losing revenue accruing from own resources collected directly on behalf of the Communities, or by an unjustified item of expenditure.

The general rule is that an irregularity will involve the withdrawal of the wrongly obtained advantage by an obligation to pay or repay the amounts due or wrongly received and by the total or partial loss of the security provided in support of the request for advantage granted or at the time of the receipt of an advance (Article 4). These measures, however, are not to be regarded as penalties. Article 5 of the Regulation deals with the penalties which may be imposed in the event of intentional irregularities or those caused by negligence. The possible penalties include, *inter alia,* the payment of an administrative fine, the total or partial removal of an advantage, exclusion from an advantage for a period subsequent to that of the irregularity, the loss of a security or deposit, or other penalties of a purely economic type provided for in the sectoral rules adopted by the Council for specific sectors.

The imposition of such administrative penalties may be suspended by a decision of the competent authority if criminal proceedings have been initiated against the person concerned in connection with the same facts. The Regulation also deals with various limitation periods for the initiation of proceedings based on the irregularities referred to. The limitation period is a four-year one but Article 13 of the Regulation provides that the sectoral rules may make provision for a shorter period which, however, may not be less than three years. Lastly, the Regulation imposes on the member states an obligation to carry out checks to ensure the regularity and reality of transactions involving the Community's financial interests (Article 8).[22]

POSSIBLE FUTURE DEVELOPMENTS

The European Council,[23] meeting in Madrid, laid considerable emphasis on the importance of the protection of the financial interests of the Community. On the strength of the encouragement provided by the European Council, the Commission has adopted an ambitious 1996 action plan for fighting fraud.[24] However, undoubtedly most of the actions envisaged by the Commission will be based on the EC Pillar rather than on Title VI. With regard to the Third Pillar area, the Commission simply adds that it will encourage all EU countries to ratify the Convention and will push for a second protocol to the Convention in order to cover, *inter alia,* the criminal liability of legal persons, judicial cooperation and money laundering.[25] The Commission indicates that it is of the view that the only effective way to combat transnational fraud is to create a *judicial space* providing for improved cooperation between investigators, prosecutors and judges.[26] It is questionable whether or not Title VI will provide an adequate basis for such an initiative.

Since the Fraud Convention is one of only four conventions adopted since Title VI came into force, it immediately constitutes one of the successes of justice and home affairs cooperation. However, it will inevitably be some time before it is ratified by the member states and enters into force. Any protocols to the Convention will also have to go through the ratification procedure (a significant delay is inherent in any action based on Title VI since unanimity is required for any measure to be adopted and ratification is also necessary in the case of conventions).

The problems which arise in relation to the fight against fraud are compounded by the fact that there is inevitably some overlap even within the Third Pillar, specifically, between Article K1(5) which deals with fraud and Article K1(7) which deals with judicial cooperation in criminal matters. This creates problems because while the Commission shares the power to initiate measures with the member states for fraud matters, it has no power of initiative in relation to criminal matters. Consequently, the Commission would be obliged to take a back seat with regard to any proposals for legislation that fall within the realm of cooperation in criminal matters rather than fraud. As the member states will doubtless be slow to propose any harmonising measures, or even measures allowing for procedural cooperation, in the criminal sphere, progress in this area will certainly not be quick.

In view of (a) the somewhat artificial nature of the distinction between the competence to impose administrative sanctions on the one hand (regarded as falling within the Community domain) and criminal sanctions on the other (regarded as coming within the Third Pillar) and (b) the problem of overlap between the two Pillars, a possible solution could be the use of the "passerelle" provision provided for at Article K.9 of the TEU. This allows the Council to communitarise certain of the matters of common interest dealt with under the Third Pillar, including the combating of fraud. However, Article K.9 is not without problems: it is in itself quite cumbersome in that unanimity is required and the member states must adopt the decision according to their respective constitutional requirements. In addition, even if the combat of fraud were to be brought within the EC Pillar by way of Article K.9, judicial cooperation in *criminal matters* would still be left in the intergovernmental pillar since the passerelle provision cannot be used for certain matters within the Third Pillar, including cooperation in criminal matters.

Otherwise, of course, the Commission could attempt to overcome the opposition of the member states in order to propose more swingeing measures on the basis of the pre-existing provisions in the EC Pillar, in particular using Article 209(a) of the EC Treaty as a real legal basis for action as opposed to its current attitude of viewing that Article as merely setting out the principle of assimilation, according to which the member states are obliged to treat fraud against the financial interests of the Community as they would cases of purely national fraud.[27] The Parliament would be an ally in such a venture.[28] The matter could be referred to the ECJ for a ruling as to the scope of the provisions in the EC Pillar and the possible legal bases for anti-fraud measures. Thus the ECJ would have an opportunity to decide on certain matters which have given rise to debate, such as the question as to whether the EC has competence to impose criminal sanctions.

It cannot be denied that the fight against fraud must be one of the priorities of the Community. The Commission correctly argues,[29] however, that the legal bases and instruments for fighting fraud are too limited. In particular, it urgently needs more than Title VI can provide.[30]

NOTES

1. 5th report, Session 1988/1989, HL Paper 27.
2. 12th report, Session 1993/1994, HL Paper 75.
3. Press release on Commission's Launch of 1996 Action Plan for Fighting Fraud IP/96/104. When presenting this action plan to the Parliament, President Santer promised to change the financial and administrative culture of the Commission. To this end, the Commission has launched an action programme called "Sound and Efficient Financial Management" or "SEM 2000". The first two phases of this programme deal with the Commission itself while the last phase is based on partnership with the member states. The first phase is to be an attempt to replace a "spending" culture with a "performance" culture. See generally address by Commissioner Gradin, "Achieving Better Value from EC Funds", given to European Federation of Accountants, 21-22 March 1996.
4. See generally, Ann Sherlock, "Controlling Fraud within the Community", (1991) *E.L. Rev. 16,* p.20.
5. Most of which are illustrated by the Report of the Tribunal of Enquiry into the Beef Processing Industry.
6. See Simone White, "A variable geometry of enforcement? Aspects of European Community budget fraud" in *Crime, Law and Social Change 23,* p.235.
7. *Ibid,* at p.239.
8. In particular, Regulation 4045/89 on scrutiny by member states of transactions of the system of financing by the guarantee section of the European Agricultural Guidance and Guarantee Fund, O.J. L338, 21 December, 1989, p.18.
9. White, *op. cit.* at p.240.
10. Case 68/88 [1989] ECR 2965.
11. The Report of Government Advisory Commitee on Fraud (PL9409) found that Irish legislation in the area of fraud was consistent with the principles defined by the ECJ.
12. Case C-240/90 [1992] ECR 1 5313 confirmed recently by case C-1904/94, *Cereol Italia Srl.-v-Azienda Agricola Castello SAS.*
13. For a general discussion on this case, see Van Gerven, "Legal protection of the Community's financial interest and the case law of the Court of Justice", in the Commission's publication on *The Legal Protection of the Financial Interests of the Community: Progress and Prospects since the Brussels Seminar of 1989.*
14. See for example, Van Gerven, *op cit,* at p.195 and Professor Verwaele, "Criminal law in the European Community: about myths and taboos", in *Agon,* the Review of the Associations of Lawyers for the Protection of the Financial Interests of the European Community, where Verwaele argues that the view that the Community does not have the right to prescribe criminal sanctions is unfounded. See also Sevenster in "Criminal law and EC law" (1992) *CMLR,* who argues that while the existence of a Community system of criminal law is still generally denied, nonetheless the absolute sovereignty of member states with regard to criminal law has become illusory. The rules of Community law can, in fact, constitute preconditions imposed on national criminal law. She goes on to argue for the harmonisation of certain aspects of criminal law, and, in particular, the economic penal law for the enforcement of EC law.
15. O.J. C316 at p.48, 27 November 1995.

16. No. 2988/95, O.J. L312 at p.1, 23 December 1995; note also now the Protocol to this Convention signed by the justice ministers on 27 September 1996, relating, in particular, to corruption.

17. As regards the legal basis, the regulation sets out that the Treaty makes no provision for the specific powers necessary for the adoption of substantive law of horizontal scope on checks, measures and penalties with a view to ensuring the protection of the Community's financial interests. This is debatable, given the existence of Article 209(a) of the EC Treaty which arguably could provide the legal basis for such a measure. However, the view taken of Article 209(a) appears to be that since this Article contains no enabling provisions for subordinate legislation, it cannot be relied upon for this type of measure. Professor Verwaele takes the view that "this interpretation is legally questionable, as well as constituting a missed opportunity to base enforcement harmonisation measures on a legal basis of Articles 100, 100(a) and 209(a)."

18. *Op. cit.,* p.4.

19. See Missir di Lusignano, "La protection des interets financiers de la Communaute: perspectives et realites", to appear in *Journal des Tribunaux, Droit European,* April 1996. Missir argues that while the provisions of Article K1.5 should be considered as complementary to the goal of the achievement of Community integration, the tendency has been the exact opposite. The intergovernmental provisions have been considered to be autonomous and free-standing, and not as merely complementary to the Community Pillar. He questions whether this was in fact the development envisaged by the drafters of the TEU.

20. For a discussion on the background to both the Convention and Regulation, see Missir di Lusignano, *op. cit.*

21. See Document 5502/96 JUSTPEN 21 dated 14 March 1996.

22. The Commission has proposed a draft regulation on controls and checks carried out by the Commission for the purpose of establishing frauds and irregularities against the financial interests of the Community to supplement Regulation 2988/95. See COM (95) 690 final adopted on 20 December 1995. This regulation is also based on Article 235.

23. See the Conclusions of the Madrid Summit, 15-16 December 1995.

24. See Press Release IP/96/104.

25. Such a draft protocol was adopted by the Commission on 20 December 1995. See COM (95) 693 final.

26. With this aim in mind, the Commission has asked the national Associations for the Protection of the Financial Interests of the Community to conduct a study on the current obstacles to the creation of such a "judicial space". Note that the justice ministers at their informal meeting held at Dublin on 27 September 1996 signed the Protocol to the Convention for the Protection of the Financial Interest of the Community, which relates in particular to corruption.

A draft joint action for the creation of a framework for the exchange of "liaison judges" with a view to improving judicial cooperation between member states is however, the subject of negotiations at Council level, having been approved by the K.4 Committee. "Liaison Judges" are defined in Article 1 of the draft, as judges or civil servants who are experts in judicial cooperation procedures. See Council documents 5331/96 JUST 4.

27. See Missir di Lusignano, *op. cit.,* at p.19.

28. See the resolution of the Parliament, O.J. L154 18 of 23 January 1995 where the Parliament indicated that Articles 43, 100(a) and 209(a) were the appropriate legal bases for the Regulation and the Convention.

29. See Commission Report for the Reflection Group on the Intergovernmental Conference 1996.
30. Doubtless there is also some truth in the point made by Mogele, "The financing System of the Common Agricultural Policy and its legal framework", (1995) 4, *IJEL 134* to the effect that "one of the most efficient means of improving fraud prevention would be the substantive simplification of the CAP schemes and the agricultural legislation of the Community". However, he adds that the complex nature of CAP schemes is often the result of political compromise in the Council and simplification would thus firstly require the political will of the governments.

PART III

EUROPEAN UNION INTERVENTION IN THE FIELD OF IMMIGRATION, ASYLUM AND BORDER CONTROLS

Chapter 9

Immigration, Visa and Border Controls in the European Union

Diarmaid McGuinness and Eileen Barrington

Introduction

The subjct of immigration, visa and border control in the European Union is, unfortunately, a complex one. The free movement of persons was, of course, one of the cardinal principles on which the Treaty of Rome was based. The introduction into this Treaty of the notion of the internal market upon the coming into force of the Single European Act in 1987 immediately gave rise to controversy as to how the concept of a single market would impact on the movement of persons and, in particular, on the continued existence of internal border controls. This controversy continues today. With the coming into force of the Treaty of Maastricht in November 1993, the addition of the provisions of Article K.1 of the Third Pillar, which relate *inter alia* to immigration policy and border controls, and the amendment of the First European Community (EC) Pillar to cover visa policy, complicated matters further. One question therefore that now emerges concerns the aspects of immigration and border control that fall within the EC Pillar of the European Union and those that fall within the Third Pillar. Another question which must be asked concerns the effect, if any, of the measures that fall entirely outside European Union structures, which have been entered into by certain member states and which also relate to free movement of persons, the Schengen Agreement being the prime example here. Answers to these questions are of interest to Union citizens, of course, but even more so to the nationals of third countries.

The purpose of this chapter is thus to attempt to provide inevitably sketchy answers to some relevant questions. For the sake of clarity, the issues will be dealt with under three sections, the first dealing with Title VI and the acts adopted thereunder, the second dealing with the EC Pillar and EC acts, and the third dealing, very briefly, with non-EC acts of relevance to the theme of external border controls, immigration and visa policy.

Immigration, Visa and Border Control under Title VI

Title VI of the Treaty of Maastricht sets out the provisions on cooperation in the fields of justice and home affairs. Article K.1 provides, *inter alia,* that:

> For the purposes of achieving the objectives of the Union, in particular the free movement of persons, and without prejudice to the powers of the European Community, member states shall regard the following areas as matters of common interest:
>
> (1) asylum policy;
> (2) rules governing the crossing by persons of the external borders of the member states and the exercise of controls thereon;
> (3) immigration policy and policy regarding nationals of third countries;
>
> > (a) conditions of entry and movement by nationals of third countries on the territory of member states;
> > (b) conditions of residence by nationals of third countries on the territory of member states, including family reunion and access to employment;
> > (c) combating unauthorised immigration, residence and work by nationals of third countries on the territory of member states.

As is clear from the terms of Article K.1, the thrust of the authority given to the Union to act in this area is premised upon the fundamental importance of ensuring free movement throughout the Union and combating the problems which such free movement might throw up. The purpose of this chapter is to address the issues referred to at K.1(2) and K.1(3), i.e. essentially the questions of the external borders and immigration policy. The question of asylum policy is addressed in chapter 10. It is therefore not proposed to examine questions relating to asylum policy and refugees in this article. None the less, there is clearly an inevitable overlap in some areas between paragraph K.1(1) and paragraphs K.1(2) and K.1(3).

Title VI – a recipe for disappointing results

It is interesting to note that Article K.1 does not use the word "competence". Rather, the member states agree to regard certain matters as being of "common interest". The avoidance of the use of the word "competence" can be viewed as illustrating the limited enthusiasm of certain member states to the idea of conferring any exclusive authority on the Union to act in the sensitive areas dealt with under Title VI. This point is all the more striking when account is taken of the fact that such matters could only, in any case, be dealt with according to the intergovernmental procedures provided for under that Title – with the safeguard of unanimity which that entails.

It is generally acknowledged that the results of cooperation in the fields of justice and home affairs have been disappointing. The European Commission, in its report for the Reflection Group for the 1996 Inter-governmental Conference, has taken the view that while the very fact that these issues were included in the Treaty of Maastricht was a major innovation, the legal and institutional framework erected has nonetheless proved to be ineffective.[1] The institutional and legal arrangements for Title VI are designed to fall somewhere between the classic EC model and simple intergovernmental cooperation, which was the manner in which these matters were dealt with up until the entry into force of the Treaty of Maastricht and which continues to be the predominant influence.[2] The institutional and legal framework is discussed in greater detail elsewhere in this work. Suffice it to say here that the major features distinguishing Title VI from the EC pillar are, *inter alia,* that the Commission and European Parliament have a much less significant role in the legislative process and that certain new legal instruments (common positions, joint actions and conventions drawn up by the Council) have been introduced. In addition, the European Court of Justice (ECJ) does not have automatic or any jurisdiction over Title VI matters unless and until it is accorded to it by Convention.

A number of problems common to all the subject matters covered under Title VI have been identified by the Commission,[3] such as the complexity of the institutional framework and the requirement of unanimity. However, the last major problem identified by the Commission in its Report impacts in the most significant manner on the subject matter of this chapter. This problem is one of demarcation between Community matters and Third Pillar matters under Title VI. The Community or EC Pillar, governed by the classic supra-national EC procedures, has the free movement of persons as one of its basic premises. The Third Pillar, added to the EC Pillar by the Treaty of Maastricht, also claims to govern aspects of the free movement of persons. However, matters falling within the Third Pillar will be dealt with according to the entirely separate intergovernmental procedures provided for under that Pillar. Thus, as the Commission puts it:

The difficulties inherent in the Treaty's pillar design have come home to roost: Article K.1 states that the aim is to achieve "the objectives of the Union, in particular the free movement of persons,.... without prejudice to the powers of the European Community". However, for the purposes of completing the single market and removing border controls, the free movement of persons is already a Community objective.[4]

The potential overlap between the provisions of the EC Pillar and of Title VI is a source of legal controversy which can inevitably give rise to even further delay in adopting Title VI measures. An example of overlap is given by the Commission itself in its Report. It takes the view that the Council was mistaken in its choice of Article K.1(3)(b) as a legal basis for one of the very few joint actions adopted under Title VI, concerning travel facilities for school pupils from third countries resident in a member state.[5] This, according to the Commission, is a Community matter.[6] The Commission takes the same view regarding the proposed Convention on Controls on Persons Crossing External Frontiers which is discussed below and for which the proposed legal basis is Article K.1(2) of Title VI. Visa policy is clearly another area where the demarcation line between Title VI and the EC Pillar is anything but clear. The unhappiness aired by the Commission regarding the Council's choice of legal basis for certain measures illustrates the fears which have been expressed elsewhere of a possible "decommunitarisation" of certain aspects of free movement of persons. The fear is that there could be a leakage of competence from the Community Pillar to the Third Pillar where, of course, the member states retain greater individual control over the adoption of measures.

The Commission itself suggests that the possibility of using the "bridge" provided for in Article K.9 of the EU which allows for the application of Community rules to certain areas formerly covered by Title VI, could be a solution to this overlap problem. In view of the significant overlap in the area of free movement, immigration and visa policy appear to be the Title VI areas of common interest best suited to being first across the bridge. This was the view of the majority reflected in the Westendorp report on the 1996 Intergovernmental Conference.[7]

ACTS ADOPTED UNDER TITLE VI

The member states have availed of Title VI in order to attempt to "approximate" the rules on immigration of foreign nationals by way of adopting a number of rather vague measures. In 1994, resolutions were adopted on the entry of students into the EU, on access to the EU labour market for the employed and the self-employed, and on the rules of family reunification. These resolutions are not published in the *Official Journal* and are, in any event, non-binding. In November 1995, the Ministers also agreed a resolution on the integration of third country nationals permanently resident in member states.

One joint action has been adopted on the basis of Article K.3(2)(b) concerning travel facilities for school pupils from third countries resident in a member state.[8]

The most important measure, however, is still in draft form. This is the draft Convention on the Crossing by Persons of the External Frontiers of Member States of the European Union (the draft External Frontiers Convention), modelled to some extent on the Schengen framework. The Convention has been blocked for some time due to disputes over the role to be given to the Court of Justice and to a dispute between the United Kingdom and Spain over the status of Gibraltar. The draft Convention contains rules concerning the crossing of the external frontiers, controls, the nature of controls and surveillance of the external frontiers, including special arrangements for airports. Article 7 of the draft Convention governs controls on persons "not entitled under Community law". This phrase is defined to include not only citizens of the Union but, in addition, two further categories of third country nationals with (albeit in some cases limited) rights of free movement. They are, firstly, family members benefiting from a right of entry and residence by virtue of EC secondary legislation and, secondly, nationals of third states who by agreement between the EC and its member states and such countries have rights of entry and residence.

Article 8 governs the crossing of frontiers by third country nationals residing in a member state. Persons who propose to stay in a member state for a period of over three months enter that state under the conditions laid down in its national law and, in that case, access is restricted to the territory of that state. The draft Convention at Articles 17–25 deals with visas. Article 17 provides that the member states undertake to harmonise their visa policies progressively, while Article 18 provides for uniform visas.

Article 29 provides that the European Court of Justice shall have jurisdiction to give preliminary rulings concerning the interpretation of the Convention and shall also have jurisdiction over disputes concerning the implementation of the Convention on application by a member state or the Commission. It is the latter provision that is still the subject of some dispute between the member states.[9]

O'Keeffe points out[10] that "perhaps the most important criticism levied on the Schengen Convention, the lack of a supra-national judicial control, is remedied [in the draft External Borders Convention] by the attribution of jurisdiction to the Court of Justice".[11]

IMMIGRATION, VISA AND BORDER CONTROL UNDER THE COMMUNITY PILLAR

BACKGROUND BEFORE MAASTRICHT: IMMIGRATION, VISA AND BORDER CONTROLS UNDER THE TREATY OF ROME

That the member states have always been reluctant to give up their prerogatives in the field of home affairs and internal security is readily apparent.[12] It is particularly true that the politically sensitive issues of immigration policy and visa requirements have generally been the subject only of intergovernmental cooperation. Under the EEC Treaty, the Community had no express power to prescribe rules for the entry by third country nationals into the territory of member states. It seemed that no competence for the Community to regulate the entry of third country nationals could be derived from Articles 48 *et seq.* which govern the rules on the free movement of workers, since these are expressly based on the idea of abolition of any discrimination based on nationality between workers "of the member states". However, the view taken by the member states that immigration was within the exclusive domain of the member states was, to a certain extent, challenged by the actions of some of the European institutions.

In particular, in a number of cases the European Court of Justice rejected the argument that the EEC Treaty did not provide for a competence to regulate the entry and stay of nationals of states which were associated with the EEC.[13] The ECJ also decided[14] that the Community had limited competence to regulate the legal status of third country nationals as part of the Community's social policy. Thus, immigration policy was capable of falling within the scope of application of Article 118 EEC to the extent that it concerned the impact of workers from non-member countries on the employment market and on working conditions in the Community.[15] However, it was never quite clear how far the Community competence under such provisions extended.

One category of non-nationals of member states quite clearly derived rights under the EEC Treaty. The family members of a worker benefit from certain secondary legislation implementing the rules on the free movement of workers.[16]

Third country nationals and the impact of the Single European Act

That the member states considered that they had each retained sovereignty in the area of movement of third country nationals was, however, clear from the Declarations appended by the member states to the Single European Act (SEA). On the one hand, Articles 13 to 15 of the SEA inserted Articles 8a, 8b and 8c into the EC Treaty.[17] It was true that Article 8a provided for the setting up of the internal market, stating that:

the Community shall adopt measures with the aim of progressively establishing the internal market over a period expiring on 31st December, 1992....

The internal market shall comprise an area without internal frontiers in which the free movement of goods, persons, services and capital is ensured in accordance with the provisions of this Treaty.

However, lest Article 8a be seen as warranting what, in the view of some member states at least, would be an excessive incursion into their sovereign rights, care was taken to state expressly in the General Declaration on Articles 13 to 19 of the SEA that the member states agreed that:

Nothing in these provisions shall affect the right of member states to take such measures as they consider necessary for the purpose of controlling immigration from third countries.

A similar modification could perhaps be seen to underlie at least partly the political Declaration by the governments of the member states on the Free Movement of Persons attached to the SEA, whereby the states agreed that:

In order to promote the free movement of persons, the member states shall cooperate, without prejudice to the powers of the Community, in particulars as regards the entry, movement and residence of nationals of third countries....

However, it was inevitable that the desires of the member states to complete the internal market on the one hand, and to conserve sovereignty over questions of immigration on the other, would at some stage come into conflict. The issue could not be avoided. As has been pointed out by one commentator:

There is one important factor which necessitates dealing with non-nationals of member states: the completion of the internal market. If the EC is seriously considering the abolition of internal borders then it is difficult to conceive of systems of systematic internal border checks which allow nationals of member states to pass blindly and which would still include the controls of third country nationals.[18]

The Commission took the view that a right of free circulation flowed from the obligation (arising as a result of the insertion by the Single European Act of Article 8a into the EC Treaty) to create an internal market and the consequent requirement to remove internal frontiers. All third country nationals legally resident in one member state could logically benefit from this development. At least some of the member states, however, took the view that Article 8a was dependent on the nationality-based and economically-based rights granted under the original free movement provisions of the EC Treaty. Article 8a, according to this view, did not create a separate concept of free movement of all persons within the internal market.[19]

Thus, the views of the Commission and these member states seemed bound to come into conflict. The Commission originally took the position that the declarations made by the member states could not change the binding force of a Treaty provision and did consider taking action against the countries which had not implemented Article 8a or interpreted the provision in such a way as to exclude third country nationals from freedom of movement within the internal market. However, the Commission subsequently proved itself reluctant to take action in this area. The failure by the Commission to press for Community measures in compliance with Article 8a led to an action for failure to act being brought by the European Parliament against the Commission before the ECJ.[20] After the commencement of these proceedings, the Commission finally did propose a package of measures to end controls on persons crossing the border between one member state and another in July 1995. These texts are discussed below.

AMENDMENT OF THE EC PILLAR BY THE TREATY OF MAASTRICHT

The TEU, in addition to granting the Union certain authority in the Title VI areas, also amended the EC Pillar in order to extend the scope of the Community in the area of immigration policy. Article 3 of the EC Treaty, which sets out the activities of the Community, was amended to provide that the activities of the Community "shall include measures concerning the entry and movement of persons in the internal market as provided for in Article 100c".[21]

Article 100c was also inserted by the Treaty of Maastricht into the EC Treaty. Article 100c provides that the Council shall determine the third countries whose nationals must be in possession of a visa when crossing the external borders of the member states. It goes on to allow for special measures to be adopted in the event of an emergency in a third country posing a threat of sudden inflow of nationals from that country into the Community. Article 100c is stated to be "without prejudice to the exercise of the responsibilities incumbent upon the member states with regard to the maintenance of law and order and safeguarding of internal security". The member states were clearly conscious of the fact that certain of them had already entered into arrangements relating to visas, in particular under the Schengen Agreement, to be discussed below. Consequently, Article 100c provides that the provisions of the Conventions in force between the member states governing the areas covered by the Article shall remain in force until their content has been replaced by Directives or measures adopted.

As a result of the introduction of Article 100c it is clear that visa policy now lies at least partly in the Community pillar. However, it also seems to fall in part within the remit of the Third Pillar for Article K.1(2) and (3), governing as they do the crossing by persons of the external borders, and immigration policy clearly also could be thought to encompass visa policy. The precise degree of the overlap is still unclear.[22]

STRUCTURAL PROBLEMS IN IMMIGRATION, VISA AND BORDER CONTROL UNDER THE COMMUNITY PILLAR

Hailbronner[23] points out that Article 100c appears to cover only some aspects of a common visa policy. The wording of the Article places the member states under an obligation to agree a list of third countries whose nationals require a visa, but it does not refer to the material requirements governing the granting of a visa, which therefore seem to fall outside the Community sphere. Consequently, he argues that visa policy falls under *both* Article 100c and Article K.1 of the Third Pillar.

On the other hand, it can also be argued that the scope of intergovernmental cooperation under Article K.3 is limited to those areas which are not already within the competence of the Community, as Article K.1 attributes the achieving of the objectives of the Union, in particular the free movement of persons, to the Third Pillar but without prejudice to the powers of the European Community.

Obviously, the introduction of Article 100c also affects the meaning to be given to Article 7a EC (formerly Article 8a EEC referred to above). The separate existence of Article 100c would appear to bolster the arguments made by some member states that Article 8a EC was never intended to serve as a legal basis for measures relating to the abolition of internal controls on nationals of non-member states. The Commision, however, continues to insist that the objective set by Article 7a is a frontier-free area for *all* persons – including nationals of non-member states. This view would appear to be shared by the European Parliament, which has indicated that the provisions of Articles 3, 7a(2) and 235 of the Treaty of Rome confer upon the Community sufficient regulatory power to extend freedom of movement to third country nationals legally registered within the Community and to enact common entry and visa regulations.

ACTS ADOPTED UNDER THE EC PILLAR SINCE ITS AMENDMENT BY THE TREATY OF MAASTRICHT

In September 1995 the Council of Ministers adopted a Regulation (No. 2317/95) determining the third countries whose nationals must be in possession of visas when crossing the external borders of the member states.[24] The legal basis for this measure is Article 100c of the Treaty of Maastricht. The Regulation specifies in an Annex a total of 126 countries or territorial entities whose nationals are to be subject to a visa requirement when seeking to cross the external frontier of a member state. Although this action was taken on the basis of Article 100c, the recitals contained in the preamble also refer to Article 7a of the EC Treaty and go on to provide that "other aspects of the harmonisation of visa policy, including the conditions for the issue of visas, are matters to be determined under Title VI of the TEU". The limitations of this measure should be noted. The list of countries set out in the Regulation is only a negative list, i.e. countries for whom visas *are* required. No positive list has been drawn up, i.e. a list of countries whose nationals are to be exempted from visa requirements.[25] Article 5 of the Regulation defines visa as meaning an authorisation given for entry onto the territory of a member state with a view to a stay of less than three months or with a view to transit through that member state. Longer stays are thus subject to national visas, which are valid only in the issuing state.

It should be noted that the Commission has also adopted a package of measures proposing the ending of all controls on persons crossing the border between one member state of the European Union and another.[26] The purpose of the package is to move towards a complete removal of internal frontiers and build upon the Schengen Agreement. The first proposal is for a Council Directive on the elimination of controls on persons crossing internal frontiers.[27] The Directive would establish the general rule that all persons, whatever their nationality, must be able to cross member states' frontiers within the Community at any point, without such crossing being subject to any frontier control or formality. The proposed legal basis for this Directive is Article 100 of the EC Treaty. The second proposal is for an ancillary Directive amending previous Directives in order to bring same into line with the abolition of internal frontier controls.[28] The third proposed Directive relates to the right of third country nationals to travel in the Community.[29] This Directive would provide for third country nationals who are lawfully in a member state to be granted the right to travel in the territories of the other member states. This right would be quite narrowly circumscribed. The detailed conditions for the exercise of the right (set out in Article 3 and 4 of the Directive) are designed to ensure consistency with the draft Convention on Controls on Persons Crossing the External Frontiers of the member states and with the regulation determining the Third Countries who must be in Possession of a Visa. It essentially extends to the internal frontiers the principles found in the External Frontiers Convention. Again, the proposed legal basis for this Directive is Article 100 of the EC Treaty. Cremona points out that the Directive would not create a right of permanent residence throughout the Community through a complete mutual recognition of residence permits – still less any rights of access to the labour market. The Directive, she argues, is designed, not primarily to improve the position of third country nationals, but rather to make possible the abolition of internal frontier controls, a result which will primarily benefit Union citizens.[30]

Clearly, these proposals would be quite politically sensitive. These texts would serve to implement within the Community sphere provisions covering the same project matter as the draft External Frontiers Convention and the Visa Regulation. Clearly, by basing the Directives on Article 100 of the EC Treaty, the Commission takes the view that these matters fall squarely within the Community Pillar. It also takes the view that Article 7a must be interpreted so as to allow for the regulation of movement of third country nationals to come within the EC Pillar. Whether or not the Council would agree to using these legal bases is an entirely different matter. The prospects for the adoption of the Council of Ministers of the Commission's border control package seem far from certain.[31]

ACTS ADOPTED OUTSIDE THE EU FRAMEWORK

No examination of the question of border controls within the European Union would be complete without mention of the existence of non-EU measures which also govern such matters within part of the territory of the EU. The most important of these arrangements is the Schengen Agreement on the Gradual Suppression of Border Controls. The Schengen Agreement is made up of the original Convention signed on 14 June 1985 and the Schengen Implementing Convention of 19 June 1990. The latter agreement entered into force on 26 March, 1995 for a trial period and was due to be fully in force from the end of July of that year.[32] The Agreement aims at creating a common territory without border control but it also provides, *inter alia,* for the harmonisation of rules governing the crossing of the common external frontiers, visa policy and the issuing of visas (including the creation of a uniform visa), conditions for entry and residence and movement of foreigners in the territory.

The common travel area established by the Agreement provides for the free movement of persons crossing internal borders (defined as common land borders, certain airports and sea ports) without any passport or identity card checks except where public policy and national security so require.

External borders are defined as being the "Contracting Party's land and sea borders and their air ports and seaports, provided they are not internal borders". The Agreement goes on to envisage the introduction of uniform visas valid for the entire Schengen area for aliens visiting for less than three months. The contracting parties have agreed on the visa status for a list of some 130 states.

As regards the relationship of the Schengen Agreement with Community law, two articles of the Schengen Implementing Convention are important. Article 134 provides that the provisions of the Convention will apply only insofar as they are compatible with Community law. Article 142 provides that when the member states of the European Communities have concluded conventions to achieve the area without internal frontiers, the Contracting Parties of Schengen will determine which provisions of the Schengen Convention require to be modified or replaced as a result, but it adds that the provisions of the Schengen Convention might provide for closer cooperation than that resulting from such future conventions.

It is clear that Schengen is largely the model on which the Union is now basing its own efforts in the area of free movements of persons (i.e. the draft Convention on the crossing of the external frontiers of the member states, the visa regulation etc.) However, Article K.7 of the Treaty of Maastricht allows for the establishment or development of closer cooperation between two or more member states insofar as such cooperation does not conflict with or impede that provided for in Title VI of the Treaty of Maastricht. Thus, where no conflict existed, a Schengen-like arrangement could continue to co-exist. Presumably, however, in the event of conflict, the Schengen states would concede in favour of the work done at Union level.[33] Eventually, therefore, Schengen could shrivel away in favour of the Title VI action.

Lastly, the suggestion that the Schengen system be brought into the *acquis communautaire* does not appear to have met with any significant opposition within the Reflection Group on the 1996 Intergovernmental Conference from a majority of member states. However, the UK would of course be opposed to such a development. Adopting this suggestion would therefore probably mean another possible variable geometry arrangement whereby certain member states could opt in to the Schengen arrangement.

CONCLUSION

In view of the significant overlap between the EC Pillar and Title VI, in particular in the area of immigration policy and border controls, the latter areas would appear to be likely candidates to be brought at least to some extent within the Community sphere. As indicated, this was the view taken by the majority of the members of the Reflection group on the 1966 Intergovernmental Conference.[34] From a purely legal perspective this solution would have the advantage of putting an end to some of the tortuous soul-searching on the question of the correct legal bases for measures harmonising visa policy, the crossing of internal borders by non-EU nationals and the crossing of external borders by non-EU nationals. In political terms, however, these areas are immensely sensitive and the objections of some states to communitarism in this area make it difficult to anticipate whether or not the intergovernmental conference will in fact reach agreement on any such step.

NOTES

1. For criticism of the operation of the Third Pillar and proposals for reform see O'Keeffe, "Recasting the Third Pillar", *CML Rev.* (1995) p.893.
2. In effect, as of the 1980s, the member states started to cooperate on immigration-related issues at an intergovernmental level. In 1986 an Ad Hoc Group on Immigration was set up to deal with the subject of asylum, controls at external borders and visa matters: see O'Keeffe, "The emergence of a European immigration policy", 20 *E.L. Rev.* (1995).
3. See Commission Report for the Reflection Group on the Intergovernmental Conference, p.52.
4. *Ibid.*, p.53. Commentators have noted that Articles 3, 7a, 100 and 235 of the EC Pillar already provide potential legal bases for Community competence to take measures to ensure the fulfilment of this objective.
5. Decision 94/795/JHA of 30 November, 1994, O.J.L327, 19 December 1994.

6. Commission Report for the Reflection Group on the Intergovernmental Conference, p.55.
7. See also Gavin Barrett, "A litmus test for Jacques Santer", in *European Brief,* October 1995.
8. Decision 94/795/JHA, O.J. L327, 19 December 1994.
9. For a more detailed discussion of the draft Convention see O'Keeffe, "The emergence of a European immigration policy", *op. cit.*
10. "The emergence of a European immigration policy", *op. cit.*
11. Ireland does not seem to take the view that the conferral of jurisdiction on the European Court of Justice would pose any constitutional problems for this country. The Conventions formerly adopted by the EC member states under the EC Pillar which were not expressly envisaged in Article 220 of the Treaty required the holding of a constitutional referendum in Ireland to permit ratification. This was the case for the Patents Convention. However, the view now appears to be that since Title VI expressly envisages the adoption of Conventions in the areas listed at K.1 and since Article 29.4.5 provides a constitutional immunity for measures necessitated by the obligations of Ireland's membership of the Union, no constitutional referendum would be required for Title VI Conventions. It is interesting to note that the Constitution Review Group, in its provisional report dealing with Article 29, does not expressly deal with the question of whether or not a referendum would be required for Title VI Conventions but simply points out that it would not approve of the idea of inserting a general blanket provision into the Constitution which would afford protection for any Conventions adopted under the EC or Third Pillar.
12. See, for example, Peers, "Towards equality: actual and potential rights of third country nationals in the European Union", *CML Rev.* (1996), 1 at p.3.
13. See case 12/86, Demirel (1987) *ECR* 3719, which concerned the provisions of the association agreement entered into by the Community with Turkey. See, generally, for discussion on this area, Kay Hailbronner, "Visa regulations and third country nationals in EC Law", 1994, *CML Rev.* Vol. 31, p.969 and Marise Cremona, "Citizens of third countries: movement and employment of migrant workers within the European Union", *LIEI* 1995/2 p.87 and pp.90–92.
14. Joined cases 281/283-285/85, Germany, France, Netherlands, Denmark and UK-*v*-Commission, 1987, *ECR* 3203.
15. The Treaty of Maastricht Agreement on Social Policy confirms that working conditions of third country nationals are within EU (less UK) competence.
16. See, for example, the provisions of Article 10 of Council Regulation 1612/68 on the free movement of workers within the community (O.J. 1968 (2) p.475) and Council Directive 68/360 on the abolition of restrictions on movement and residence within the Community for workers of member states and their families (O.J. 1968 (II) p.485).
17. The Treaty of Maastricht inevitably complicated matters by changing the numbering of these Articles to 7a, 7b and 7c respectively. I will refer to the Articles as 8a, 8b and 8c when I am discussing the law as it was before the Treaty of Maastricht entered into force.
18. See Hans Ulrich Jessurun D'Oliveria, "Expanding external and shrinking internal borders: Europe's defence mechanisms in the area of free movement, immigration and asylum" in *Legal Issues of the Maastricht Treaty,* O'Keeffe & Twomey, 1994.
19. See Cremona, *op. cit.* at p.96.
20. Case C-445/93, Parliament-*v*-Commission.
21. See Article 3, paragraph (d).
22. This potential overlap in the area of immigration and external border controls has given rise to confusion not only regarding the extent of overlap between EC and Title VI competence but also between these two pillars and the conventions which are

currently in force between the member states or some of them – the Schengen Agreement and the Dublin Convention of 1990 – to which reference is made in Article 100(c)(7) and which will remain in force until their content has been replaced by Directives or measures adopted by the Community.

23. See Hailbronner, *op cit.,* p.973.

24. Council Regulation EC No. 2317/95 of 25 September 1995, O.J. L234 of 3 October, 1995.

25. Article 2 of the Regulation provides that the member states shall determine the visa requirements for nationals of third countries not on the common list. This would seem to imply that Article 100C would also provide the legal basis for any "positive" list which was to be drawn up.

26. See editorial "Legislating free movement: an over ambitious commission package?", (1996) *CML Rev.* 33, p.1

27. Comm (95) 347 final.

28. COM (95) 348 final.

29. COM (95) 346 final.

30. The decision by the Commission to justify its choice of Article 100 of the Treaty of Rome as the legal basis, as opposed to Article K.1, seems to constitute evidence for this point.

31. As has been pointed out, the package of border control proposals "graphically illustrates the problems and uncertainties of legislating on a matter that straddles the First and the Third Pillars. It does seem a pity that a subject so politically fraught should be further complicated by the difficulty of drawing clear lines between the Union's different areas of competence." See "Legislating free movement: an over ambitious commission package?", *op. cit.,* at p.5.

32. Seven countries have implemented Schengen – Belgium, France (although France delayed implementation), Germany, Luxembourg, the Netherlands, Portugal and Spain. The Convention did not enter into force for the other parties to Schengen, Italy and Greece, which have implementation problems. The UK and Ireland have not adhered to Schengen since the former is opposed to the abolition of frontier controls and Ireland is concerned because of the common travel area it shares with the UK. See David Conlan Smyth, Eurlegal News, *Gazette of the Incorporated Law Society,* July 1995 and "Schengen: The pros and cons", Editorial, *CML Rev.* (1995) p.673.

33. See editorial, *CML Rev.* 1995 p.673.

34. See report published on 24 August 1995 by Carlos Westendorp, the Chairperson of the Reflection Group and, generally Gavin Barrett, "A litmus test for Jacques Santer", *op. cit.*

# CHAPTER 10

ASYLUM POLICY AND TITLE VI OF THE TREATY ON EUROPEAN UNION

BILL SHIPSEY

INTRODUCTION

International cooperation in the field of refugees and asylum seekers has a relatively long history in Europe. As far back as 1951, the Geneva Convention Relating to the Status of Refugees was signed, although this was a measure which (as well as being confined to refugees within Europe) was limited by the fact that it applied only to events occurring before 1 January 1951.

Also of relevance here is the New York Protocol Relating to the Status of Refugees, which entered into force on 4 October 1967, expanding the scope of the Convention's definition to include refugees from all regions of the world. Further and more recent international treaties containing measures of importance to the question of asylum in Europe were the Schengen Agreement of 19 June 1985 on the Gradual Abolition of Border Controls at Common Frontiers and its Implementing Convention of 19 June 1990, both of which have now been adhered to by all member states of the European Union except Ireland and the United Kingdom.

Finally, on 15 June 1990, all EEC member states (except Denmark, which signed it the following year) signed the Dublin Convention Determining the State Responsible for Examining Applications for Asylum Lodged in One of the Member States of the European Communities.

BACKGROUND TO SCHENGEN AGREEMENT AND DUBLIN CONVENTION

In the process of abolishing the internal border control within the area of the EU countries, the matter of asylum seekers and refugees had already received considerable attention before the Maastricht Treaty. It had been assumed that harmonisation of asylum law was necessary for the open market. This is of course not necessarily the case. In a unified European market, the fact that there are different asylum practices ought not to be any more of a problem than it is now.

The rationale behind the Schengen Agreement (to a lesser extent) and the Dublin Convention (to a greater extent) appears to have been a desire on the part of the countries concerned to ensure that an asylum seeker who has been rejected in one of the EU countries cannot go to another EU country and try his or her luck there. It can be easily seen that this has little to do with the desire to create a unified market and is and was a political choice of the countries involved. The Schengen Agreement and the Dublin Convention were brought about through intergovernmental treaties and not within the existing EC framework. As a consequence, the European Commission, the European Parliament and the European Court of Justice do not play any role in the conclusion or the application of the treaties. The conventions of Dublin and Schengen stipulate the following criteria. In principle, only one of the parties to these conventions is responsible for handling a request. In other states, a second request by the same person is inadmissible. Although the systems of Schengen and Dublin are slightly different, they can, in general, be summarised as follows. Responsibility for determining an asylum application rests with:

- the state which earlier granted a resident's permit to the asylum seeker
- if this does not exist, the state which granted a transit visa
- if this does not exist, the state where the asylum seeker first crossed the external border of the whole Schengen or EU area
- if this cannot be established, the state where the asylum seeker submitted his or her request.

It will be apparent from the above list that this system itself calls for harmonisation of the substantive law of asylum of the states which are parties to these conventions. As has been pointed out by Spijkerboer,[1] harmonisation is necessary for two reasons:

- Differences in the material law of asylum will result in different recognition rates for groups of asylum seekers which, in other respects, are comparable. It is to be expected that asylum seekers will react to this by turning to the state with the (supposedly) most favourable interpretation of refugee law.... Effects of this kind (different recognition rates for comparable groups), which burden some states and relieve others of their responsibility for a concerted European asylum policy, are of course, undesirable. They can only be prevented by harmonisation of the material law of asylum in the states which are parties to the conventions of Dublin and Schengen.

The basic rule of international refugee law is the prohibition of refoulement. This rule is binding upon all parties to the conventions, and is recognised as such. The rule not only prohibits direct refoulement, but also "indirect" refoulement, i.e. sending someone who can invoke the protection of the 1951 Geneva Convention to a third state, which will return the person concerned to a country where he has a well-founded fear of being persecuted. Therefore, each party to one of the conventions mentioned will, under present circumstances, have to decide if someone who invokes the 1951 Geneva Convention is considered as a refugee under its own interpretation of the 1951 Refugee Convention, and if so, if the country to which deportation is considered (even if this is the responsible state under the rules of the conventions of Dublin and Schengen), will give the person concerned the protection of the 1951 Refugee Convention. This obligation on each state which is a party to the 1951 Refugee Convention to assess a request for asylum individually is incompatible with the system as set out in the conventions of Dublin and Schengen, and threatens to make it ineffective. It must be feared that some national courts, confronted with the system of distribution as set out in the conventions of Dublin and Schengen, will find it impossible to apply these rules if they have no guarantees that there is a harmonised definition of the concept of refugee. These conventions, therefore, can only be effective if the material law of asylum is harmonised.

EVALUATION OF RECENT INTERGOVERNMENTAL COOPERATION

The main products of intergovernmental cooperation in the field of asylum policy, under the system set up by Title VI of the Treaty (the so-called Third Pillar of the European Union), have been the 1992 London and the 1993 Copenhagen Resolutions, the Resolution on "Minimum Guarantees" (referred to above) for Asylum Procedures, and the recommendation concerning a specimen bilateral re-admission agreement between a member state of the European Union and a third country, a 1996 joint position on the harmonisation of the implementation of Article 1 of the 1951 Geneva Convention (refugee definition), and various resolutions on "burden sharing" in situations of mass influx. The paucity of measures adopted reflects the difficulty of making progress through the inefficient, five-layer, decision-making structure of the Third Pillar, in particular where there are fundamental differences in approach by various member states. Such agreements as are eventually reached tend to be non-binding and inevitably contain the lowest common denominator of member state practice. Moreover, decision making has been dominated by security and border control concerns, rather than social or humanitarian concerns.

The secrecy of decision making has reinforced alarming tendencies in our societies: the increasing fear among segments of public opinion that state authorities are losing their grip on immigration has been fostered by xenophobic political statements concerning aliens, including asylum seekers. The lack of democratic scrutiny available within the intergovernmental framework reinforces this misperception that asylum policy needs to be based solely on the short-term, defensive interests of national states.

National parliaments are not in a position to control the negotiations and results of the intergovernmental cooperation under the Third Pillar. The preparation of the decisions and the decision-making meetings have been secret and the status of the resolutions unclear. While presenting the results to their national parliaments, governments have urged them to incorporate the content of the resolutions into national legislation in order to avoid the arrival of more asylum seekers to the state concerned. The erosion of the legislative function of parliaments throughout Europe has frustrated an open and well-informed public debate.

The lack of transparency and the requirement of unanimous voting in the Council of Ministers responsible for immigration and asylum, in addition to the lack of competency given to the European Court of Justice, have severely limited the scope for cooperation.

Intergovernmental cooperation has appeared unable to resolve some of the most urgent problems related to forced migrations. It has not, for example, taken any measures to guarantee the necessary protection for those displaced as a consequence of civil war or generalised violence. It has shown itself unable to relate asylum policies to a comprehensive approach. It has not developed a common policy for resettlement, and has not functioned as a genuine regional partner to the United Nations High Commissioner for Refugees (UNHCR) in terms of policy development or joint action.

The Position of Ireland

Ireland's position in relation to refugee policy on an EU level was, until very recently, unique. In the first instance, Ireland (uniquely among EU member states) had no legislation (either primary or secondary) regulating asylum policy until the enactment of the Refugee Act 1996. Immigration in Ireland until then was governed by the Aliens Act of 1935 which contained no reference to the term "refugee" or "asylum". Procedure in Ireland over the past decade has been regulated by an understanding agreed in writing between the Minister for Justice and the Representative of the United Nations High Commissioner for Refugees (exchanged in letter form in December 1985) under which a ten-point procedure for determining refugee status was agreed. This was implemented (and modified slightly) to a greater extent in more recent years, particularly since the High Court decision in *Fakih* v. *Minister for Justice*[2] in which the December 1985 letter was held to create a "legitimate expectation" that asylum applications would be determined in accordance with the terms of the letter and in accordance with the obligations imposed on Ireland as a party to the 1951 Refugees Convention and the 1967 Protocol. It should be noted, however, that the Supreme Court, in *Gutrani* v. *Minister for Justice*,[3] held that the Minister, having established a scheme under the December 1985 letter, was bound to apply it to appropriate cases, not under any principle of legitimate or reasonable expectation but simply because it was the procedure which the Minister had undertaken to enforce.

For reasons which are both geographical and historical, Ireland has never attracted a very large number of asylum seekers. Figures published by the Irish Refugee Council show the number of new arrivals having increased from 1991 to 1996 as follows:

1991	31
1992	39
1993	91
1994	355
1995	424
1996	1,179

One could argue, therefore, that Ireland is in a very good position to argue for a radical change in EU asylum policy, since it is unlikely, mostly for geographic reasons, that large numbers of asylum seekers will ever make their way to our borders. This is a cynical view, but one which no doubt encouraged our legislators to opt for a Refugee Act which is quite liberal and progressive by EU standards.

The present writer would argue that (despite the likely limited exposure of Ireland to large influxes of asylum seekers) it must be in Ireland's interest to try to create a unified EU asylum policy since mere attempts to harmonise will always leave the impression (if not the reality) that there are "hard" countries as opposed to "soft" countries within the EU in which to apply for asylum, and Ireland may be perceived as a "soft" country. It is of course to be hoped that Ireland will adopt a *communautaire* approach. The risks for Ireland are not great, and it is to be hoped given our own historical experience that our Government, if not actually giving the lead, will at least support moves towards the unification of asylum policy.

REVISION OF THE MAASTRICHT TREATY

It is the view of the present writer (and of almost every NGO concerned with refugees and asylum) that the Maastricht Treaty as it applies to asylum policy needs to be revised radically. The existing "means" to achieve the desired "ends" in Title IV (which are virtually identical to the provisions provided in Title V) are, as already stated, wholly inadequate and inappropriate for the development of a common asylum policy. What is needed, as already stated, is not so much the harmonisation of asylum policy as its unification across the entire EU. Only such a unified system can ensure the certainty and consistency that are the essential prerequisites of an asylum policy that can ensure compliance with the Refugees Convention. At the very minimum every effort must be made to address the failings of the current system, through:

- preventing harmonisation at the lowest common denominator
- ensuring transparency and openness
- addressing the effects of the "safe third country" policy
- ensuring respect for existing international standards.

PREVENTING HARMONISATION AT THE LOWEST COMMON DENOMINATOR

As laid down in Article K.1 of the Treaty on European Union, EU member states consider asylum policy as a matter of common interest and have reinforced their cooperation with a view to harmonising their legislation in this area. Member states tend to agree only on the lowest common denominator and, as a consequence, persons seeking protection against persecution are confronted with more and more restrictive asylum policy in the European Union, such as that under the Schengen Agreement. Any revision of the Maastricht Treaty should prevent further erosion of the system of international protection for asylum seekers and refugees in the European Union, and should ensure that the harmonisation of asylum policies corresponds to the highest protection standards.

THE NEED FOR TRANSPARENCY AND OPENNESS

Transparency and openness in the decision-making process are particularly necessary as regards EU asylum policy, as the decisions taken may directly affect the fundamental rights of people seeking protection from human rights violations in the European Union. The right to seek and enjoy asylum is itself protected by Article 14 of the Universal Declaration on Human Rights.

There should be clear provisions in the Treaty on European Union guaranteeing that asylum policy is open to public discussion and scrutiny. Such transparency would also assist human rights and refugee organisations in defending the rights of asylum seekers and refugees.

Moreover, a transparent and open process in this area is needed to allow for the involvement of the UNHCR as the agency responsible for supervising the implementation of the 1951 Geneva Convention relating to the status of refugees in order to ensure that member states of the European Union respect their international obligations and meet international standards as laid down in conclusions of Anchor's Executive Committee. The necessity for close cooperation between EU member states and the UNHCR should be mentioned expressly in the revised Treaty on European Union.

ADDRESSING THE EFFECTS OF THE "SAFE THIRD COUNTRY" POLICY

The 1992 London Resolution on a harmonised approach to questions concerning host third countries and the 1995 recommendation concerning a specimen bilateral readmission agreement between a member state of the European Union and a third country clearly reveal the will of EU member states to return asylum seekers to third countries in as many cases as possible without taking responsibility to examine their asylum applications.

The revision of the Treaty could provide the opportunity to set up a proper consultation with third countries in the area of asylum policy in order to address issues in respect of international standards on refugees and in a spirit of international solidarity and burden sharing.

ENSURING RESPECT FOR EXISTING INTERNATIONAL STANDARDS

With the draft convention on the crossing of their external borders and the regulation establishing third countries whose nationals must be in possession of a visa when crossing their external borders, EU member states attempt to restrict access to their territory as far as possible without taking account of the specific protection needs of asylum seekers and refugees. They deter asylum seekers from entering their territory by imposing strict visa requirements and carrier sanctions and therefore risk undermining the right to seek and enjoy asylum by preventing asylum seekers from reaching safety. Such measures are contrary to Article 31 of the Geneva Convention.

Furthermore, the recently adopted resolution on minimum guarantees for asylum procedures provides for a number of exceptions which put the general principles into question. In as far as the resolution does not provide for the suspensive effect of a decision on an asylum claim in all cases, it falls short of international standards such as conclusions of the Executive Committee of the UNHCR. Moreover, international standards call for decisions on asylum applications to be taken by a centralised and specialised authority and not by border officials, something that the resolution allows.

Another current project of EU member states, the discussions on the harmonisation of the refugee definition, contained in Article I of the Geneva Convention, underlines the need for full respect of existing international standards. The 1951 Geneva Convention is an international – not a European Union – instrument which was signed by more than a hundred states, and a handbook on procedures and criteria for determining refugee status according to this convention provides guidance to signatory states. The revision of the Maastricht Treaty should ensure that any harmonisation of the refugee definition conforms fully to the standards set out in the Geneva Convention, conclusions of the Executive Committee of the UNHCR and the handbook of the UNHCR.

In Article K.2 of the Maastricht Treaty EU member states have committed themselves to respect the 1950 European Convention on Human Rights and the 1951 Convention Relating to the Status of Refugees. However, the policy of EU member states so far shows that this commitment in the Treaty is not enough to ensure that decisions taken at EU level comply with international standards. When revising the Treaty on European Union EU governments should take all necessary steps to ensure that laws, policies and administrative procedures in the European Union fully respect the principle of non-refoulement as set out in Article 33 of the 1951 Convention. One positive sign would be if a revised Treaty on European Union made reference to international standards such as those contained in the conclusions of the Executive Committee and the handbook of the UNHCR.

CONCLUSION

The nature of the legal structures of Title VI and the failure to make significant use of the legal instruments provided in it have been the subject of widespread and sustained criticism in respect of all Title VI's specified justice and home affairs issues. Arguably, however, it is only in the case of asylum policy that the situation has been rendered much worse since the adoption of the Treaty. It has been the misfortune of asylum as an issue, and the consequent effect on asylum seekers, that it has been joined with such issues as the fight against drugs trafficking, fraud and terrorism. All the member states of the EU are signatories to the UN Convention on Refugees and its 1967 Protocol and therefore, superficially at least, one might expect that each of the member states would wish to ensure a common policy with regard to refugees and asylum seekers. Unfortunately this has not happened in practice, and the situation since the adoption of the Treaty and indeed for some time prior to its adoption has, as already stated, deteriorated. The present writer would argue that it was wholly unrealistic to expect that the intended objectives of Title VI – namely, the facilitation of greater consistency of action; the provision of a single institutional framework; the creation of the possibility of enhanced parliamentary consultation and supranational jurisdiction – were achievable on an intergovernmental basis.

The intergovernmental cooperation which has occurred to date has, perhaps understandably, been marked by a concern to control illegal immigration, rather than the search for a consistent and coherent asylum policy. There has to date been a marked failure or inability to distinguish between immigration policies on the one hand and asylum policies on the other. Recent efforts to streamline and adjust some of the procedural aspects of asylum law, in the form of the resolution on "minimum guarantees" applicable to asylum procedures, have served only to illustrate the inherent shortcomings and failings in the current system. By allowing for "opt-outs" and exceptions to be submitted by individual EU member states in order to reflect their own policy and practice, the resolution has become in the words of UNHCR, "a missed opportunity to formulate a comprehensive set of essential principles to guide the asylum procedures throughout the European Union".

It is the hope of the present writer that legislative powers will be granted to the European Union institutions since, otherwise, the probability is that any agreement reached on asylum policy on an intergovernmental basis will be based on the lowest common denominator. In the absence of a supra-national European Court with binding jurisdiction in this field, states at present have a legitimate fear of attracting asylum seekers if the criteria they use are more liberal than those applied by the other parties to the treaties. In such circumstances, it is easy to see how the lowest common denominator could become the norm for all.

What is required above all else in relation to asylum policy is certainty and consistency. It is the view of the present writer that the provisions contained in the Treaty for the implementation of the objectives of Title V1 are wholly unsuited to achieving the certainty and consistency that are required.

What is absent, and what is urgently required, is a transparent, democratic (i.e. subject to debate and control by the EU institutions) and judicially controlled European asylum policy. Asylum policy as it has evolved in the European Union both prior to the Maastricht Treaty (including the Schengen Agreement and the Dublin Convention) and since, and the so called "white lists", have in practice seriously eroded the position of refugees and asylum seekers fleeing to Europe. Notwithstanding the aspirations of Article K.1 of Title V1 and the requirement under Article K.2 to comply, *inter alia*, with the Convention relating to the status of refugees, the only result of intergovernmental "cooperation" so far has been a non-binding set of policy recommendations and resolutions, often codifying existing variations in member states' national practices. Member states have implemented these policy recommendations differently and outside any community framework, so that standards of refugee protection continue to vary.

NOTES
1. *A Bird's View of Asylum Law in Eight European Countries* (1993, Dutch Refugee Council).
2. [1993] 2 IR 406.
3. [1993] 2 IR 427.

PART IV

JUSTICE AND HOME AFFAIRS COOPERATION:
OTHER MAJOR THEMES

■ CHAPTER 11

RACISM AND XENOPHOBIA IN EUROPE

WILLIAM DUNCAN

RACISM AND XENOPHOBIA IN EUROPE: THE CURRENT PROBLEM

No doubt, we have built up Europe, used the Council of Europe to maintain the basic values on which our democracies are founded, made the first step towards political union with the European Union and gathered the continent around the democratic ideal after the fall of the Berlin wall. But we have also let poverty and violence, negligence and egoism, fear and hatred find a way in. Profanations, arson, racist murders, ethnic cleansing (in ex-Yugoslavia) are all there to remind us that "the belly of the vile creature is yet fertile." [1]

The manifestations of racism and intolerance are ever changing. In modern Europe they tend mostly to affect third country nationals as well as certain national religious or ethnic minorities. In 1992 roughly 3 per cent of the total population of the then twelve European Community states was made up of third country nationals (11 million). This was largely the product of the wave of immigration from southern Europe, North Africa and the former colonies of European States, which occurred during the 1950s and 1960s in response to the demand for unskilled labour. This was supplemented during the 1970s and 1980s by secondary immigration through family reunification, and more recently as a result of the great increase in the numbers of refugees and asylum seekers.[2] As regards non-immigrant ethnic minorities one of the largest groups to suffer systematic discrimination is that comprising the various travelling communities in Europe.[3]

The principal modern forms of racism and intolerance[4] may be summarised as follows.

Racial violence and incitement to racial violence – against immigrants, asylum seekers, blacks, Jews, Gypsies and other Travellers.[5]

Discrimination – particularly against non-nationals in relation, e.g. to the right to work, travel, the provision of services.

Exploitation – of immigrant workers, particularly black and migrant women.

The growth of political extremism [6] – growing support for far-right parties in several European countries, centring on anti-immigrant sentiment and intolerance of refugees and asylum seekers. Racial hostility and anti-Semitism are persistent themes. Principal targets tend to be the most vulnerable minority groups.

Internationalisation of racial hatred – developing cooperation and coordination between far-right groups, use of new technologies (Internet etc.), coordinated violence at football matches, etc.

Cross-border publication of racist materials – facilitated by new technologies (computer games, modems, bulletin boards, etc.).

Current concern over the level and persistence of racist and xenophobic sentiment has been expressed as follows by the European Union Commission in its 1995 Communication on Racism, Xenophobia and Anti-Semitism:[7]

> The continuing presence of racism, xenophobia and anti-Semitism across the European Community presents a major challenge for our societies. Although the exact scale of the problem is hard to quantify, it is impossible to ignore. Violent, racist crimes are reported throughout the Community with sickening regularity. What is more, an undercurrent of prejudice and discrimination can be seen in many walks of life, and the language of racism has become increasingly common in public, political manifestations in all the member states of the Community.

As regards the growth of political extremism, the situation has been summarised thus by the European Centre for Research and Action on Racism and Anti-Semitism:

> The current threat to democracy posed by the far-right in Western Europe is not that of a revolutionary force about to overturn democratic institutions. The danger is rather that of the growing influence in some countries of xenophobic, racist and anti-democratic parties which promote authoritarian solutions to perceived problems of immigration, refugees and rising levels of crime. Few far-right groupings pose a real threat to the democratic process at present. Instead they threaten the civil and constitutional rights of certain minorities (whose members may be citizens or residents) and contribute to a worsening climate of racial intolerance.[8]

SOME CAUSES

Among the causes of the modern phenomenon of racism and intolerance are political alienation and disillusionment with mainstream political parties in certain countries, and insecurity accompanying rapid social change. There have always been, and will remain, certain personality types attracted by authoritarian structures. These tend to be drawn from a cross-section of the population in terms of age, gender and socio-economic groupings. The EU Consultative Commission, in its interim Report (November, 1994), reminds us of the linkage with economic depression.

> The rise of racism, xenophobia and intolerance is connected to a large extent with the worsening of the economic and social living conditions of certain disadvantaged sectors of the population, and in particular with unemployment, which marginalises both the potential victims and perpetrators of racial incidents.

INTERNATIONAL AND REGIONAL BACKGROUND

UNITED NATIONS

It is worth briefly painting the international background to the work currently being undertaken by the European Union to combat racism and xenophobia. First there is the work of the United Nations, and in particular the International Convention on the Elimination of All Forms of Racial Discrimination, adopted on 21 December 1995, and ratified by all EU member states[9] with the exception of Ireland. Ireland's ratification awaits the passage into law of the new Employment Equality Bill. The legislation will prohibit, in employment and in the provision of various services, discrimination based on gender, marital or parental status, sexual orientation, religion, age, disability, race, colour, national or ethnic origin and membership of the Travelling community.[10]

In the Vienna Declaration and Programme of Action, arising from the World Conference on Human Rights, held in Vienna on 14–25 June 1993, the "speedy and comprehensive elimination of all forms of racism and racial discrimination, xenophobia and related intolerance" was declared to be "a priority task for the international community" (Para. 1.15).

COUNCIL OF EUROPE.

The Vienna Declaration of the Heads of State and Government of the Member States of the Council of Europe (9 October 1993) condemned "in the strongest possible terms racism in all its forms, xenophobia, anti-Semitism and intolerance and all forms of religious discrimination". This was followed by the establishment of a Committee of Governmental Experts (known as the European Commission against Racism and Intolerance or ECRI) to "review member states' legislation, policies and other measures to combat racism, xenophobia, anti-Semitism and intolerance, and their effectiveness." The Council of Europe also launched in 1994 a European Youth Campaign to mobilise public opinion, under the banner "All different, all equal."

ECRI is currently engaging in a review of the law operating in the member states of the Council of Europe, with a view to identifying successful policies and practices.[11] It has also been examining the possibility of a new Protocol to the European Convention on Human Rights, with a view to the more effective application of the principle of non-discrimination, currently contained in Article 14 of the Convention. A proposal was submitted to the Committee of Ministers at the end of 1995, and it has been referred for further examination to the competent Steering Committee for Human Rights.[12]

THE EUROPEAN PARLIAMENT

The European Parliament has been at the forefront of the campaign to involve the Union more directly and more effectively in the fight against racism and xenophobia. A Committee of Inquiry was established by the Parliament, to study the rise of fascism and racism in Europe, and produced the Evrigenis Report in December 1985.[13] A Joint Declaration against Racism and Xenophobia was signed on 11 June 1986 by the Presidents of the European Parliament and the Council, the representatives of the member states meeting within the Council and the Commission. A second Committee of Inquiry into Racism and Xenophobia was established by the Parliament, which led to the Ford Report, 1991.[14] There have also been a number of resolutions of the Parliament expressing concern and condemnation, notably that of 21 April 1993.

THE COMMISSION

The Commission has taken the view that the Community has at present no mandate or competence to legislate against racism. In the *White Paper on European Social Policy*, 1995, the Commission declared its intention to press, at the 1996 Intergovernmental Conference, for specific Treaty powers to combat racial and other forms of discrimination. In its *Communication on Racism, Xenophobia and Anti-Semitism* (13/12/95), which contained a proposal that 1997 be designated "European Year Against Racism", the Commission again addressed the question of Treaty amendment, and suggested the inclusion of a general non-discrimination clause – a possibility also mentioned in the final report of the Reflection Group on the 1996 Intergovernmental Conference. (1997 was in fact designated "European Year Against Racism" – see "Recent Progress" at the end of this chapter.)

The Commission has also been able to adopt a number of measures which indirectly impact on the problem. These have included measures taken in respect of the integration of migrants (e.g. funding of the Migrants' Forum) and on inter-cultural education, a Report (subsequently updated and re-issued) on "legal instruments available in the member states to combat racism and xenophobia", an examination of systems to monitor incidents of racial harassment, and the development of a code of practice prohibiting racial discrimination in employment. A full description of the Commission's activities in this area appeared in its December 1995 *Communication on Racism, Xenophobia and Anti-semitism*.[15]

THE EUROPEAN COUNCIL

Four declarations condemning racism and xenophobia have been issued by the European Council.[16] The Council, meeting in Corfu on 24–25 June 1994, in response to a Franco-German initiative on racism and xenophobia, decided to establish The Consultative Commission on Racism and Xenophobia with the remit to make recommendations on cooperation between governments and the various social bodies to encourage tolerance, understanding and harmony with foreigners. The Council further decided to develop a global strategy at Union level aimed at combating acts of racist and xenophobic violence, and to promote training for national administration officials most concerned with the phenomenon.[17]

The Justice and Home Affairs Committee was also asked to report, and did so on 3 March 1995, recommending the strengthening of controls over illegal immigration, measures concerning police cooperation and training, and a further examination of state laws with a view to removing obstacles to judicial cooperation.

At the time of writing, there is no indication that the European Council is close to realising its ambition of formulating a global policy.

THE CONSULTATIVE COMMISSION ON RACISM AND XENOPHOBIA

The Consultative Commission was established as described above. It is composed of independent "eminent persons" (one from each member state), and, as observers (taking full part in discussions) two MEPs, two Commission representatives and two Council of Europe representatives. Its first meeting was on 19 September 1994. It produced its Interim Report in November 1994,[18] and a Final Report in April 1995.[19] It has engaged in a process of consultation which has included the holding of national round tables, attended locally by non-governmental organisations and others involved in the fight against racism and intolerance.[20]

THE PROPOSAL FOR A EUROPEAN OBSERVATORY ON RACISM AND XENOPHOBIA

Under its first heading of "Information, Communication and the Media", the Consultative Commission's most important proposal was for the establishment of a European Observatory on Racism and Xenophobia. The objectives of the Observatory would be:

- to gather statistical, documentary and technical information concerning the extent, causes and manifestations of racism and xenophobia throughout Europe
- to establish reliable bases for comparison of statistical, legal and other data from member states
- to assess the efficacy of measures taken to combat racism and xenophobia
- to establish a network of national research in these areas
- to provide information and make proposals to Community institutions which may assist in the development and assessment of Community policies in the area
- to disseminate research findings as appropriate and publish an annual report.

This proposal was accepted by the Council (at its meeting in Cannes on 26–27 June 1995), and the life of the Consultative Commission was extended to enable it to conduct a feasibility study in respect of the Observatory. That work was completed, and the Consultative Commission's Report was considered at the European Council meeting in Florence, in June 1996. (See "Recent Progress" at the end of this chapter.)

Unfortunately, the proposal for the establishment of an Observatory has run into some difficulty because of disagreement over the relative responsibilities of the European Union and the Council of Europe. The Council of Europe has argued that the Observatory should be a joint venture of the two European bodies, on the basis that this would make sense scientifically (given the work already being carried out by ECRI, and given that problems of racism and xenophobia have pan-European dimensions), and that this would be a better way of using limited resources. The EU Consultative Commission, on the other hand, has taken the view that the Observatory should be firmly established, at least in the first instance, within the Union. It should cooperate closely with ECRI, but it should have as its focus the serious problems which currently affect the Union, and it should concentrate on the development of effective policies within the Union.

Other proposals of the Consultative Commission under the heading of "Information Communication and the Media" included:

- measures to improve cooperation between NGOs and governments
- measures to control the flow of inflammatory publications from third countries into the EU
- consciousness-raising initiatives
- the establishment of SOS hotlines
- measures to improve advertising standards (including advertising by aid organisations) and to encourage balanced reporting
- measures to ensure more access to the media for members of ethnic minorities
- more youth exchange programmes

EDUCATION, TRAINING, POLICE AND JUSTICE

The main headings of the Consultative Commission's Report under "Education and Training" were:

- education towards respect for diversity and mutual loyalty
- training of occupational groups
- other measures specifically addressed towards "difficult districts".

Under "Police and Justice" the main headings were:

- employment and unemployment
- freedom of movement
- harmonisation of legislation and the role of the police
- the criminal justice system
- distribution of racist material.

The matters dealt with under these headings were selective, in view of the work being done in this area by other bodies, such as the Council of Europe. But the proposals concerning freedom of movement are of particular interest. It was recommended that there should be:

- a right for all persons legally resident within a member state to travel freely within the Union
- a right for a non-EU citizen, residing and working legally in a member state, to travel within the Union for purposes connected with such work
- a full right of free movement within the Union for persons permanently resident (based on five years' legal residence) in a member state
- further consideration to the extension of "Union" citizenship based on five years' permanent residence in a member state.

TREATY AMENDMENT AND INSTITUTIONAL QUESTIONS

The Final Report of the Consultative Commission firmly recommended amendment of the Treaty to provide explicitly for Community competence in respect of the elimination of discrimination based on race, colour, national or ethnic origin, and set out detailed supporting arguments, which may be summarised as follows:

(a) There is need for legal underpinning of Community action.

(b) There is need for discussion around moral and political arguments, including the threat posed to stability and democracy, and the necessity of respect for fundamental human rights.

(c) Community action will reinforce political will in states where there is resistance to firm action.

(d) Action against racism and xenophobia is required to underpin free movement.

(e) The same action is needed to avoid distortions in the labour market which inhibit free competition (compare *Defrenne v Sabena* [21]).

(f) Action at Community level would help to advance the social objectives of the Community which include social progress and the improvement of the living and working conditions of its peoples (compare *Defrenne v Sabena*).

(g) Community institutions are well placed to assess what action is needed and likely to be effective.

(h) Community action in respect of sex discrimination, taken under Art. 119, provides a compelling precedent.

The main objection to giving the Community a clear competence in this area is the argument that the objectives of combating racism and xenophobia can be better achieved by action taken at national level, which may take better account of local conditions. Where cooperation is needed, it may take place under the Third Pillar. To give the Community a clear competence would be to breach the subsidiarity principle. The counter-arguments adduced by the Consultative Commission may be summarised as follows:

- Vital Community interests are involved.
- Action by individual states is not always sufficient or effective.
- Principles of tolerance and non-discrimination should be established as basic principles of Community law, with little margin for departure or variation by individual states.
- A Treaty amendment would be in harmony with the respect accorded by European Court of Justice to fundamental rights principles, and with the adherence by member states to the European Convention on Human Rights.
- It is important that the European Court of Justice be given the role of overseer.

Support is growing for the idea of broader anti-discrimination provisions in the Treaty. The European Parliament[22] and the Commission[23] have long been in favour. More recently the Reflection Group on the 1996 Inter-governmental Conference has noted general support for inclusion in the Treaty of express condemnation of racism and xenophobia, as well as for a general clause prohibiting discrimination on grounds of gender, religion, opinion, sexual preferences, etc. Several non-governmental organisations have also called for Treaty amendment, some of them proposing specific forms of wording.[24]

The Consultative Commission repeated and reinforced its proposals for Treaty amendment in the Report considered at the Florence summit in June 1996. It added specific proposals for amendment of Article 3 of Title II of the Union Treaty (to add the prohibition of racial discrimination to the tasks set out in Article 3 of the EC Treaty), and for a new Article in Title II giving clear competence for the adoption of Community measures to combat racism and xenophobia, which would also place direct obligations on member states.

In this author's opinion, these proposals are of great importance and call for reflection about the type of Europe that we wish to create for future generations. The proposal for a Treaty amendment is much more than a simple proposal for legal change. It poses a challenge for the European Union. It raises questions about the very nature of that Union and of the great European enterprise. How serious is the intent, in the face of growing racism and xenophobia, to preserve the democratic values which helped to inspire its creation?

The proposal for an amendment of the Treaty is in essence a proposal that the European Union should take the fight against racism and xenophobia to its heart – that this fight should no longer be simply the subject of protestations, declarations and aspirations.

RECENT PROGRESS

THE EUROPEAN MONITORING CENTRE ON RACISM AND XENOPHOBIA

At a meeting in Dublin in December 1996 the European Council called for the speedy establishment of the Monitoring Centre on Racism and Xenophobia. It is expected that the Centre will be established during the 1997 European Year Against Racism (declared in July 1996 during the Irish Presidency). Following the feasibility study prepared by the Consultative Commission on Racism and Xenophobia in 1996, the project is now being progressed by a working committee. There remain certain problems concerning the legal basis for establishing the Centre. The use of Article 235 of the EC Treaty, proposed by the Consultative Committee, remains controversial, and the issue has been raised of whether the use of that Article would prevent the Centre from exercising a monitoring function in relation to criminal law matters. Clearly such a restriction would seriously limit the effectiveness of the Centre. There is also some concern in the Consultative Commission (which continues to meet pending the setting up of the Centre) that the powers recommended for the Centre may, in the working group, be undergoing a process of dilution. It is particularly important that the Centre be established as an independent body, with the ability to determine research priorities and to publish findings freely, and with the freedom when necessary to raise issues which may cause some embarrassment to individual states. If it is to be an effective body it must be capable of ringing warning bells.

TREATY AMENDMENT

The draft Treaty for the European Union, which was put forward in December 1996 during the Irish Presidency, contains important provisions concerning racism and xenophobia.

The proposed Article K.1 of the Treaty of Maastricht would make "preventing and combating racism and xenophobia" a specific area of common interest with a view to cooperation and common action, i.e. under the Third Pillar. More significantly, a new Article 6a in the TEU would give the Council clear competence for the first time to take action against discrimination based, *inter alia,* on racial, ethnic or social origin. Such action would unfortunately be subject to the unanimity principle, and the new Article would not give the principle of non-discrimination direct effect. Despite these restrictions, the new provision, which was seen by the Irish Presidency as being the maximum that is at this stage politically possible, represents a considerable achievement and advance.

The Consultative Commission has concluded, in its Declaration on "1997 – European Year Against Racism", that "[t]he setting up of the Monitoring Centre, together with appropriate amendments to the Treaty, will secure the basis necessary for developing firm, effective and sustained action by the European Union against racism and xenophobia over the years to come."

NOTES

1. Mme Catherine Lalumiere, former Secretary General of the Council of Europe, from a speech given at an International Symposium "Europe Against Discrimination; Vigilant for Democracy and Freedom", Strasbourg, 20/21 October 1994, Final Report (Foundation International Symposium Strasbourg 1994), at p. 35.

2. See e.g. Martin Mac Ewan, *Tackling Racism in Europe; An Examination of Anti-Discrimination Law in Practice,* Berg, 1995.

3. In 1992 the Romany/Gypsy/Travelling population of greater Europe was estimated to be twelve and a half million, with two and a half to three million in the European Union. *Eurostat,* 1 January 1992.

4. See, e.g. the European Parliament, Committee of Inquiry into the Rise of Fascism and Racism in Europe, *Report on the Findings of the Inquiry* (the Evrigenis Report), Strasbourg, December 1986; European Parliament, Committee of Inquiry on Racism and Xenophobia, Report on the Findings of the Inquiry (the Ford Report), Luxembourg (OOPEC) 1991.

5. For the situation in Ireland, see especially Marian Tannam, *Racism in Ireland, Sources of Information,* Harmony (Ireland), 1991; Dublin Travellers Education & Development Group, Irish Council for Civil Liberties, Irish Traveller Movement, *Anti-Racist Law and the Travellers,* Irish Traveller Movement, Dublin, 1993.

6. See especially the following publications of the European Centre for Research and Action on Racism and Antisemitism (CERA) – *Political Extremism and the Threat to Democracy in Europe. A Survey and Assessment of Parties, Movements and Groups,* Paris, 1994, and *Extremism from the Atlantic to the Urals,* editions de l'aube, 1996.

7. Commission of the European Communities, Brussels 13.12.1995, 95/0355 (CNS).

8. *Political Extremism and the Threat to Democracy in Europe, op. cit.,* at p. x.

9. Ratified by 146 states as of February 1996.

10. Speech by Mervyn Taylor T.D., Minister for Equality and Law Reform at a Conference on "Developments in Discrimination Law in Ireland and Europe", Dublin, 26 April 1996.

11. Council of Europe, European Commission against Racism and Intolerance, *Legal Measures to Combat Racism and Intolerance in the Member States of the Council of Europe*. Report prepared by the Swiss Institute of Comparative Law, Strasbourg, 2 March 1995.

12. Statement by Jane Dinsdale, Deputy Director of Human Rights, Council of Europe, "Combating Discrimination: A View from the Council of Europe", given at the Irish Centre for European Law Conference on Developments in Discrimination Law in Ireland and Europe, Dublin, 26 April 1996.

13. See footnote 4.

14. See footnote 4.

15. See footnote 7.

16. At Dublin (May 1990), Maastricht (December 1991), Edinburgh (December 1992), and Copenhagen (June 1993).

17. European Council at Corfu, 24–25 June 1994, Presidency Conclusions.

18. Noted by the European Council at its meeting in Essen, 9–10 December 1994.

19. Considered by the European Council at its meeting in Cannes, 26–27 June 1995.

20. Three such round tables have been held in Dublin, under the present author's chairmanship.

21. [1976] ECR 455.

22. Most recently, in its Resolution of 17 May 1995 (at para. 7), there is a proposal that the Treaty should contain a clear rejection of racism, xenophobia and anti-Semitism, and legal protection against discrimination for all individuals resident within the Union.

23. See the *Communication on Racism, Xenophobia and Anti-Semitism* of 13 December 1995, and the *White Paper on Social Policy* of 27 July 1994.

24. See e.g. the Starting Line Group of NGOs, whose proposals are available from the Starting Line Group, 174 rue Joseph II, B- 1040 Brussels; the Utrecht Standing Committee of Experts on International Immigration, Refugee and Criminal Law, *Proposals for the Amendment of the Treaty on European Union at the IGC in 1996.* (March 1995); and Justice, *The 1996 Inter-Governmental Conference* (June 1995).

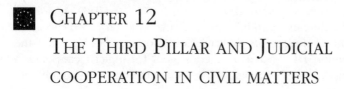

CHAPTER 12
THE THIRD PILLAR AND JUDICIAL
COOPERATION IN CIVIL MATTERS

SEAMUS WOULFE

INTRODUCTION

Article K.1 of the Treaty on European Union (the TEU) obliges member states to regard certain listed areas as "matters of common interest", one area being judicial cooperation in civil matters. The obligation is stated to be for the purposes of achieving the objectives of the Union (set out in Article B), and in particular the free movement of persons.

It may be useful to approach this topic by asking three questions.

1. What is meant by "judicial cooperation"?

2. What has been the effect of including an express reference to the topic of judicial cooperation in the TEU?

3. What are the prospects for future developments in this area?

MEANING OF JUDICIAL COOPERATION

Most Irish lawyers would, I think, consider the scope for judicial cooperation in civil matters as arising primarily in three interlocking areas. Firstly, the jurisdiction of courts – which member state's courts should determine a dispute with a cross-border element? Secondly, service of legal documents – will judges in other member states accept the method of service adopted in their own state? Thirdly, recognition and enforcement – will such judges recognise and enforce a judgment given in another member state?

The above approach, of viewing judicial cooperation in terms of cooperation between the various judiciaries, may not be shared by lawyers in civil law jurisdictions where the role of judges is a broader one. It appears that judicial cooperation in criminal matters is viewed in far wider terms by European lawyers, and this may flow from the fact that a judge in a continental European country also has prosecutorial functions, unlike in Ireland.

In fact judicial cooperation in the above areas pre-dates the TEU. As regards jurisdiction and enforcement, the Brussels Convention on Jurisdiction and the Enforcement of Judgments in Civil and Commercial Matters ("the Brussels Convention") set out a detailed system for judicial cooperation between the original member states of the European Economic Community as far back as 1968.

Although the term "judicial cooperation" was not used in the Treaty of Rome, Article 220 of that Treaty provided a basis for the Brussels Convention. It provided that member states should enter into negotiations with a view to securing for the benefit of their nationals the simplification of formalities concerning the reciprocal recognition and enforcement of judgments of courts or tribunals and of arbitration awards. The Brussels Convention has been in force in Ireland since 1988[1] and has proved highly significant for all lawyers engaging in litigation.

IMPACT OF THE BRUSSELS CONVENTION ON JURISDICTIONAL RULES

The Convention gives rise to judicial cooperation at the jurisdictional stage in that judges in the member states now decide on which member states' courts should have jurisdiction pursuant to a common set of rules set out in the Convention rather than each state's judges applying their own national rules. The Convention applies generally to "civil and commercial matters", but that expression is not defined. It is clear from Article 5 that the term includes matters relating to a contract, to maintenance, to tort, and to a trust. It does not extend to revenue, customs or administrative matters and Article 1 contains other express exclusions, such as certain matrimonial matters, wills and succession, bankruptcy, certain insolvency matters, social security and arbitration.

As regards the remaining civil and commercial matters, Article 2 lays down a general rule that a defendant shall be sued in the courts of his domicile, and domicile is defined in terms of ordinary residence. So a defendant ordinarily resident in Ireland should, in general, be sued in the Irish courts. Article 5 lays down rules of special jurisdiction which depend on the nature of the claim. For example in a tort claim, such as a motor vehicle accident claim, a defendant may be sued "in the courts for the place where the harmful event occurred". Other Articles go on to deal with insurance matters, consumer contracts, rules of exclusive jurisdiction, agreements between the parties as to a particular court having jurisdiction, the obligation on one court to decline jurisdiction where a court of another Contracting State has exclusive jurisdiction, the staying of proceedings where similar proceedings are brought in different Contracting States, and provisional measures.

THE CONVENTION AND RECOGNITION AND ENFORCEMENT OF JUDGMENTS

Recognition and enforcement of judgments, perhaps the most obvious form of judicial cooperation, is also governed by common rules with the emphasis on facilitating enforcement. Limited grounds are set out which can operate to prevent recognition, and Article 29 of the Convention provides that under no circumstances may a final judgment be reviewed as to its substance.

The Convention sets out a simplified enforcement procedure and adopts a system based on an *ex parte* application subject to certain Convention rules. The application for enforcement is enabled to proceed rapidly providing all the procedural formalities are met, without prior warning to the defendant. Enforcement can be refused only if there is a ground for refusing recognition.

THE HAGUE CONVENTION AND THE SERVICE OF DOCUMENTS

As regards service of documents, clearly it is important for litigants to be able to operate uniform modes of service in different countries and for judicial cooperation in accepting such service. A Convention in this area was drawn up in 1965, not under the auspices of the European Communities, but by the Hague Conference on Private International Law, a more diverse international body. The Hague Convention on the Service Abroad of Judicial and Extrajudicial documents was implemented into Irish law in 1994.[2] The scheme for service abroad under the Convention, as implemented in Irish law, is quite complex, involving an application by a "competent authority or judicial officer" to a "Central Authority" for certification of certain matters. If the Central Authority, in Ireland the Master of the High Court, grants certification it returns the application to the applicant with such a certificate for transmission by the applicant directly to the Central Authority of the foreign state addressed. The Central Authority of the state addressed then itself serves the document or arranges to have it served by an appropriate agency.

EFFECT OF EXPRESS TREATY REFERENCE

It is clear from the above that judicial cooperation in civil matters between the member states did not await the TEU. However, the topic now has an express foundation in the TEU, and thus may in principle have a wider sphere of operation than was possible when relying on Article 220 of the Treaty of Rome. The Article 220 root was limited to recognition and enforcement of judgments, and matters ancillary thereto.

The topic of judicial cooperation in civil matters is located in Title VI of the Treaty, which covers provisions on cooperation in the fields of justice and home affairs. While such cooperation in general has gone on between the member states for many years, Title VI attempts to strengthen it and to provide for institutional arrangements and for new legal instruments. It is not necessary to review here the complex institutional and legal framework, as this is fully dealt with elsewhere in this publication. One might just say that the problems of cumbersome operational structures, the uncertain overlap between the Third Pillar and Community competences and the requirement of unanimity have all hindered action in the area of judicial cooperation in civil matters just as in other Third Pillar areas.

PROPOSALS RELATING TO JUDICIAL COOPERATION IN CIVIL MATTERS

Two of the working parties under the Title VI multi-tier structure are dealing with topics relating to judicial cooperation in civil matters, one on the extension of the Brussels Convention and one on transmission of acts, i.e. service of documents. While the Brussels Convention applies in general to civil and commercial matters, Article 1 excludes its application to a number of areas, the most important exclusion probably being matrimonial matters. The Council Presidency has proposed a draft Convention on jurisdiction and the enforcement of judgments in matrimonial matters.

The draft Convention seeks to provide for judicial cooperation by laying down a common rule for assuming jurisdiction in actions relating to divorce, separation and annulment of marriage. Article 2 stipulates that in general the member state where both, or in certain circumstances one, of the spouses habitually reside shall have jurisdiction. Alternatively, the member state of nationality of both spouses or of joint domicile established on a permanent basis may assume jurisdiction and member states must choose one or the other of these alternative criteria. The Convention also seeks to lay down a common rule as regards ancillary proceedings relating to the exercise of parental authority over the children of both spouses. Under Article 3 the member state where the children of both spouses are habitually resident will normally have jurisdiction to take ancillary decisions on the exercise of parental authority, i.e. regarding child custody. Provisions are included for cases where one or more but not all of the children are habitually resident in another member state or where none of the children resides in the member state with jurisdiction in the main marital proceedings.

Article 10 deals with the obligation on one member state to stay proceedings where proceedings involving the same cause of action and between the same parties have already been brought in another member state having jurisdiction. Article 12 enables application to be made in one member state for urgent provisional, including protective, measures, even if another member state has jurisdiction as to the substance of the matter. Title III of the draft Convention seeks to provide for recognition and enforcement of matrimonial judgments throughout the European Union in a manner similar to the Brussels Convention.

This draft Convention is being considered by the Working Party on extension of the Brussels Convention. A press release from the Council meeting in November 1995 referred to the draft Convention as having been held up for years by substantive issues, and stated that the main obstacle continued to be whether or not the exercise of parental authority and the custody of children should be included in the scope of the Convention. It noted that the Council had affirmed its political will to press ahead with this Convention "which is of paramount importance for all European citizens", and that it had instructed the working party to adopt a more flexible approach towards harmonising the rules of jurisdiction regarding the exercise of parental authority.

Another proposed measure in the area under discussion is a draft Convention on the Service in the Member States of the European Union of Judicial and Extrajudicial Documents. Reference was made above to the Hague Convention on the Service Abroad of Judicial and Extrajudicial Documents, which has been ratified by most of the member states. The scheme for service abroad under the Convention, as implemented in Irish law, is quite complex, as described above. Following certification, the request for service abroad must be transmitted by the Applicant directly to the Central Authority of the state addressed. The new draft Convention aims to facilitate the application of the Hague Convention between the member states which have ratified it, by decentralising the transmission of documents and providing that transmission and service are carried out in the shortest possible time. Article 2 provides that each member state should designate one or more public officers, authorities or other persons competent in all or part of its territory for the transmission and receipt of judicial or extrajudicial documents which must be served in another member state. Article 3 provides that judicial or extrajudicial documents shall be transmitted directly between the public officers, authorities or other competent persons designated on the basis of Article 2. As regards service, Article 6 provides that the competent public officer, authority or other person that has received a document shall effect or cause to be effected service of the document, either in accordance with the relevant national law or in the particular form requested by the applicant, provided that it is compatible with the law of the state of destination. All steps required for service of the document are to be effected as soon as possible.

In October 1995 the Council presidency put forward a fresh presentation of the draft Convention for consideration by the Working Party on Simplification of Document Transmission. The fresh presentation involves a two-stage approach, whereby the European Union Convention would supersede the Hague Convention in certain respects but aspects not dealt with in the European Union Convention would remain as settled by the Hague Convention. In 1996 work continued towards concluding the European Union Convention.

A third draft Convention was also relatively recently transferred into the Third Pillar domain under the rubric of judicial cooperation in civil matters. The draft Convention on Insolvency Proceedings began life within the Community sphere rooted in Article 220 of the Treaty of Rome, the terms of which are set out above. It is easy to envisage how problems might arise where a debtor who owns assets in different member states becomes insolvent, and the need for common rules to regulate orderly insolvency.

The draft Convention seeks to determine the jurisdiction of the courts or authorities of the member states with regard to the intra-Community effects of insolvency proceedings, to create certain uniform conflict of laws rules for such proceedings, to ensure the recognition and enforcement of judgments given in such matters, to make provision for the possibility of opening secondary insolvency proceedings and to guarantee information for creditors and their right to lodge claims.

The basic jurisdictional rule is found in Article 3, whereby the courts of Contracting States within whose territory "the centre of a debtor's main interest" is situated shall have jurisdiction to open insolvency proceedings. The courts of another Contracting State shall have jurisdiction to open secondary insolvency proceedings only if the debtor possesses an establishment within the territory of that other Contracting State. Any such secondary proceedings shall be restricted to the assets of the debtor situated in the territory of that Contracting State.

Article 4 provides that the law applicable to insolvency proceedings shall be that of the Contracting State where such proceedings are opened and that law shall determine the conditions for the opening of those proceedings, their conduct and their closure. As regards recognition and enforceability of insolvency judgments, Article 25 states that judgments which concern the course and closure of insolvency proceedings, and compositions approved by the proper court, shall be recognised with no further formalities and applies the relevant provisions of the Brussels Convention on enforcement to such judgments. Finally, Chapter IV seeks to guarantee the provision of information for creditors throughout the European Union and the right to lodge claims.

PROSPECTS FOR FUTURE DEVELOPMENTS

The area of judicial cooperation in civil matters is a less contentious area than some of the other areas listed as matters of common interest in Article K.1, such as asylum policy and immigration policy. The general Third Pillar concerns regarding cumbersome structures and lack of use of the new legal instruments apply in principle, but perhaps with less immediate force, since the wide differences between the laws and legal systems in the different member states have arguably necessitated slow movement. Judicial cooperation in civil matters between common law and civil law countries outside the areas attempted to date may well be difficult, because of those wide differences and the problems of moulding same into common rules.

The progress report published in 1995 by Carlos Westendorp, the Chairperson of the Reflection Group on the IGC, agreed that the results under Title VI have so far been disappointing – a conclusion which was ultimately echoed in the Group's final Report.[3] The majority felt that some of the Title VI matters should be brought into the Community sphere, but accepted that the areas of police cooperation and judicial cooperation in both civil and criminal matters ought to be developed by means of closer intergovernmental cooperation. Future developments in the area of judicial cooperation in civil matters will probably include further extension of the Brussels Convention, to cover the types of proceedings now excluded from the Convention's scope and which have the greatest cross-border relevance. Note, however, that further extension is likely to be by way of Conventions as before. The Commission has noted that "the adoption and implementation of Conventions is a slow and complicated business",[4] and this will doubtless remain the case, although some reforms at least in this area are apparently under consideration in the ongoing Intergovernmental Conference.

NOTES

1. Jurisdiction of Courts and Enforcement of Judgments (European Communities) Act, 1988, s.3.
2. Rules of the Superior Courts (No. 3), 1994: S.I. No. 101 of 1994.
3. SN 520/95 (Reflex 21) (Brussels, 5 December, 1995).
4. Commission of the European Communities, *Report on the Operation of the Treaty on European Union*, Brussels, 1005 1995 SEC (95) 731 final, at paragraph 121.

PART V

THE LINK BETWEEN JUSTICE AND HOME AFFAIRS COOPERATION AND FUNDAMENTAL RIGHTS

CHAPTER 13
FUNDAMENTAL RIGHTS, DEMOCRACY AND THE RULE OF LAW IN THE THIRD PILLAR

ANTHONY WHELAN[1]

INTRODUCTION

When they were first established, it was not anticipated that the three European Communities[2] would have a significant impact on fundamental human rights. It soon transpired, however, that the essentially economic concerns of those Communities did not prevent their laws and policies from affecting, potentially at least, the fundamental rights of individuals as they were understood in the legal systems of a number of member states and under international treaties. Such effects could be felt without the mediation of national implementing measures (which might be subject to national judicial review) due to the direct effect of many Treaty provisions and legislative and executive acts under Community law. On the other hand, it was evident from the outset that the subject matter governed by Title VI of the Treaty on European Union (TEU) – the Cooperation in Justice and Home Affairs, or the Third Pillar of the Union – was intimately related to the "classical" sphere of application of fundamental rights concerning, in particular, the liberty of the person, privacy and the fairness of criminal procedures. It is ironic, and a matter for concern, therefore, that while the TEU – and especially Title VI thereof – is littered with references to fundamental rights, on which the EC Treaty is mute,[3] their judicial protection is assured under the latter Treaty and is virtually excluded under the former. The fact that measures adopted by the Council in the Third Pillar are unlikely to be directly effective may, however, mitigate the practical effects of that exclusion.

FUNDAMENTAL RIGHTS, DEMOCRACY AND THE RULE OF LAW IN THE EC LEGAL ORDER[4]

The sole basis in the EC Treaty for a general fundamental rights jurisdiction is Article 164, which states that "[t]he Court of Justice shall ensure that in the interpretation and application of this Treaty the law is observed".[5] The Court has relied upon this provision to develop general principles of Community law common to the laws of the member states, regarding equality, proportionality, legitimate expectations and legal certainty, as criteria for judicial review of legislative and executive acts. The Court of Justice included fundamental rights among those principles in 1969;[6] in 1970, the Court stated that it derived inspiration from the constitutional traditions common to the member states,[7] to which it added, in 1974, guidelines from international treaties on which the member states have collaborated or of which they are signatories.[8] The European Convention on Human Rights (ECHR) was expressly cited in 1975,[9] and has now been accorded "special significance" [10] other international instruments have also been referred to in judgments.[11] These fundamental rights principles apply only within the scope of application of Community law: to control Community acts, member state acts implementing Community law,[12] and member state acts derogating from Community law.[13] However, the EC is not competent to adhere to the ECHR, as there is no express provision empowering it to take positive measures in this field, and such a step would be of such constitutional significance as to preclude using the residual legislative basis provided by Article 235 of the EC Treaty.[14]

The Court of Justice has also developed principles of democratic legitimacy, transparency and the rule of law, which have important consequences for the individual. The Court of Justice has stated that the EC is based on the rule of law, which entails a complete system of legal remedies and procedures to permit it to review the legality of measures adopted by the institutions in the light of the basic constitutional charter, the Treaty.[15] This led the Court, for example, to review Acts of the European Parliament which had legal effects *vis-à-vis* third parties, even though this was not originally provided for in the EC Treaty.[16] The rule of law also underlies the principles of the direct effect of Treaty provisions[17] and of unimplemented directives,[18] and of member state liability for failure to comply with Community law obligations.[19] The Court has also policed rigorously the division of competences – the "institutional balance" – between the political bodies of the Communities,[20] the requirement that every act should have an appropriate legal basis in the Treaty,[21] and the obligation to give reasons for Community measures.[22] The Court of Justice has indicated that where an act can potentially be adopted on more than one legal basis, that which affords the greater participation to the European Parliament should be preferred, as such participation "reflects the democratic principle that the peoples should take part in the exercise of power through the intermediary of a representative assembly".[23] Thus, while the political system of the Communities is often characterised as suffering from a "democratic deficit" (a question too large to be addressed in the present discussion), such democratic elements as have been included in that system are judicially enforceable. As regards transparency, the Court of First

Instance has interpreted Council Decision 93/731 on public access to Council documents as requiring a genuine and reasoned balancing of the interest of citizens in access to documents against any interest of the Council in their confidentiality.[24] It is also worth noting the right of citizens and residents of the Union to address petitions to the European Parliament on matters within the Community's fields of activity which affect them directly, the right of the Parliament to establish Committees of Inquiry into contraventions or maladministration of Community law, and the role of the Ombudsman in investigating complaints of maladministration in the activities of the Community institutions or bodies.[25]

These developments have been endorsed by the member states, although chiefly in a rhetorical fashion. The preamble to the Single European Act (SEA) cites their determination "to work together to promote democracy on the basis of the fundamental rights recognized in the constitutions and laws of the member states, in the [ECHR] and the European Social Charter". Article F(1) of the TEU states that "[t]he Union shall respect the national identities of its member states, whose systems of government are founded on the principles of democracy" (without, however, indicating whether the subsidiary statement is a formal condition of membership or merely a factual observation). Article F(2) states that "[t]he Union shall respect fundamental rights, as guaranteed by the [ECHR] and as they result from the constitutional traditions common to the member states, as general principles of Community law". However, these provisions were not made enforceable by the Court of Justice, even though they essentially reflect its case-law.[26]

FUNDAMENTAL RIGHTS, DEMOCRACY AND THE RULE OF LAW IN THE THIRD PILLAR

The Third Pillar is part of the general framework of the European Union established by the TEU. The provisions of Article F of the TEU regarding democracy and fundamental rights have already been mentioned. In Title VI itself, Article K.2(1) states that the matters of common interest referred to in Article K.1 "shall be dealt with in compliance with the [ECHR] and the [Geneva] Convention relating to the Status of Refugees of 28 July 1951 and having regard to the protection afforded by member states to persons persecuted on political grounds". Article K.2(2) states that Title VI "shall not affect the exercise of the responsibilities incumbent upon member states with regard to the maintenance of law and order and the safeguarding of internal security". Article K.3(2) provides for the unanimous adoption of different measures in the Third Pillar: (a) joint positions and cooperation; (b) joint actions (which may be implemented by a qualified majority); and (c) conventions, to be adopted by the member states in accordance with their respective constitutional requirements (to be implemented by a two-thirds majority of the parties). The third subparagraph of Article K.3(2)(c) states that "[s]uch conventions may stipulate that the Court of Justice shall have jurisdiction to interpret their provisions and to rule on any dispute regarding their application, in accordance with such arrangements as they may lay down". Article K.4(2) provides that the Commission shall be fully associated with the work in the Third Pillar. Article K.6 states that the Presidency and the Commission shall regularly inform the European Parliament of discussions in the Third Pillar. The Presidency shall consult the Parliament on the principal aspects of activities in the Third Pillar and shall ensure that the Parliament's views are duly taken into consideration. The Parliament may ask questions of the Council or make recommendations to it. Article K.8 provides for the application in the Third Pillar of certain institutional provisions of the EC Treaty, thus ensuring the single institutional framework referred to in Article C of the TEU. Articles 138c, 138d and 138e of the EC Treaty are not included in this list. In the Final Provisions of the TEU, Article L provides that the Court of Justice shall exercise the powers conferred by the Community Treaties in respect of the TEU only as regards those provisions which amend those Treaties, the Final Provisions and the third subparagraph of Article K.3(2)(c).

In one sense, the inclusion of Title VI in the TEU constitutes a step forward for the rule of law and fundamental rights.[27] It replaces a secretive, informal set of cooperative arrangements, operating on an exclusively intergovernmental basis, such as the TREVI committees and the Ad Hoc Group on Immigration, by a formal, legal structure. The Commission, traditional guardian of the Treaties and of individual rights thereunder, is fully associated with Third Pillar activity, and has a partial right of initiative. The European Parliament has a right, albeit an ill-defined one, to be consulted about the principal aspects of activity in the field, while its right to ask questions can underpin its right to information. There is at least the potential for partial judicial supervision by the Court of Justice. However, the Third Pillar remains deeply flawed from the perspective of democratic legitimation, the rule of law and fundamental rights.

DEMOCRATIC LEGITIMATION

This assessment is based on the premise that the European Parliament can afford to Union measures a degree of democratic control and legitimation that the national parliaments, in their relations with the individual member state governments which are represented in the Council, are, both in principle and in practice, unable to guarantee.[28] The competences of the Parliament's Petitions Committee, its Committees of Inquiry and the Ombudsman have not been extended to the Third Pillar. There were complaints from the outset about the quality and immediacy of the information provided to the European Parliament, although the Commission has undertaken to improve this.[29] Although Article K.6 clearly envisages consultation of the Parliament before the adoption of decisions,[30] this does not occur systematically.[31] In part, as will be seen below, this is because the Council retains a preference for informal measures. Article K.8 gives the Parliament some degree of political control, as administrative expenditure in the Third Pillar is charged to the Communities' budget, over which it has significant power, and operational expenditure may be so charged. The significance of this potential power is undermined by the tendency of the Council to favour the alternative of charging expenditure to the member states. For example, the budget of the European Police Office (Europol), probably fiscally the most significant initiative in the Third Pillar, is charged to the member states in accordance with their respective GNPs.[32] The Parliament's resulting lack of effective influence is reflected in Article 34 of the Europol Convention, which provides simply for an annual report to Parliament by the Council Presidency (although it does also provide for the consultation of the Parliament in respect of any future amendments). The Parliament proposed an inter-institutional agreement on the Third Pillar in December 1993, regarding provision of information, question-time at parliamentary committees, follow-up information on Parliament recommendations and a general right of consultation on draft texts, but this was rejected by the Council in February 1994.[33]

Ironically, the Parliament's power was substantially increased by the TEU in some fields of EC activity which are related to the Third Pillar. Thus, the EC measures adopted in 1991 regarding money laundering and weapons would be subject, if decided upon today, to the procedure of co-decision by the Parliament and the Council.[34] On the other hand, the Parliament is merely consulted under Article 100c of the EC Treaty, regarding third country visa requirements and the uniform visas (but which potentially extends, through the operation of the *passerelle* in Article K.9 of the TEU, to all the matters of common interest referred to in Article K.1(1) to (6)), although that right to consultation is at least legally enforceable.[35] Furthermore, it is possible that the introduction of Article 100c into the EC Treaty by the TEU has reduced EC competence regarding the free movement of persons by making express, but very limited, provision for it.[36] Recourse to Article 235 of the EC Treaty as a residual legal basis may be precluded by the fact that Article 3(d) of that Treaty provides as one of the Community's activities "measures concerning the entry and movement of persons in the internal market *as provided for in Article 100c*".[37]

THE RULE OF LAW

The two chief problems regarding the rule of law in the Third Pillar are the uncertain status of the legal instruments provided for and the exclusion of the jurisdiction of the Court of Justice regarding many aspects of it. On the first point, a joint position is probably simply declaratory or recommendatory in character,[38] while a convention is clearly binding once it comes into force. The status of a joint action is entirely unclear; there is reportedly a difference of view between the United Kingdom and the Netherlands regarding whether a joint action is binding, the latter taking the view that it is similar in nature to an EC directive.[39] It seems unlikely that a joint action is capable of direct effect (if only because the Court of Justice has no jurisdiction to address the question); a convention may, on the other hand, have direct effect in member states with monist legal systems.[40] What is most striking is that the member states have avoided even the least constraining "soft-law" measure, the joint position, in favour of undefined resolutions, recommendations, conclusions, texts and guidelines, most of which are not even published in the *Official Journal* and appear only in press releases.[41]

In the field of asylum, for example, minimum guarantees for asylum procedures are provided for in a resolution, which states that such procedures "will be applied in full compliance with the 1951 Geneva Convention and the 1967 New York Protocol relating to the Status of Refugees and other obligations under international law in respect of refugees and human rights" (Article II.1), but also states merely that "member states will *strive* to bring their national legislation into line with these principles by 1 January 1996" (Article VIII.31).[42] It is not at all clear that the member states are under anything other than a moral obligation to give effect to this measure. It can hardly derive binding force from the TEU, which does not provide for resolutions. At the same time, it is difficult to characterise it as an implicit international agreement of the member states, as it is, in form, an act of the Council rather than of its members, and is, in any event, couched in less than compelling terms. A document approved the same day, on the means of proof in the framework of the Dublin Convention of 15 June 1990 determining the state responsible for examining applications for asylum lodged in one of the member states of the European Union, is described as a "text adopted by the Council".[43] As is also the case with regard to the resolution discussed above, this text is of enormous importance to asylum-seekers, as it sets out types of probative and indicative evidence for determining the country responsible for examining their application which, if ignored, could give rise to the phenomenon of "refugees in orbit", and yet its status is entirely unknown. Some member states may apply it consistently, others at their discretion, and others not at all, thus confirming the established Community-law principle that merely administrative measures provide insufficient guidance and security to individuals regarding their rights.[44] It is certainly a matter of speculation whether an aggrieved individual could invoke the "text" before a national court.

The above problem of uncertainty is exacerbated by the fact that the Court of Justice has no jurisdiction to resolve disputes or doubts about the legal effect of the provisions of Title VI or of most measures adopted under it. The exceptional case of conventions adopted under Article K.3(2)(c) of the TEU has proved to be a political battlefield, giving rise to very varied compromises. For example, the Commission's proposal for a Convention on controls on persons crossing external frontiers provides, in Article 29, for the Court of Justice to have jurisdiction (a) to give preliminary rulings concerning its interpretation and (b) in disputes concerning its implementation, on application by a member state or the Commission. On the other hand, Article 40 of the Europol Convention provides that disputes between member states on its interpretation or application shall in an initial stage be discussed by the Council with the aim of finding a settlement and that, where such disputes are not settled within six months, the member states who are parties to the dispute shall decide, by agreement among themselves, the modalities according to which they shall be settled.[45] In an accompanying declaration, fourteen member states (all but the United Kingdom) state that they will systematically submit the dispute in question to the Court of Justice. It is open to question whether this declaration, combined with the text of Article 40, satisfies the requirements of Article K.3(2)(c) of the TEU, as no jurisdiction is stipulated, nor are arrangements laid down, in the Europol Convention itself.[46] A subsequent protocol provides for interpretation of the Europol Convention by the Court of Justice by way of a preliminary ruling procedure.[47] However, acceptance of this jurisdiction by the member states is optional.[48] Furthermore, the member states have the option of permitting the making of references only by courts against whose decisions there is no judicial remedy under national law.[49] These arrangements leave the settlement of inter-state disputes primarily in political hands, with the resulting likelihood that the practical application of the Convention will be varied by administrative fiat in the light of compromise solutions, while the protection of the individual in national courts and the uniform interpretation by them of the Convention is undermined by varying degrees of permitted recourse to the jurisdiction of the Court of Justice.[50] Thus, for example, individuals who are aggrieved about the denial to them of the right of access to data held by Europol, or to have that data checked, and who wish to challenge decisions of the relevant national supervisory body or of the joint supervisory body in their national courts, or to seek compensation for ensuing damage, may encounter widely varying conditions in the different member states.[51]

The sole (and very limited) source of legal certainty in the Third Pillar outside the case of conventions which grant jurisdiction to the Court of Justice is Article M of the TEU, which states that nothing in that Treaty, other than the relevant amending provisions, shall affect the Community Treaties. This Article is subject to the jurisdiction of the Court of Justice. Thus, that Court can ensure that measures adopted in the Third Pillar do not encroach on Community competences and, arguably, can annul Council measures which have that effect.[52] However, this grants the Court of Justice merely the role of frontier guard of the Community Pillar, rather than that of policeman of the Third.

FUNDAMENTAL RIGHTS

In the limited case of Third Pillar conventions which grant jurisdiction to the Court of Justice, it is likely that the Court will seek to interpret the relevant provisions in the light of fundamental rights.[53] It is not clear, however, what standard the Court should apply. Article F(2) of the TEU states that "[t]he Union shall respect fundamental rights, as guaranteed by the [ECHR] and as they result from the constitutional traditions common to the member states, as general principles of Community law",[54] which confuses somewhat the scope of the obligation. In Title VI itself, only compliance with the ECHR and the Geneva Convention is mentioned, in Article K.2(1), as a condition of Union activity. This suggests a more direct obligation to comply with such international human rights treaties than is normally acknowledged by the Court of Justice in Community law, while omitting any separate reference to national traditions.

The Court of Justice may subject to the principles of substantive fundamental rights, proportionality and fair procedures decisions which invoke the grounds of public policy or security, as it has done in Community law. Thus, for example, the Court may review decisions under Article 10(3) of the draft Convention on controls on persons crossing external frontiers which exclude entry by persons on those grounds in the case of past serious crimes or contemplated serious crimes.[55] However, the exclusion of a preliminary ruling procedure under certain conventions exposes individuals to serious threat. For example, the draft Protocol to the Convention on the protection of the European Communities' financial interests provides for certain conduct by Community or national officials to be criminalised by the member states,[56] and to be punishable by "effective, proportionate and dissuasive criminal penalties".[57] If the member states' measures in this regard are not subject to review by the Court of Justice consequent upon cases arising in the national courts, it will be virtually impossible to ensure uniform compliance with either the express requirement of proportionality or the overriding obligation under Article K.2(1) of compliance with the ECHR.[58] This will depend, essentially, on whether the ECHR is enforceable in the domestic law of the member states concerned, which is not the case in at least two of them.[59] The degree of judicial review for compliance with fundamental rights will also vary according to whether there is a *national* constitutional tradition of such review of acts of the executive or the legislature.[60] The principle of supremacy which has excluded such purely national review of Community acts can hardly apply with the same force in the Third Pillar in the absence of the general jurisdiction of the Court of Justice.

The protection of fundamental rights in fields of activity falling within the Third Pillar is undermined, therefore, in the Irish context, by the terms of Article 29.4.5 of the Constitution.[61] That provision, as amended by the Eleventh Amendment consequent upon the signing of the TEU, extends to laws enacted, acts done and measures adopted by the state which are necessitated by the obligations of membership of the European Union the same constitutional immunity which was provided from the outset for state laws, acts and measures necessitated by the obligations of membership of the Communities. The fatal difference is that the Court of Justice does not, in the former case, assure consistently the protection of fundamental rights. Furthermore, the lack of certainty about the binding force of the measures – joint positions and joint actions – referred to in Article K.3(2)(a) and (b) of the TEU (not to mention resolutions, recommendations, conclusions, guidelines and texts) leaves the precise scope of this constitutional immunity decidedly unclear.[62]

Recourse by individual or state application to the European Commission and Court of Human Rights at Strasbourg provides one potential avenue by which fundamental rights principles could be applied uniformly to measures adopted in the Third Pillar which fall outside the jurisdiction of the Court of Justice. Such applications could be taken against the member state responsible for an alleged breach of the ECHR. In the context of Community law, the Commission on Human Rights has declined jurisdiction to review acts of the Council, as the Community is not a party to the ECHR, or the participation of individual member states in the adoption of such acts.[63] The Commission on Human Rights later suggested that it might accept applications against Community organs which entailed the responsibility of all the member states collectively, all of whom are parties to the ECHR.[64] The Commission on Human Rights has also indicated that the member states remain bound by their obligations under the ECHR when they implement Community law; as this is the case regarding most Community measures, these could in effect be reviewed at the point of application. However, it added that "the transfer of powers to an international organisation is not incompatible with the [ECHR] provided that within that organisation fundamental rights will receive an equivalent protection". It accepted that such protection was afforded by Community law and declined jurisdiction.[65] Such protection is not, for the most part, provided in the Third Pillar. Furthermore, there are no directly applicable Union measures: conventions, although drawn up by the Council, are acts of the member states, while joint positions and joint actions require implementation by national authorities. Therefore, there is nothing to exclude the jurisdiction of the ECHR organs regarding the compatibility with the ECHR of member state acts adopted consequent upon Council deliberations in the Third Pillar.[66] However, in the absence of application of the ECHR by national courts, or of the enforcement by those courts of autonomous national fundamental rights standards, aggrieved individuals face a long battle to vindicate their rights, first exhausting national remedies and then facing the long delays endemic in proceedings before the ECHR organs themselves. This will be the unfortunate fate of individuals in the United Kingdom and Ireland.

OUTLOOK FOR THE FUTURE: THE INTERGOVERNMENTAL CONFERENCE AND THE IRISH DRAFT TREATY

The draft Treaty amendments prepared by the Irish Presidency of the Council contain much that may be significant to the promotion of fundamental rights, democracy and the rule of law in the Third Pillar, even though certain key institutional questions are not addressed. The draft adopts as the Union's objective in this field the development of the Union "as an area of freedom, security and justice, in accordance with the principle of the rule of law".[67] Article F(1) of the TEU would be amended to read that "[t]he Union is founded on the principles of liberty, democracy, respect for human rights and fundamental freedoms, and the rule of law, principles which are upheld by the member states", while the confusing reference to principles of *Community* law in Article F(2) would be removed.[68] These provisions would be of greater assistance to the Court of Justice (and to national courts in cases where they are the sole competent jurisdiction) in determining the criteria for interpretation of Third Pillar measures in the light of the Union's fundamental rights commitments.

Interestingly, the draft would also commit the political organs of the Union to supervising the observance of fundamental rights principles by the member states, a task which the Court of Justice has shied away from even in the Community pillar save in areas where the member states implement or derogate from Community law. Article O would commence, "[a]ny European State, which respects the principles set out in Article F(1), may apply to become a member of the Union". Furthermore, a new Article Fa of the TEU would permit the Council to determine the existence of a serious and persistent breach by a member state of those principles, which could lead to the suspension of certain rights deriving from the application of the provisions of the Treaties to the state in question. Given this potential new activism on the part of the Council regarding the behaviour of the member states, for which a considerable degree of support exists in the Intergovernmental Conference (IGC), it is interesting to note the limited degree of independent judicial supervision of the Council's own activities in the Third Pillar which is envisaged.

A new Title on free movement of persons, asylum and immigration is proposed in order to bring about the free movement of persons provided for in Article 7a of the EC Treaty. The Presidency did not prejudge whether it should be a Title of the EC Treaty or of the TEU, and it combines competences from the Third Pillar and from Article 100c of the EC Treaty. As a result, the potential roles of the Court of Justice and of the Commission and Parliament are left open. Legal certainty would be advanced somewhat by such a Title, however, because it sets out in greater detail the scope of the measures which the Council would be empowered to adopt, and would avoid much of the present uncertainty about the relationship of the Community and Third Pillars. On the other hand, the draft Title refers throughout to the Council adopting "measures", a term even vaguer than many of those used at present to describe the acts of the Council in this field, but this may arise simply from the fact that the place of this Title in the overall scheme of the Union's constitutional Treaties is, as yet, undecided.

A number of changes are also proposed for what would remain of the present Third Pillar. Again, the draft goes into much more detail about the substantive scope of measures which might be adopted in this field, going far beyond the rather laconic present content of Article K.1 of the TEU. It refers expressly to the possible approximation of laws, which would require legal instruments more compelling than most of those currently employed in the Third Pillar. Regarding Europol, the draft Article K.1b(2) provides for it to assist in operational actions of joint teams and for its technical units to assist national police forces in their investigations. Such operational competence, greatly exceeding Europol's present role of coordinating intelligence data, would require a much more comprehensive judicial review procedure than that currently envisaged by the Europol Convention and Protocol.

The draft Article K.3(2) of the TEU provides for a satisfying advance in the realm of legal certainty and democratic legitimation. It provides formally for the consultation of the European Parliament before the adoption of any measure, thus improving upon the present rather vague obligations of the Presidency of the Council and the Commission under Article K.6 of the TEU. The proposed Article K.3(2) sets out three possible Council measures: (a) decisions, which, whether for the purpose of establishing a common position or of setting up an operational action of the Union, are stated to be binding on the member states; (b) framework decisions for the purpose of approximation of laws. These are conceived of in terms similar to EC directives, as they "shall be binding upon the member states as to the result to be achieved but shall leave to the national authorities the choice of form and methods". Furthermore, "[t]he Court of Justice shall have jurisdiction to interpret their provisions"; (c) conventions, whose role remains unchanged. However, the draft goes into greater detail about the jurisdiction of the Court of Justice. This is still, in principle, optional, save where reference is made to concepts of Community law, in respect of which a preliminary ruling jurisdiction would be mandatory. In a formula reminiscent of some of the conventions already drawn up and discussed above, mandatory jurisdiction is also provided for in the case of a dispute between member states regarding the interpretation or application of a convention which cannot be settled by the Council within six months. While these elements would represent an advance on the present *ad hoc* arrangements, it is curious that the jurisdiction of the Court of Justice should remain optional, in part, regarding conventions (and in particular preliminary rulings thereon), while framework decisions would be subject to a compulsory interpretative jurisdiction. The fact that conventions are acts of the member states rather than of the Council appears to be too formalist a point of distinction. It is also worth noting that the Court's jurisdiction is in neither case described as extending to the validity of measures adopted in the Third Pillar, in contrast with Articles 173, 174 and 177 of the EC Treaty.

Taken as a whole, the draft Treaty provisions of the Irish Presidency of the Council represent progress regarding fundamental rights, democratic legitimation and the rule of law in what is now the Third Pillar of the Union, but many issues remain open: the ultimate regime regarding the free movement of people, the interpretation and validity of decisions and conventions, the fundamental rights standard to be applied by the Court of Justice, the judicial supervision of Europol, the enforceability of the slender consultative competence of the Parliament, the use by the Council of legal instruments not provided for in the TEU. Issues external to the TEU, but of particular continued interest in Ireland, are the scope of application of the constitutional immunity in Article 29.4.5 of the Constitution (which will probably be extended by the provision for explicitly binding instruments in the draft Article K.3(2) of the TEU), and the jurisdiction of the European Commission on Human Rights and Court of Human Rights in the persistent absence of a comprehensive fundamental rights review jurisdiction of the Court of Justice.

NOTES
1. All views expressed are personal.
2. The European Coal and Steel Community, the European Atomic Energy Community and the European Economic Community (now the European Community (EC)).
3. The sole exception is Article 130u(2), on development cooperation, which states that "Community policy in this area shall contribute to the general objective of developing and consolidating democracy and the rule of law, and to that of respecting human rights and fundamental freedoms". However, this provision, inserted by Article G(38) of the TEU, governs only the Community's external relations with third countries, and not its internal activities. On the rather extensive scope of this provision, see Case C-268/94 *Portugal* v *Council*, judgment of 3 December 1996, not yet reported. The Treaty also contains a number of anti-discrimination provisions, regarding nationality (Article 6) and sex (Article 119), and in the field of agriculture (Article 40(3)).
4. For a more extensive review of the law in this field, see J. Weiler & N. Lockhart, "Taking rights seriously: the European Court and its fundamental rights jurisprudence" (1995), 32, *Common Market Law Review* 51, 579; K. Bradley, "Fundamental rights and the European Union: a selective overview" (1994), 21, *Polish Yearbook of International Law*, 187.
5. The political institutions of the Communities have adopted non-binding measures, such as the Joint Declaration of the Parliament, Council and Commission of 5 April 1977, OJ 1977 C103, p. 1, and the Parliament's Declaration of Fundamental Rights and Freedoms of 12 April 1989, OJ 1989 C 120, p. 51, but these have followed the lead given by the Court of Justice.
6. Case 26/69 *Stauder* v. *Stadt Ulm* [1969], ECR 425.
7 Case 11/70, *Internationale Handelsgesellschaft* [1970] ECR 1134.
8. Case 4/73, *Nold* [1974], ECR 507.
9. Case 36/75, *Rutili* [1975], ECR 1219.
10. Case C-260/89, *ERT* [1991], ECR I-2963.
11. The Universal Declaration of Human Rights, in Case 41/74, *Van Duyn* [1974], ECR 1351; the European Social Charter and an ILO convention, in Case 149/77, *Defrenne* [1978], ECR 1378; and the International Covenant on Civil and Political Rights, in Case 374/87, *Orkem* [1989] ECR 3283.
12. Case 5/88, *Wachauf* [1989] ECR 2639.

13. *ERT*, cited above.
14. Opinion 2/94, [1996], ECR I-1759.
15. Case 294/83, *Les Verts* v. *Parliament* [1986], ECR 1339; Case C-314/91, *Weber* v. *Parliament* [1993], ECR I-1093.
16. Article 173 of the EC Treaty was amended *ex post facto* by Article G(53) of the TEU to provide expressly for such review.
17. Case 26/62, *Van Gend en Loos* [1963], ECR 1.
18. Case 41/74, *Van Duyn* v. *Home Office* [1974], ECR 1337.
19. Joined Cases 6/90, 9/90, *Francovich* v. *Italy* [1991], ECR I-5357; see, most recently, Joined Cases C-178/94 *et al.*, *Dillenkofer* v. *Germany*, judgment of 8 October 1996, not yet reported.
20. On the consultation of the Parliament, see, for example, Case 138/79 *Roquette* v. *Council* [1980] ECR 3333; on the requirement of Council assent to Commission decisions on production quotas under Article 58(1) of the ECSC Treaty, see Case 119/81, *Klöckner-Werke* v. *Commission* [1982] ECR 2627; on Parliament's right to take proceedings in order to protect its prerogatives, see Case 70/88 *Parliament* v. *Council (Chernobyl)* [1990], ECR I-2041 (since expressly acknowledged in the amended text of Article 173 of the EC Treaty).
21. See, for example, Case 45/86, *Commission* v. *Council (Tariff Preferences)* [1987], ECR 1493.
22. Article 190 of the EC Treaty. The Court indicated in Case 222/86, *UNECTEF* v. *Heylens* [1987], ECR 4097 that this obligation extends to member state decisions which affect Community-law rights. However, it does not appear to extend to general national legislation which affects only potentially the exercise of such rights – see the Opinion of Advocate General Fennelly of 6 February 1997 in Case C-70/95, *Sodemare* v. *Regione Lombardia*, not yet reported.
23. Case C-300/89, *Commission* v. *Council (Titanium Dioxide)* [1991], ECR I-2869. However, this line of reasoning has not been pursued in subsequent cases.
24. Case T-194/94, *Carvel and Guardian Newspapers* v. *Council* [1995] ECR II-2765. The Court of Justice declined to follow Advocate General Tesauro's recommendation that a general principle of transparency be established, in Case C-58/94 *Netherlands* v. *Council* [1996] ECR I-2169. However, the Ombudsman, Mr Soderman, has insisted that all Community institutions and agencies adopt rules on public access to documents – failure to do so will be regarded by him as an act of maladministration, having regard to Declaration No 17 on the right of access to information attached to the TEU and to the inter-institutional agreement on democracy, transparency and subsidiarity of 25 October 1993; see No 6093 (n.s.) *Europe*, 30 January 1997. On the value of free expression, see Case 100/88 *Oyowe* v *Commission* [1989] ECR 4285.
25. Articles 138d, 138c and 138e(1) of the EC Treaty respectively.
26. See the Court's remarks on the SEA in Case 249/86, *Commission* v. *Germany* [1989], ECR 1290.
27. See P. Twomey, "Title VI of the Union Treaty: Matters of common interest as a question of human rights", in J. Monar & R. Morgan (eds.), *The Third Pillar of the European Union* (Brussels, 1994) 49, at p. 50; W. de Lobkowicz, "Intergovernmental cooperation in the field of migration – from the Single European Act to Maastricht" in the same volume, 99, at p. 118.
28. See e.g. Twomey, *op. cit.* at p. 53; Curtin & Pouw, *op. cit.* at p. 14.
29. J. Monar, "The evolving role of the Union institutions in the framework of the Third Pillar" in Monar & Morgan, (eds.), *op. cit.*, 69, at p. 76.
30. D. Curtin & J. Pouw, "La coopération dans le domaine de la justice et des affaires intérieures au sein de l'Union européenne: une nostalgie d'avant Maastricht?" (1995), *Revue du Marché Unique Européen* 13, at p. 20.

31. The Robles Piquer Report of the European Parliament Committee on Civil Liberties and Internal Affairs of 1 July 1993 on cooperation in the fields of justice and home affairs under the TEU, EP Doc. No. A3-0215/93, described the obligation of the Presidency of the Council to ensure that the Parliament's views are duly taken into consideration as "almost moving in its naivety"; quoted by Twomey, *op. cit.* at p. 52.

32. Article 35(2) of the Convention of 26 July 1995 on the establishment of a European Police Office (the Europol Convention), OJ 1995 C 316, p. 2.

33. EP Doc. 207.086. See Monar, *op. cit.* at p. 79.

34. Council Directive 91/308/EEC of 10 June 1991 on the prevention of the use of the financial system for the purpose of money laundering, OJ 1991 L 166, p. 77 and Council Directive 91/477/EEC of 18 June 1991 on control of the acquisition and possession of weapons, OJ 1991 L 256, p. 51. These measures were adopted on the basis of, in the first case, Articles 57(2) and 100a of the EC Treaty and, in the second, Article 100a. The co-decision procedure is set out in Article 189b of the EC Treaty.

35. The Parliament has sought to enforce its right to reconsultation in cases of substantial change to a Commission proposal in Case C-392/95 *Parliament* v. *Council* regarding a measure adopted under Article 100c, Council Regulation (EC) No. 2317/95 of 25 September 1995 determining the third countries whose nationals must be in possession of visas when crossing the external borders of the member states, OJ 1995 L 234, p. 1. The Opinion of Advocate General Fennelly in this case was due to be given on 20 March 1997 – too late for account to be taken of it in the present work.

36. This argument is independent of the existence of the Third Pillar, as Articles M and K.1 of the TEU indicate that the provisions of that Treaty, and those on the Third Pillar in particular, do not affect the powers of the EC. However, at the oral hearing in Case C-392/95, *Parliament* v. *Council*, mentioned above, the agent for the Council did suggest that the Court should bear in mind the Union's competences in the Third Pillar when interpreting Article 100c of the EC Treaty.

37. Emphasis added. While the competence provided for in Article 100c is at present greatly restricted, it is potentially very extensive because of the *passerelle* from the Third Pillar. Article 7a of the EC Treaty provides for the establishment of an internal market, in which the free movement of persons is ensured, by 31 December 1992, in accordance with a number of specified legislative bases which do not include Article 235, but which are stated to be without prejudice to other provisions of the Treaty. The post-Maastricht Article 3(d) also subsists with Article 3(c), which underpins Article 7a and speaks of "the abolition, as between member states, of obstacles to the free movement of ... persons...". The Parliament commenced an action against the Commission for failure to act to give effect to Article 7a by the date indicated (Case C-445/93, OJ 1994 C 1, p. 22), which was withdrawn when the Commission made a joint proposal of a Convention on controls on persons crossing external frontiers and of what was to become Council Regulation No 2317/95, OJ 1995 C 11, pp. 8 and 15 respectively. The Convention has not yet been adopted. The Community is also competent to regulate certain aspects of the establishment of and provision of services by third-country nationals under Articles 52 and 59 of the EC Treaty (see Opinion 1/94 on GATS and TRIPS [1994] ECR I-5267) and to require consultation by the member states regarding the promotion of the integration of third-country migrant workers in economic and social life pursuant to Article 118 of the EC Treaty (see Joined Cases 281/85 *et al. Germany et al.* v. *Commission* [1987] ECR 3203).

38. P.-C. Müller-Graff, "The legal bases of the Third Pillar and its position in the framework of the Union Treaty" in Monar & Morgan (eds.), *op. cit.* 21, at pp. 33-6; G. Hogan & A. Whelan, *Ireland and the European Union* (London, 1995) at pp. 92-93. Council Joint Position No. 96/196/JHA of 4 March 1996 on the harmonised application of the definition of the term "refugee" in Article 1 of the Geneva

Convention of 28 July 1951 relating to the status of refugees, OJ 1996 L 63, p. 2, states that it is "without prejudice to member states' caselaw on asylum matters and their relevant constitutional positions" and that it is adopted "within the limits of the constitutional powers of the Governments of the member states; it shall not bind the legislative authorities or affect decisions of the judicial authorities of the member states".

39. Curtin & Pouw, *op. cit.* at p. 30.

40. It is also possible, in principle, that the Court of Justice, if given jurisdiction to interpret a convention, could find that it had direct effect in all the member states.

41. *Ibid.*, at p. 29. These are sometimes published at a later date. For example, the Council decided on 23 November 1995 to publish in the *Official Journal* acts and other texts adopted in the field of asylum and immigration dating back to 20 June 1994. This decision was implemented only on 19 September 1996; see OJ 1996 C 274, p. 1.

42. Council Resolution of 20 June 1994 on minimum guarantees for asylum procedures, OJ 1996 C 274, p. 13, emphasis added.

43. OJ 1996 C 274, p. 35.

44. On the invocation of "soft" legal commitments in Ireland in the field of asylum law, see *Fakih* v *Minister for Justice* [1993] 2 IR 406 and *Gutrani* v *Minister for Justice* [1993] 2 IR 427.

45. A similar provision is contained in two other conventions drawn up on the same day, 26 July 1995, the Convention on the use of information technology for customs purposes (Article 27) and the Convention on the protection of the European Communities' financial interests (Article 8), OJ 1995 C 316, pp. 34 and 49 respectively, as well as in the Protocol to the latter convention drawn up on 27 September 1996 (Article 8), OJ 1996 C 313, p. 5. However, they all provide expressly for referral of a dispute to the Court of Justice by one of the parties if no solution is found within six months.

46. Article 182 of the EC Treaty provides that the Court of Justice shall have jurisdiction in any dispute between member states submitted to it under a special agreement between the parties, but only where it relates to the subject matter of that Treaty.

47. Protocol of 23 July 1996 on the interpretation, by way of preliminary rulings, by the Court of Justice of the European Communities of the Convention on the establishment of a European Police Office, OJ 1996 C 299, p. 2.

48. All but four of the member states made simultaneous declarations accepting the jurisdiction of the Court of Justice. Sweden stated that it would make a declaration in the autumn of 1996; Denmark and Spain stated that they would make declarations at the time of adoption of the Protocol. The United Kingdom's stance indicates that it does not intend to accept the Court's jurisdiction. Four member states (Belgium, the Netherlands, Luxembourg and Italy) also declared their hope that a similar solution could be found regarding preliminary rulings on the Convention on the use of information technology for customs purposes and the Convention on the protection of the European Communities' financial interests.

49. France and Ireland exercised this option in their declarations. All the other declarant member states reserved the right to require such courts of ultimate national jurisdiction to make a reference in appropriate cases.

50. The Commission has acknowledged, in an answer by Commissioner Gradin on 17 January 1996 to a parliamentary question by Claudia Roth MEP, OJ 1996 C 161, p. 5, that measures adopted in the Third Pillar which are not subject to the jurisdiction of the Court of Justice are to be interpreted and applied by the courts of the member states, when seised.

51. See Articles 19, 23, 24, 38 and 39 of the Europol Convention.

52. This question arises in Case C-170/96, *Commission* v. *Council*, in which the Commission, supported by the Parliament, seeks the annulment of Council Joint Action No. 96/197/JHA of 4 March 1996 on an airport transit regime, OJ 1996 L 63, p. 8, which it is argued should have been adopted pursuant to Article 100c of the EC Treaty. The written stage of the hearing of this case has not yet been completed.

53. See e.g. D. O' Keeffe, "The new draft External Frontiers Convention and the draft Visa Regulation" in Monar & Morgan, (eds.), *op. cit.* 135, at p. 145.

54. Emphasis added.

55. See O' Keeffe, *loc. cit.*

56. Articles 2 and 3 of the draft Protocol.

57. Article 5 of the draft Protocol.

58. The British Prime Minister, John Major MP, has suggested that the International Court of Justice could be seised of cases regarding the non-Community pillars of the TEU, *Hansard*, H.C. Vol. 208, col. 267, but this seems scarcely credible.

59. Ireland and the United Kingdom. On the role of the ECHR in Irish law, see G. Hogan & G. Whyte (eds.), J.M. Kelly, *The Irish Constitution* (Dublin, 1994) at pp. 296-299.

60. This is expressly acknowledged in Council Joint Action No 96/750/JHA of 17 December 1996 concerning the approximation of the laws and practices of the member states of the European Union to combat drug addiction and to prevent and combat illegal drug trafficking, OJ 1996 L 342, p. 6, Article 9 of which states that "member states undertake, *subject to their constitutional principles and the basic concepts of their legal systems*, to make it an offence publicly and intentionally to incite or induce others, by any means, to commit offences of illicit use or production of narcotic drugs" (emphasis added).

61. Of course, it could be argued that such protection had scarcely been developed in Community law at the time of Ireland's accession.

62. See Hogan & Whelan, *op. cit.* at pp. 90–98.

63. *CFDT* v. *EC, EC member states collectively and EC member states individually* [1979] 2 CMLR 299; *D* v. *Belgium and the EC* [1987], 2 CMLR 57.

64. *Dufay* v. *EC, EC member states collectively and EC member states individually*, Application No. 13539/88, 19 January 1989.

65. *M* v. *Germany*, Application No. 13258/87, February 1990. This reasoning is reminiscent of that of the German Constitutional Court in *Wünsche Handelsgesellschaft* [1987], 3 CMLR 225.

66. See Hogan & Whelan, *op. cit.* at pp. 113-116; Twomey, *op. cit.* at p. 56.

67. Proposed Article B, fourth indent, of the TEU, on the general objectives of the Union, and proposed Article K, on the scope and objectives of action in the fields of justice and home affairs.

68. A new Article 3c of the EC Treaty would contain the present Community-specific text of Article F(2) of the TEU, substituting the Community for the Union as the subject of the provision.

CHAPTER 14

REFLECTIONS ON THE EUROPEAN UNION AND HUMAN RIGHTS

BRIAN WALSH

INTRODUCTION

It is not surprising that the question of human rights should arise in the context of the operation and government of the European Union. The activities of the European Union affect rights to property, free business activity, fair procedures and other activities or restrictions which may impinge on human dignity or family life and rights of association. It is important to bear in mind that in Union law the expression "human rights" as such does not often appear but the expression most commonly used in this field is "fundamental rights". All human rights are fundamental rights but not all fundamental rights, many of which may be purely political or civic rights, are necessarily human rights in the strict sense. Certain rights are properly called human rights because they are inherent in man because of the fact that he is human, whereas many of the rights which are called fundamental rights are themselves the creations of positive law, that is, created by some law-making civil authority.

However, one should also bear in mind that many of the so-called fundamental rights created by positive law, are often simply expressions of an undoubted human right, the human right to justice. It has been noted that the Universal Declaration of Human Rights employs both terms and recites that the member states of the United Nations have pledged themselves "to achieve....the promotion of universal respect and observance of human rights and fundamental freedoms". The full title of the European Convention is the "Convention for the Protection of Human Rights and Fundamental Freedoms". In the law of the European Union there is no catalogue of fundamental rights having constitutional or legislative status. Article 164 of the Treaty of Rome provided "[t]he Court of Justice shall ensure that in the interpretation and application of this Treaty the law is observed". Alongside all written European Union law there exists what might be called the unwritten Union law. Clearly the written law of the Union consists of the various relevant Treaties which are the foundation of the Union and the regulations and directives which have been made pursuant to those Treaties. Certain rights may be expressly granted by the various Treaties and other

Acts but the unwritten European Union law can comprise the general principles of law. The fact that a particular principle of law is not mentioned in the written law of the Community is not proof that it does not exist. The European Court of Justice in Luxembourg had declared that the guarantee of fundamental rights is an integral part of the general principles of the law of the European Union which it is its task to apply, and that in ensuring this protection it would act in accordance with both the constitutional provisions of the member states and the international instruments designed to ensure respect for the elementary rights of the individual and the fundamental rules of freedom and democracy in society. It was pointed out by Judge Pescatore, in an address he delivered to the Judicial and Academic Conference in Luxembourg in September 1976, that in practice the protection of fundamental rights was not a major preoccupation in the life of the Community, particularly as the process of European unification had not hitherto seriously touched on the basic rights of the individual. He added, "Of course the individual rights and, above all, the fundamental rights of the Community subject must be protected against unlawful encroachments which may result from .... an incorrect application of Community law. But here again, the only basis on which protection can be defined is a common one. Any attempt, at national level, to impose this protection unilaterally will inevitably result in weakening the Community system and destroy its unity. And, I repeat, it is not in the interest of our states."

He had previously warned against what he called "mental telescoping", the tendency to treat as a constitutional question what was in fact a question of Community law. He condemned approaching the problems of the application of Community law in terms of national constitutional law so as to confer jurisdiction on constitutional courts which, as he said, "ought to be reserved, in the final analysis, for review by a common court, the Court of Justice of the European Communities, for that is the Court which under Article 164 of the EEC Treaty, is responsible for determining authoritatively and finally, what imperatives are applied to the words 'the law is observed' in the application and interpretation of the Treaty established in the Community and the law derived therefrom".

The question of the protection of fundamental rights had already been raised by both the German and Italian Constitutional Courts, who appear to have expressed the view that the ultimate protection of fundamental rights where they are guaranteed by national constitutions rests with the final judicial authority of those countries. In effect the result was that the Community maintained the view that its prime purpose in the judicial sphere was to ensure that the final interpretation of the acts of law of the Community was left with the Court in Luxembourg but, in effect, with an undertaking that the fundamental rights which were "common" to the member states of the European Community would be observed.

DEVELOPMENT OF PROTECTION OF FUNDAMENTAL RIGHTS BY THE EUROPEAN UNION

The Single European Act in its preamble proclaimed that the member states were determined to work together to promote democracy on the basis of the fundamental rights recognised in the Constitutions and laws of the member states, in the Convention for the Protection of Human Rights and Fundamental Freedoms and the European Social Charter, notably freedom, equality and social justice".

In 1979 the European Commission had recommended the formal accession of the Communities to the European Convention of Human Rights and Fundamental Freedoms and this recommendation was endorsed by the European Parliament.[1] At the time it was stated by the Commission that "accession would reduce the risk of national courts using the absence of a written catalogue of fundamental rights formally binding upon the Community as justification for reviewing acts of the Council or the Commission by reference to their national institutions and possibly declaring them inapplicable in the light of these Constitutions, thus violating the principle of the uniformity of Community law". This clearly reflected views similar to those expressed by Judge Pescatore in 1976, referred to above. The matter was carried further by the Maastricht Treaty on European Union which contains the following provision: "[t]he Union shall respect fundamental rights, as guaranteed by the European Convention for the Protection of Human Rights and Fundamental Freedom signed in Rome on the 4th November 1950 and as the result from the Constitutional traditions common to the member states, as the general principles of Community law".

Furthermore the Treaty of Maastricht provides that the object of the common form and security policy of the European Union shall be "to develop and consolidate democracy and the Rule of Law, and respect for human rights and fundamental freedoms".[2] Furthermore in that part of the Treaty of Maastricht dealing with cooperation of fees of justice and home affairs it is provided as follows: "[t]he matter referred to in Article K1 shall be dealt with in compliance with the European Convention for the Protection of Human

Rights and Fundamental Freedoms of 4th November 1950 and the Convention relating to the Status of Refugees of 28 July 1951 and having regard to the protection afforded by member states to persons persecuted on political grounds". However, the three provisions referred to above are outside the jurisdiction of the Court of Luxembourg by virtue of the same Treaty. This is somewhat reminiscent of Article 45 of the Constitution of Ireland and reflects policy matters rather than statements of law. As a policy in practice it meant that respect for fundamental rights would be a necessary condition for accession to the European Communities, with a solemn declaration of respect for and the maintenance of representative democracy of human rights in each of the member states of the European Union.

The Luxembourg Court's commitment to draw inspiration from constitutional tradition common to the member states already has the built-in qualification of having to be "common" to the member states. In addition, the Court will draw inspiration from the relevant traditions but will not be bound by them. Similarly, international treaties for the protection of human rights and in which member states have collaborated or of which they are signatories will be used as guidelines which should be followed within the framework of Union law. Thus the European Union and its Court will not uphold measures which are incompatible with the fundamental rights recognised and protected by the constitutions of these states. But the question of whether an infringement of fundamental rights alleged by a member state had been brought about by a European Union law or institution can only be judged in the light of the Union law itself because to permit the introduction of special criteria for assessment stemming from the constitutional law of a particular state would in the view of the Court be damaging to the substantive unity and efficacy of [Union] law and would lead "inevitably to destruction of the unity of the [Union] and the jeopardising of the cohesion of the [Union]".[3]

Thus the last word on the subject lies with the Court of Justice of the European Union, which will decide whether the protection claimed is one which may be held to be a common standard of protection taking account of all the legal systems of the member states and not just the one of the complaining state. The ultimate assessment entails the application of a standard which represents a choice by the Court from among different potential answers, on the basis of such comparison. Such a procedure would result in some standard being set by the Court, but it could also result in a declaration that no such standard exists as a fundamental right in the legal order of the Union. Thus the claim to inviolability of business premises to be on the same basis as the inviolability of the home guaranteed in many countries was rejected by the Court on the grounds that there were many divergencies between the legal systems of the member states in regard to the nature and degree of protection offered to business premises against intervention by public authorities. Nevertheless the Court held that any intervention by public authorities in the private activities of a person, whether a natural or legal person, must have a legal basis and be justified on grounds laid down by law. The need for protection against arbitrary or disproportionate intervention would be recognised as a general principle of the law of the European Union as distinct from recognising the existence of a fundamental right to the inviolability of business premises in the Union's legal order. However, it is interesting to note that the Court of Justice has held in relation to the powers of the European Commission when carrying out an investigation under competition rules, and where the Commission seeks the assistance of the national authorities to carry out an investigation with which the undertaking being investigated does not agree, that it is, in principle, for the national law of the state in question to decide what are the appropriate procedural rules to ensure respect of the rights of that undertaking.

EFFECT OF THE EUROPEAN CONVENTION ON HUMAN RIGHTS ON EU LAW

There are thirty-six member states of the Council of Europe. These states have adopted the European Convention on Human Rights and Fundamental Freedoms. Only fifteen of these states are members of the European Union. The European Union itself is not a state within the meaning of the statutes governing the Council of Europe. The European Union and its institutions have never held that the European Convention on Human Rights was binding on the European Union. While the provisions of the European Convention on Human Rights may provide a useful check-list of the fundamental rights which have been agreed to by almost virtually every European state, it must be recalled that the European Court of Human Rights is subsidiary to the national courts of the member states whereas the contrary is the case in the European Community in that, insofar as European law is concerned, the ultimate authority on what is or is not European Community law resides in the Court of Justice at Luxembourg. It is also to be borne in mind that the European Convention on Human Rights is not part of the national law of two of the states which are members of the European Community, Ireland and the United Kingdom.

In the view of the present author, in respect of those states it cannot really be argued that the European Convention on Human Rights can be pleaded against them in cases before the Court of Justice at Luxembourg because the obligation they have undertaken in respect of the European Convention lies only in international law and is not part of the national law. Thus, for example, in Ireland the European Convention of Human Rights operates outside the sphere of the Irish courts in its direct application as it is not part of the domestic law of Ireland. The view expressed by the late Professor R.F.V. Heuston in 1976 that one effect of Ireland's accession to the European Communities had been to incorporate into the Constitution of Ireland and into Irish law "all the human rights in the European Convention" is not, in the present author's view, correct. Likewise, one cannot accept as being correct the suggestion that the European Convention of Human Rights would apply to Ireland in the Community sphere but not in purely national law cases.[4]

Indeed if the Convention were to be enacted into Irish law it would be subordinate to the Constitution itself unless the Constitution were amended to give it a place similar to that occupied by the European Union Treaties under the amendment of Article 29 of the Constitution. The above suggestions seem to have been prompted by the fact that the Courts of Justice in Luxembourg have on more than one occasion noted that rights guaranteed in the European Union legal order are in accord with ideas common to the constitutions of member states and with those reflected in the European Convention on Human Rights. It is to be borne in mind as set out before that the Luxembourg Court was not unaware of the fact that there are mutual inconsistencies and contradictions lurking in these sources and in fact insofar as it has committed itself to anything it is only to look for the ones which are common to all these possible sources. The present author believes that the most that at best can be said is that the European Court of Justice at Luxembourg would look on the decisions of the Courts in Strasbourg as persuasive authorities. It is quite clear they do not regard the judgments of Strasbourg as binding on the legal opinions of the Union.[5]

CONCLUSION

As indicated above, it is abundantly clear that the primary purpose and indeed the primary function of the European Court of Justice at Luxembourg is to defend the supremacy of Community law over national law and to be sympathetic to the defence of fundamental rights. It is also abundantly clear that in drawing inspiration from various national constitutions and international conventions the European Court of Justice at Luxembourg was not committing itself to adopting formally any of the provisions to be found in these sources but in fact was searching for what might be regarded as a norm common to the member states of the European Union insofar as that norm did not threaten the supremacy of the European Union law. Indeed, the European Convention on Human Rights, which has been in force since 1953, was not specifically referred to by the Luxembourg Court until 1975. The reference in the preamble of the Single European Act and later in the Maastricht Treaty was a recognition of the European Convention of Human Rights as a source of inspiration for what has been described as an unwritten Bill of Rights to be observed in the development of European Union law so that as a general principle the protection and guarantee of fundamental rights would be considered an integral part of the legal principles which the Court of Justice at Luxembourg guaranteed to respect. The reactions of the German Constitutional Court and the Italian Constitutional Court to the protection of fundamental rights was a significant contribution to the adoption of this outlook by the European Court of Justice and the European Union. The reaction of these Courts reflected the recognition that fundamental rights are, to adapt the words of the late Chief Justice O'Dálaigh, "declared not alone because of the bitter memories of the past but no less because of the improbable, but not to be overlooked, perils of the future".[6]

As mentioned above, in this article, human rights are distinct from the generality of fundamental rights. Human rights are rights which are inherent in man because he is man and which are priceless in economic terms. By definition they cannot be sacrificed to serve economic interests. While it may well be argued that it is not possible to identify a uniform European conception of morals it must be conceded that each state has a responsibility in this field and this is expressly recognised in the European Convention on Human Rights. In a truly democratic society, which the Union is pledged to uphold as one of its ideals, the essential objective of all economic and social progress is for the benefit of the peoples of the member states without damaging or endangering their inherent human rights. All laws, whether of the Union or of the member states, must be measured against those standards. The law exists for the protection of society. It exists not only to protect the individual from injury, exploitation and corruption; it must also protect the institutions and the community of ideas, political and moral, without which people cannot live together. Many laws have specific ethical significance. Thus laws against racial discrimination have as their aim the shaping of people's moral thinking by legal sanction. The European Union entry into the field of justice and home affairs cannot be successful without a proper recognition of the fact that morality is properly the concern of the law. That has been the common heritage of the peoples of Europe. The periods where that has been rejected, particularly in the present century, have left indelible stains on the history of mankind.

NOTE
1   Note now however that on 28 March 1996 the Court of Justice held an advisory opinion that the Union could not accede to the European Convention on Human Rights in the absence of an appropriate amendment to the Treaty of Rome. It must follow therefore that membership of the Union cannot of itself incorporate the Convention into the national law of the Member States of the Union.
2. The statements in the Single European Act and in the Treaty of Maastricht were assurances prompted by the reactions of the Constitutional Courts of Germany and Italy.
3. Case 44/79 Hauer [1979] ECR 3727.
4. See here, e.g. article by J.T. Lang (1983) *Dublin University Law Review*, 3.
5. Judge Pescatore in his contribution in 1988 to *The Protection of Human Rights: the European Dimension* (Carl Heymans Verlage K G-Koln) suggests that the Court at Luxembourg when applying the provisions of the European Convention should explicitly state that it does so because it is bound by international law to do so. He said the procedural provisions of the Convention are matters solely for the Strasbourg Court.
6. *McMahon v. Attorney General* 1972 IR 69 at p. 111.

● INDEX

IEA FOUNDATION MEMBERS

The Institute is particularly indebted to its *Foundation Members* which enable it to operate independently on a financially secure basis.

Aer Lingus
Aer Rianta
Agra Trading
AIB Bank plc
An Bord Tráchtála
An Post
Arthur Andersen
Avonmore Foods plc
Bank of Ireland
Bord Gáis
Bord na Móna
Bristol-Myers Squibb Co.
Cityjet
CRH plc
Deloitte & Touche
Dublin Port
Electricity Supply Board
FBD Insurances plc/*Irish Farmers Journal*/IFA
First National Building Society
FitzPatrick Hotel Group

Forbairt
FORFÁS
Glen Dimplex
Guinness Ireland Ltd
IBEC
IDA Ireland Ltd
Independent Newspapers plc
Irish Distillers
Irish Life
Irish Permanent plc
National Irish Bank
National Treasury Management Agency
New Ireland Assurance Company plc
RTÉ
Siemens Ltd
SIPTU
Smurfit (Ireland) Ltd
Telecom Éireann
The Irish Times
Ulster Bank
Waterford Crystal plc

IEA CORPORATE MEMBERS

Agriculture, Food and Forestry, Department of • Arthur Cox • Arts, Culture and the Gaeltacht, Department of • ASTI • Attorney General/Chief State Solicitors Office, Office of the • Bizquip • British Embassy • Central Bank • Centre for International Co-operation • Church of Ireland Working Group on Europe • Committee on European Affairs of the Irish Episcopal Conference • Construction Industry Federation • Defence, Department of • Director of Public Prosecutions, Office of the • Dublin City University • Dublin Corporation • Education, Department of • Employment Equality Agency • Enterprise and Employment, Department of • Environment, Department of the • Equality and Law Reform, Department of • Equity Bank • European Commission Library Service • European Foundation for the Improvement of Living & Working Conditions • FÁS • Finance, Department of • Foreign Affairs, Department of • Fyffes • Government of Quebec, London Office • Gypsum Industries plc • Health, Department of • Henley Centre • Howmedica • ICOS • ICTU • IMPACT • INTO • Irish Management Institute • Irish Pensions Board • Justice, Department of • Lansdowne Market Research Ltd • Léargas • Marine, Department of the • McCann FitzGerald • NCB Group • NESC • Ombudsman, Office of the • Revenue Commissioner, Office of the • Social Welfare, Department of • Taoiseach, Department of the • Tourism and Trade, Department of • Transport, Energy and Communications, Department of • UCC • UCC, Department of History • UCD • Údarás na Gaeltachta • University of Dublin, Trinity College • USIT • Wavin Ireland Ltd

IEA PUBLICATIONS

Studies in European Union
Political Union
Editor: Patrick Keatinge
ISBN 1 874109 00 1, 200 pages, IR£12.95, 1991
Economic and Monetary Union
Editor: Rory O'Donnell
ISBN 1 874109 01 X, 148 pages, IR£12.95, 1991
Maastricht and Ireland: What the Treaty Means
Editor: Patrick Keatinge
ISBN 1 874109 03 6, 180 pages, IR£10.00, 1992
Social Europe: EC Social Policy and Ireland
Editor: Seamus Ó Cinnéide
ISBN 1 874109 06 0, 176 pages, IR£15.00, 1993
Constitution-building in the European Union
Editor: Brigid Laffan
ISBN 1 874109 21 4, 256 pages, IR£15.00, 1996
Britain's European Question: the Issues for Ireland
Editor: Paul Gillespie
ISBN 1 874109 22 2, 224 pages, IR£15.00, 1996
European Security: Ireland's Choices
Patrick Keatinge
ISBN 1 874109 24 9, 224 pages, IR£15.00, 1996

Implications for Ireland
Political Union
Paul Gillespie and Rodney Rice
ISBN 1 874109 02 8, 60 pages, IR£5.00, 1991
EMU and Irish Fiscal Policy
Donal de Buitléir and Don Thornhill
ISBN 1 874109 05 2, 74 pages, IR£7.50, 1993
Ireland and the IGC
Dermot Scott
ISBN 1 874109 19 2, 64 pages, IR£3.95, 1996

Understanding Europe
Eastern Exchanges
Interchange of Education, Training and Professional Formation between
Ireland and Czechoslovakia, Hungary and Poland.
Miriam Hederman O'Brien
ISBN 1 874109 04 4, 48 pages, IR£5.00, 1992
Managing the Finances of the EU: the Role of the European Court of Auditors
Barry Desmond
ISBN 1 874109 35 7, 80 pages, IR£5.00, 1996

Occasional Papers

No. 1 **Irish Public Opinion on Neutrality and European Union**
Michael Marsh IR£4.00, 1992

No. 2 **The Economic Consequences of Maastricht**
Paul Tansey IR£5.00, 1992

No. 3 **Subsidiarity: Its Application in Practice**
Ciaran F. Walker IR£5.00, 1993

No. 4 **Ireland's Contribution to the European Union**
Dermot Scott ISBN 1-874109-08-7, 48 pages, IR£7.50, 1994

No. 5 **Knowledge of the European Union in Irish Public Opinion: Sources and Implications**
Richard Sinnott ISBN 1-874109-09-5, 48 pages, IR£7.50, 1995

No. 6 **Citizenship of the European Union**
Niamh Hyland, Claire Loftus, Anthony Whelan
ISBN 1-874109-13-3, 64 pages, IR£7.50, 1995

No. 7 **The Role of the Commission and Qualified Majority Voting**
John Temple Lang and Eamonn Gallagher
ISBN 1-874109-14-1, 48 pages, IR£7.50, 1995

Final Reports
Maastricht: Crisis of Confidence
Paul Gillespie • *Brendan Halligan* • *Philip Halpin* • *Patrick Keatinge*
• *Brigid Laffan,* IR£4.00, 1992

What Price CAP? Issues and Challenges Facing Agricultural and Rural Policy in the European Union
Editor: Brendan Kearney ISBN 1 874109 15 X, IR£30.00, 1995

The 1996 Intergovernmental Conference: Issues, Options, Implications,
IEA Bureau ISBN 1-874109-18-4, 288 pages, IR£30.00, 1995

IGC Conference Report
Edited by Ben Tonra ISBN 1-87109-32-X, 80 pages, IR£5.00, 1997

Interim Reports
Europe – Community and Continent: the enlargement of the European Union and its relationships with its continental neighbours
Tony Brown, 250 pages, IR£12.50, 1994

Towards a Safer Europe – Small State Security Policies and the European Union: Implications for Ireland
Editor: Patrick Keatinge ISBN 1-874109-10-9, 160 pages, IR£30.00, 1995

Summary of Interim Reports
Europe — Community and Continent
Tony Brown ISBN 1-874109-10-9, 48 pages, IR£4.00, 1994
Towards a Safer Europe
Editor: Patrick Keatinge ISBN 1-874109-11-7, 56 pages, IR£7.50, 1995

Research Papers
A European Cultural Identity: Myth, Reality or Aspiration
Ben Tonra and Denise Dunne, ISBN 1-874109-27-3, 32 pages, IR£5.00, 1997
Social Policy and the IGC
Joe Larragy, ISBN 1-874109-28-1, 32 pages, IR£5.00, 1997
EMU – The Third Stage (Treaty & Non-Treaty Basis of EMU)
Gavin Barrett, ISBN 1-874109-31-1, 104 pages, IR£15.00, 1997
Hungary, Ireland and the European Union,
Editor: Marton O'Donoghue ISBN 1-874109, 32 pages IR£5,00, 1997

Seminar Papers
Recent Changes in Multilateral Security
Foreword: Patrick Keatinge
Facsimile pages, IRIR£10.00
Britain's European Question: the Issues for Ireland – Seminar Papers
Editor: Paul Gillespie
ISBN 1-874109-23-0, 176 pages, IR£20.00, 1996

Seminar Reports
Austria our New Partner
Tony Brown (Rapporteur) ISBN 1-874109-15-X, 44 pages, IR£7.50, 1995
Sweden in the European Union
Tony Brown (Rapporteur) ISBN 1-874109-17-6, 48 pages, IR£7.50, 1995
Finland in the European Union
Tony Brown (Rapporteur) ISBN 1-874109-16-8, 48 pages, IR£7.50, 1995
Norway and the European Union
Tony Brown (Rapporteur) ISBN 1-874109-20-6, 48 pages, IR£7.50, 1996
Report on the Netherlands Presidency of the Council of Ministers
Ben Tonra (Rapporteur) ISBN 1-874109-29-X, 16 pages, IR£5.00, 1997
Published on behalf of the European Commission Representation in Ireland
European Social Policy – Options for the Union
David Gardner (Raporteur): Free distribution

Periodicals
Contemporary/Historic Documents Archive
European Document Series
Editor Tony Brown ISSN 0791-8097, c. 64 pages an issue, 297 x 210 mm
Annual subscription (4 issues) IR£40.00
Annual subscription to members IR£25.00, Individual issues IR£15.00
Back issues available – No. 1 spring 1993 to No. 16 winter 1996-97

German Commentary
Editor: Jill Donoghue, ISBN 1-874109-30-3, 32 pages, IR£5.00, 1997
Newsletter for Members
IEA NEWS
Editor: Dermot Scott
Quarterly
Forthcoming issue No. 17, summer 1997